No, no, not more of those damned whores!

Lt Ralph Clark, 1790

Some of our convicts I have heard even to boast of the crimes and murders committed by them and their accomplices, but the far greater number were harmless unfortunate creatures....

John Nicol, of the female convicts
on the *Lady Juliana* 1790

This project was assisted through Arts Tasmania
by the Minister for the Arts

The Regional Arts Fund is a Commonwealth
Government initiative through the Australia
Council, its arts funding and advisory body

Published by
Esperance Press
Editor: Edith Speers

Cover Design: Meryl Moscrop & Edith Speers

PO Box 52
Dover Tasmania
Australia 7117
www.esperancepress.com.au

female factory
female convicts

the story of the more than 13,000 women
exiled from Britain to Van Diemen's Land

Tony Rayner

'The valley of the shadow of death'

Cascades Female Factory between Hobart Rivulet and Mount Wellington, Tasmania

Photograph [c1890] courtesy of the Archives Office of Tasmania

Dedication:

In memory of:

Kay Daniels Ph.D., D.Lit., 1941-2001
Teacher, mentor, friend

&

Ann Holmes 1815-1878
7 years transportation
per *William Bryan* 1833
My paternal grandmother's grandmother

The Currency Lads may fill their glasses,
And drink to the health of the Currency Lasses;
But the Lass I adore, the lass for me,
Is a lass in the Female Factory

Author's Acknowledgments

This book would not have been possible without extensive assistance from the late Kay Daniels to whom this book is dedicated, from Jill Roberts and from my editor and friend Edith Speers. Staff of the History Department of the University of Tasmania both past and present including Professor Michael Roe, Richard Ely and Stefan Petrow were extraordinarily helpful as were other members of the staff. I wish to acknowledge the assistance of the following people: Ian Pearce and the staff of the Archives Office of Tasmania; Tony Marshall and the staff of the Tasmanian Collection, State Library of Tasmania. Stefan Petrow and Tansy Rayner Roberts read and commented on the manuscript.

Most of the information on the female convicts of Van Diemen's Land, their names, ships and colonial records were sourced from *Notorious strumpets and dangerous girls* by Phillip Tardif. I have relied heavily on this book for the facts from which I could recreate the stories of individual women and their lives.

Special thanks must go to Dianne Phillips, David Woodward, Miranda Morris and Christine Woods each of whom allowed me extensive and generous use of their unpublished material, though Christine's book *The Last Ladies: female convicts on the Duchess of Northumberland, 1853* has since been published and is highly recommended to the reader.

Publisher's Acknowledgment to suppliers of images

Grateful thanks must go to those institutions who are preserving the pictorial history of Australia and making it available to the publisher and the public:

Archives Office of Tasmania
 Photographs of Cascades Female Factory; front & pp130, 156
 Photograph of Dynnyrne House (Nursery); p152
Tasmanian Museum and Art Gallery
 'Figure of a girl', pencil & watercolour by GTWB Boyes (1825); on first page of book, and used to create image on back cover
 'The Old Treasury [Lower] Macquarie Street', from a sketch [?] 1833; p68
State Library of Tasmania (Allport Library and Museum of Fine Arts)
 'View of Hobart Town' by Joseph Lycett; front cover
 'Orphan School, Hobart' by Emily Bowing; p164
National Library of Australia
 'Female penitentiary, or factory at Parramata [ie, Parramatta], NSW'; undated water colour by Augustus Earle (1826?), Rex Nan Kivell Collection.
The Library of the Religious Society of Friends in Britain (London)
 'Mrs Fry reading to prisoners at Newgate', engraving by T. Oldham Barlow from painting by Jerry Barrett; p26

Additional Publisher's Acknowledgments

Thanks also to The Five Mile Press and Peter Cuffley (ed.), for quotes from 'Send the boy to sea' by James Montagu Smith; and Text Publishing for quotes from 'Life and adventures of John Nicol, Mariner 1776-1801'. The verse on the dedication page is part of a song

Table of Contents

Illustrations

Stories, quotes & out-takes

Chapter 1.   Young, noisy and light-fingered

On 21 April 1853 the last female convict ship to Australia and the second last convict ship to Eastern Australia arrived at the port of Hobart Town. Her name was *Duchess of Northumberland*, Captain George Mitchell, and she had sailed from Woolwich on the River Thames near London six months and three weeks before. On board she carried a cargo of human beings, 216 women convicts, three having died on the voyage. The women were mostly young and convicted mainly of petty crimes. These women had been forcibly exiled from their homes and families in Britain to the island colony of Van Diemen's Land, 20,000 kilometres away. The island was so infamous in the annals of exile and imprisonment that within three years of the last convict arrival its citizens would change its name to Tasmania in a vain attempt to forget its shameful history.

Over half the women sent as convicts to Australia between 1788 and 1853 in the system known as Transportation were sent to Van Diemen's Land. Throughout the colonies that received transported convicts, places of residence and incarceration were established. In the case of the women these were known as female factories because their original purpose was to produce goods. The most infamous was the Cascades Female Factory in South Hobart. Known locally as 'the Factory', its remains still stand as a reminder not only of Tasmania's history but as a personal reminder to those who trace their family histories back to any of the women transported to Van Diemen's Land. If they did not pass through its doors themselves, the threat of this place and its reputation was certainly part of their exile experience.

Although 1853 brought the last of the female convicts to Van Diemen's Land and was celebrated as 'the end of Transportation', the women did not disappear. Their presence, their offspring, and their influence continued well into the 20th Century and even now has not entirely faded away. These were the often unacknowledged and sometimes unknown founding mothers of Australia.

Australians, and Tasmanians as those Australians with the highest percentage of convict ancestry, have no need to be ashamed of their

1

heritage. Sensible people no longer believe that your distant ancestors determine your character, your abilities or your ethical base. That female convicts had to wait even longer than the male convicts to be suitably recognised, and to some extent to be rehabilitated, says more about the male historians of the 1950s and 1960s than it does about the convicts themselves. That the relative badness of the female convicts rested more on their open sensuality and sexuality, their smoking and drinking and their refusal to bow to the petty restrictions of the convict system tells us far more about the oppressive nature of gender inequities, gender hypocrisies, and the absurd nature of middle class morality between the early Victorian ages and the very recent past, than it does about the true nature of their character.

Where the women were morally reprehensible in any true sense, at least to the modern mind, it was very much along the same lines as it was for the men. They were murderers, robbers, forgers, destroyers of property, assaulters of their fellow humans. But these people were in the minority. The statistics are clear. The women were even less likely than the men to be very serious offenders and far more likely to be petty thieves. Having arrived in the colonies, and in spite of the incredibly fierce oversight of the convict system, only a few of them were ever convicted of stealing again. The economic nature of the new colonies meant that few ever had to look to theft as a means of making a living.

Some of the women, possibly as many as one in four but probably no more than one out of five, had at some time in their past been prostitutes. Prostitution in itself did not get a woman transported, but it often contributed to her being recognised as a former offender. It seems to have significantly increased her chances, once convicted of theft, of being sentenced to transportation. Having been sentenced to transportation, a woman with a known history of prostitution was then more likely to be actually transported for the theft.

By far the largest proportion of the women were young and, let's face it, in any generation a significant proportion of the young are notorious for sexual escapades, noisy high jinks and light-fingeredness. Different ages have different names for the phenomenon; in the 1950s and 1960s it was called juvenile delinquency. Our contemporary justice systems tend to look much more indulgently on such activity than did Britain of the 1780s through to the 1850s. Looking hard at the statistics of both the male and female convicts it is difficult to ignore the possibility that one in three, or at times as many as half of the convicts were of this type. Once in the colonies, although a significant number went on to be constant or regular offenders, the majority disappeared into obscurity and relative honesty, particularly once the eagle eye of the convict system was no longer focused on them.

As could be expected from a system of justice, any system of justice, many of those scooped up into the maws of the British system were constant, continuous, regular offenders and included some of the most degraded, vicious, violent and unruly persons known to mankind. But even of these, though a few seem to have continued the old ways for the rest of their lives, a surprising number committed no further offences once they left the convict system.

The only other group that stands out as continuing offenders are those who were clearly alcoholics, and a few others who can best be described as social nuisances. A few of the alcoholics don't appear to have had a problem with drinking before they were transported, but to have taken up the bottle either due to the effects of exile, or because of tragedies in their colonial life. Nevertheless, many of the convicts in this category attributed their original conviction to alcoholism.

The offences committed by female convicts in the colonies were mostly offences against public order or the convict discipline system, and the severity of the punishments was a reflection of that system. However the level of punishment decreased as the convict moved through different stages towards gaining her freedom. For similar offences a woman aboard ship or in a female factory tended to be punished more severely than an assigned servant, who tended to be punished more severely than a woman with a ticket-of-leave, who was punished more severely than a woman who had a conditional pardon, who in turn was punished more severely than one who had served her sentence (free by servitude). But it was not only the severity of the punishments that altered according to the convict's status. The level of proof required to convict her also altered. An assigned servant accused of stealing (which could lead to an extension of transportation) might well be found not guilty but then immediately sentenced to twelve months in the Female Factory on 'violent suspicion' of having committed the crime. Such a course was not available to the magistrates in the case of a woman possessing a pardon or who was free by servitude.

The female factories

As time went on the colonial convict system became more and more organised, with a gradual reduction in the possibility of individual convicts being able to slip through the cracks. With regard to the women convicts, the colonial authorities had one principal tool to control, punish, and potentially to reform. That was the female factory system.

From their beginnings at Parramatta in New South Wales at the start of the 1800s, the female factories of Australia multiplied, large and small across the landscape of early colonial convict Australia, first to the small settlements of New South Wales, then to the emerging settlements of Van Diemen's Land and to those areas of New South Wales which were to become southeast Queensland.

The Parramatta Factory in New South Wales and the Cascades Factory in Van Diemen's Land were each by far the most important institution dealing with female convicts within their respective colonies, though for a few years during the Probation Period in the 1840s the numbers passing through the probation station the hulk *Anson*, moored on the River Derwent at Hobart, rivalled the numbers held at Cascades.

On the other hand, the Ross Female Factory in central Van Diemen's Land only operated as a female factory for a few years towards the latter part of the convict transportation system. However, it was extremely well planned and organised, the authorities apparently having learned their lessons the hard way.

The Cascades Female House of Correction was situated two miles (three kilometres) from the centre of the town and operated as an institution for the reception of female convicts between 1829 and 1877, a period of fifty years. Almost invariably it was known as the Hobart Town Female Factory or the Cascades Female Factory or within the local area just as *The Factory*, although it was also referred to by a crusading journalist of the time as 'The valley of the shadow of death'.

Although this book deals to some extent with all the female convicts who came to the Australian colonies and to a lesser extent with all the female factories, its main focus is specifically on the Cascades institution and to a lesser extent on how the lessons consistently acknowledged but just as consistently ignored at Cascades were finally remedied in the case of the Ross Factory.

Sex as a crime

From the 1850s to the 1970s Tasmania wanted to forget its convict origins. Like other places in the English speaking world the culture had changed. High esteem was placed on church-going, honesty and respectability. Sexual morés held a particularly high place in this culture and sexuality was covert, private, largely undiscussed and, when it was discussed, subject to a high degree of hypocrisy. Unmarried couples were shunned, unmarried single mothers were both pitied and shunned, and divorcees were similarly treated though generally not so badly as the first two groups. A child born out of wedlock was stigmatised and discriminated against. Young sexually active men were rarely considered seriously culpable, or if they were, it was soon forgotten. Young sexually active women or girls suffered not only social discrimination but were also subject to morality laws which could lead to their incarceration in institutions, sometimes for years at a time or sometimes until they reached 21 years of age. Even worse, though relatively uncommonly, such 'loose' sexuality could be deemed to be a sign of mental instability and the young women condemned to years and sometimes a lifetime in a mental institution, often at the behest of their families.

The upholders of these values of punishment and denial were not going to be reminded that in these matters they too might have had a past that was less than 'innocent'. That one or more of their grandmothers or great grandmothers had been a female convict was a much more shocking background than having a male convict ancestor, and if the female turned out to have been a prostitute, the thought of publication or dissemination of such information could be enough to threaten a person to a living hell of rumour, slander and social deprivation.

Until the late 1970s there were still quite strong taboos in Tasmania about discussing convict ancestors, particularly in small rural areas or villages where many families had lived since the convict days. This even had an official edge to it: the Archives Office of Tasmania refused access to all convict records until they received a written undertaking that no name or other material that might identify an individual convict was to be published or disseminated.

Poverty and survival

It was against this background that in the 1920s and 1930s, both in Britain and Australia, historians started to point out that the convicts were not as bad as they had been painted; they weren't as different from the general run of people in England and Ireland as people had hitherto imagined. They also pointed out the chaotic and unfair nature of British society at the time, and that many of the richest and most respected family fortunes had actually been made from outright theft from the common people, by devious and unfair oppression of ordinary people by their social betters and by the failure of British society as a whole to continue to support its poorer members. If this was so, how could people have survived without resort to some form of criminal behaviour? The fact that most seemed to have lived honest lives doesn't really help us to understand when we look at those who weren't honest. One has to survive, and help your family and friends, however best you can.

In the 1950s it was common for Australians to believe that most convicts had been sent out for 'stealing a loaf of bread', for political or union agitation, for poaching, for a minor youthful indiscretion or as a victim of the unfair British legal system or the Irish famine. Historians such as Manning Clark, AGL Shaw and Lloyd Robson (amongst others) started to look at the records and to deal with them in a statistical way using elements of social science methodology.

What they found shocked both them and their Australian readers. The convicts appeared to be criminals much like the offenders we read about in the papers today and who with a certain degree of satisfaction we are happy to see sent to gaol for a few months or a few years for their crimes. Even worse, particularly to the readers of the 1950s and 1960s, many of the women lived loose sexual lives and not a few of them had been prostitutes. They were often loud, vulgar, loose-living, ne'er-do-well, and light-fingered trollops (at least that is how my grandmother would have described them).

In short, few of the female convicts were the sort of people you would like to have living next door in your street. Though of course there is the fact, largely ignored, that it takes two to tango. In general, women can't live loud, vulgar and 'sexually-loose' lives in isolation from their menfolk or their male contemporaries. As a number of more open-minded and clear thinking colonial convict officials pointed out, it wasn't that the women were worse than the men, it was that they were expected to be better, and when they failed to be any better than the men, they were condemned as being worse.

But to a large extent, these female convicts are Australia's great-great-grandmothers; they were the women who built what they saw as a better world, on the opposite side of the earth from what had once been home. Most of them became mothers, most of them seem to have done a good job at it, and in the end they were just ordinary people getting through life as best they could. And when you read the stories contained in this book, and see the way in which the convict system operated on those who found themselves mired in its institutions, and see what happened to their children who typically did not grow up to be our ancestors because they died in the unbearable and intolerable plague pits of the Female Factory Nurseries, it is hard to remember that some of their contemporaries saw all these women, good, bad and indifferent (as they might have been described by their keepers), as utterly abandoned, unworthy of pity, irredeemable, and a permanent future blot on the history of the country they helped build.

There are over 13,000 stories of female convicts in Van Diemen's Land. Each one is different; they are all alike; each is a tragedy, a few are comedy; all are neither; most stories are accessible, few are knowable; the mass of detail is unending, the amount of information too little. 'The past is another country' where we think we know the geography and are confused by knowing the words but not the language; we see the text but fail the context.

To tell the story of an individual distorts the story of the whole. To tell the story of the whole distorts the history of the individual. If we fail to note that under certain circumstances statistics of the whole, the usual, the average can only tell us about the group and not the individual, indeed it can only warp the story and history of the individual, then the way we are forced to proceed by the nature of the evidence will fail to provide a reasonably true account. Above all, the stories of our convict predecessors (and to many of us our convict ancestors) deserve no less than a true account.

Mrs Fry reading to prisoners at Newgate Gaol: the respected and influential Elizabeth Fry was active in prison reform during the period of Transportation.

Lithograph c1860, courtesy of the Library of theSociety of Religious Friends in Britain (London)

8

Chapter 2. The City of Terror

In 1780 it was the greatest city of Europe and in June of that year it lay under a pall of smoke, fear, panic and terror. The most significant and notorious prison in the city had been stormed, hundreds of the prisoners set free and the building set alight and burnt to the bare stones.

The mob then moved on and attacked, looted and burned numerous smaller prisons. Next they turned their attention to the houses of judges, magistrates, aristocrats and wealthy industrialists and merchants. Then one of the leading rioters who had stormed the main prison performed an act typical of the use of the symbolism of the age. Accompanied by a huge crowd, he marched into the centre of one of the city's bridges in triumph. With great solemnity, ceremony and deliberation, he dropped the ancient, massive and now entirely useless keys of the gaol into the waters of the river, to the raucous cheers of the assembled multitude.

The end of the riots was to signal the beginning of a reign of retributive terror, an orgy of public slaughter and judicial mayhem. The death toll from public executions that year was to be 50, the highest in the city for thirty years. In the next ten years 1780-1789 there would be a total of 534 executions in the city and many more on its outskirts and far suburbs. Amongst those, the first persons to become objects of official terror and judicial killing would be the wretches who had so desecrated the principal gaol of the city, and looted and destroyed the homes of judges, magistrates and leading citizens. And in particular, the weight of appalling horror would fall on those who were involved in the destruction of the house of the aristocratic and notoriously severe chief judge of the land, who together with his wife and loyal servants had fled from the back door as the mob had broken down his front railings, gates, doors and windows and stormed the house.

Over the next few days of June 1780 following the riots, scores of accused were dragged before the judges and twenty-five of the rioters including four women were executed in small groups at widely dispersed streets and squares of the city. In later years one person who, as a boy, had witnessed these events wrote:

I remember seeing a whole cartload of young girls, in dresses of various colours, on their way to be executed... They had all been condemned, on one indictment, for having been concerned in ...the burning of some houses during ...[the] riots. It was quite horrible. Greville was present at one of the trials consequent on those riots, and heard several boys sentenced, to their own amazement, to be hanged. 'Never,' said Greville with great naïveté, 'did I see boys cry so.'

This was not the city of Paris, for the French Revolution was nine years in the future. The prison liberated in 1780 was not the Bastille. It was Newgate Prison in the centre of London.

The gaily dressed girls were not in a tumbril headed for the guillotine, they were in the typical cart used to take most of the London condemned to the three-legged gibbet at Tyburn. There in the midst of a largely uncaring carnival, a rope would be placed around the condemned person's neck while the cart drove away, leaving them, if they were extremely lucky, with a snapped neck and almost instantaneous death. It was with this intention that many of the condemned threw themselves from the cart, but usually to no avail. More usually they were left slowly strangling over two, three or four minutes, or if they were extremely unlucky perhaps as long as fifteen minutes, while their struggling, twisting bodies voided their bodily wastes, and often while the executioner or perhaps some of their friends dragged them down by the feet to hasten their slow and savage death.

Secret places, hasty gibbets

But the Tyburn Fair was not to be the fate of the 1780 rioters, in spite of the memories of the gentleman as a lad, and it is unlikely that he saw more than two women in a cart, for that was the most number of female rioters executed on the one day or at the one site. Perhaps his memory was based on seeing groups of young rioters being brought from distant prisons for their trials, where quite a number were given prison sentences, often with flimsy evidence, for minor roles in the riots including, more than once, for little more than being in the wrong place at the wrong time. Within a day or so, indeed sometimes within mere hours of their trial, small groups of the rioters were daily transported in carts to carefully and secretly selected squares of the city where a gibbet was hastily erected and the condemned dispatched, often to the stares of a mere dozen passers-by.

This was the plan of the authorities, to quickly and publicly execute the condemned rioters before it was possible for a large crowd to gather. Such a crowd was far too likely to demonstrate their sympathy, attempt a rescue or even to go on further riotous rampages. The authorities wished to reduce the risk of stirring up the mob again and the riskiest part of the normal process of execution was the procession to Tyburn.

The new, improved executions

When three years later, in December 1783, most public executions in London were moved from Tyburn, there was a level of concern for the efficiency, safety, and retrieval of control from the mob, as well as sheer symbolism in the fact that the new place for executions was to be outside the main gate of the newly rebuilt Newgate Prison. The new, improved execution process was to occur on a high demountable stage, with the condemned suddenly appearing from a door in the wall of the prison immediately behind the scaffold and safely out of reach of the crowd.

For the first time, attempts were deliberately made to improve the actual efficiency of the killing by implementing a sudden drop through a trapdoor so that death by the breaking of the neck might be more certain. This though was a rather forlorn hope as the use of a one-length-fits-all rope still led to many being slowly strangled. The executioners were scared to use a longer drop for fear of creating an undignified spectacle of the heavier condemned (perhaps mercifully) having their head ripped off altogether.

The role of the crowd was changed by their being positioned behind a barricade which kept them well away from the scaffold and largely restricted to an area in the front of Newgate which recently had been cleared of houses. By these physical restrictions the mob was made into a vocal but otherwise passive audience rather than a potentially active participant as had always been a possible outcome in the hurly-burly of the Tyburn procession. The mob, as witness to the terror of the state, had been curbed, restricted, crushed. And it had happened in front of the rebuilt site of its most symbolic victory against the system of horror and terror that was used to control their lives.

The new place of execution was established just in time to witness the deadliest years of the century in London.

In the first few years after the riots, the death toll from executions in the city had dropped somewhat, though not nearly to the levels of the previous two or three years. But then the amount of property crime increased and the judges and magistrates rose to the challenge. In 1783 and 1784 more citizens were executed than in the bloody riot year. But during the following three years of 1785 to 1787, it seemed as if the judicial blood-lust had gone entirely mad: a total of 239 people were executed, mainly for crimes against property.

In the peak year of 1785 the toll was 97 deaths, and only one individual out of all those killed was executed for murder. The total number of executions for the four years of 1784 to 1787 was 295, exactly equivalent to all the executions for the following fourteen years. In 1787, ninety-three people died on the scaffold. Then the storm of executions that had arrived with the riots of 1780 blew itself out just as suddenly as it had arisen. Seemingly overnight the number of executions dropped to only a third of those in the worst year, and then continued to fall for a whole generation.

What caused the violent and deadly 'Bloody Code' in the mid-1780s to suddenly become more merciful after 1787? The answer is immediately clear to any student of Australian history. The English stopped executing so many of their malefactors simply because in 1788 they had something worse for them. They transported them to Australia.

Botany Bay was a place that had only ever been visited by Europeans once, seventeen years before. People were literally being sent to the ends of the earth. Some historians have claimed that transportation was not such a terrible fate when compared with being hanged, and that as a punishment it could scarcely be expected to terrify and awe the populace to the same extent as execution. However, at the time there was no doubt in most people's minds that exile to the furthest corner of the earth, with little or no chance of ever returning, was a very severe and terrifying punishment indeed.

Chapter 3. The Bloody Code

Most Australians are well aware of the horrific punishments inflicted on those found guilty of even minor crimes under the old British regime before some measure of reform of the criminal law took place in the late 1820s and early 1830s, roughly two-thirds of the way through the Transportation period. Hanging, flogging, and transportation beyond the seas or to prison hulks was the punishment for everything from murder to petty theft. For minor offences there were the pillory, the stocks, or committal to the old unreformed gaols and castle dungeons where storms of infectious diseases regularly swept away a significant proportion of the inmates.

This tells us little about the true experience or the reality of law and order in the Britain of the time. In actual fact, the severest punishment, the death penalty, though often pronounced was enforced reasonably sparingly, and transportation had been the main punishment for most crimes for many years before 1788.

If we look at the convict experience through the eyes and the story of an ancestor, our perspective is even more likely to be distorted, for all too often we are looking at what the convict officials in particular saw as the great success of the system. After all, you are a descendant, you are the evidence that it was all for the best, it all worked out well in the end.

However this is a very skewed perspective. Firstly, only a small minority of male convicts, and possibly only a bare majority of the female convicts, ever married or had descendants in the Australian colonies. Secondly, the vast majority were never in serious danger of being executed, however scary the prospect loomed to the individual facing the possibility of the hangman. Thirdly, a considerable majority of those found guilty of crimes that could lead to transportation were not transported at all; they were either sentenced to minor punishment or even when sentenced to transportation many were never sent.

The period of transportation of female convicts to the eastern colonies lasted for sixty-five years, 1788 to 1853, while the entire period of transportation of convicts from Britain to the Australian colonies lasted for eighty years, 1788 to 1868. This was also a period of modernisation in the British legal system.

To fully understand how all these parts of the jigsaw fit together, it is necessary to look at the British system of law and order from the other end, and begin with how that system threw up some people who were eventually sent to Australia.

The Modern and the Medieval: a patchwork not a plan

In the English or more generally the British tradition, somewhere between the Glorious Revolution of 1688 and the present day the recognisably modern world emerged. But it is not always easy for us to work out just which elements of the modern are already present at a given time, as distinct from those which seem to be modern but actually are not; and those which seem on the face of it to belong in the medieval world but which can, with an adjustment of thought, be seen have modern elements of thought behind it.

During the period that affected the transportation of convicts to Australia, there were quite extraordinary changes to the British criminal laws under which convicted felons were sentenced and there were, for instance, considerable differences between English and Scottish laws as well as considerable difference between the ways laws were applied in England and Wales, Scotland and Ireland. Most of us looking back to the legal system of the 1880s, well after transportation had ended, would readily appreciate the system of criminal law and order that prevailed at that time. However, the same cannot be said of the Britain of the 1780s, the era of the Bloody Code when the American War of Independence had made transportation of convicts impossible.

The terror factor

During the mid-1700s minor offences often attracted the death penalty, and this led the parliament to consider that more horrific crimes obviously required much more serious punishments than mere death. The terror factor in the punishments becomes more obvious. In 1752 the punishment for murder was supplemented by "some further Terror and peculiar Mark of Infamy" which consisted of immediate sentence of death upon conviction (rather than waiting for the last day of the Assizes) and execution within two days (so that appeals for clemency could not be heard). Meanwhile the convicted prisoner was to endure solitary confinement on bread and water until the execution.

After death the punishment was not yet complete and the body was to be handed over to the surgeons for dissection or to be hung in chains, and the convicted were to forfeit all their lands and goods. Severe penalties were prescribed for others who assisted in any way to avoid the strict carrying out of all details of the punishment including seven years transportation for rescuing or burying the body before dissection or the completion of the period of hanging in chains. The relatively immediate execution was obviously designed to strike terror, in that it restricted the possibility of applying for mercy. Solitary confinement meant that family and friends would have no chance to visit and say farewell. The diet of bread and water struck at the traditions of a last meal, and the fact that many eighteenth century executions were carried out on people who were drunk, sometimes to the point of total insensibility. But it was the last three conditions, of expropriation of property, dissection and hanging in chains, that probably caused the most terror.

Murder of a husband: 'burnt with fire until dead'

Women could be sentenced to be dissected under the terms of the 1752 Act but did not suffer the indignity of hanging in chains, though an even more horrific fate awaited those found guilty of petty treason. Petty treason, literally the lesser forms of being a traitor, referred to murder of either a lord by a vassal, a master by a servant or a husband by a wife and also to certain crimes against the state especially coining (counterfeiting, clipping, altering or colouring coin of the realm). The penalty for male coiners had for long been hanging, but until 1790, three years after the First Fleet sailed for Botany Bay, the sentence for women was still to be "drawn to the place of execution, and there burnt with fire until she was dead".

The actual executions were usually a little more humane than the sentence suggests. For at least most of the eighteenth century it was accepted that rather than being "drawn" (that is dragged) along the street by horses, the condemned would symbolically travel on a hurdle, sled or in a cart. It was also accepted that the executioner would strangle the woman before the fire had time to reach her, though to do so was strictly against the law and was in itself the capital crime of murder. Because the original crimes covered under petty treason were derived from treason itself, the rules regarding the criminality of accessories to even a very minor degree after the fact were extremely stringent so that someone with almost no knowledge or connection to the crime could be found guilty.

Such was the case in 1777 when a fourteen year old girl was having the faggots stacked around her body when the execution was stopped by Lord Weymouth who was just passing by at the time. Her crime was to have attempted to hide, at her master's orders, some white-washed farthings, and thus be guilty of being an accessory to coining but only through an extraordinarily distant chain of connection. The *Quarterly Review* said: "a mere accident saved the nation from this crime and this national disgrace". She was reprieved, though whether to merely hang or be transported we do not know. One wonders whether Lord Weymouth would have intervened had the condemned been middle-aged, or perhaps unattractive, or perhaps had been the much more culpable person who had actually carried out the coining.

In 1789 Christian Murphy was the last woman to be strangled and burnt in front of Newgate. The executioner, perhaps learning from previous experience, heaped so much wood around the body that it was completely covered. Within Newgate, and within earshot of the crowd that gathered to watch the execution, were women who had been sentenced to death, at least one by burning. It was only later that they were pardoned and transported to Botany Bay on the *Lady Juliana*.

In the following year the law was changed to exclude burning and the punishment for petty treason was changed so that, like murderers, women were now liable to be drawn and hanged within two days of their trial and then dissected by the surgeons.

Transportation before Australia

Transportation as a punishment similar in import to the later transportation of convicts to Australia was introduced to English Law by the Transportation Act 1718, though the concept and practice of transporting convicts had a much longer history. The 1718 Act came about because punishments for aggravated and ordinary thefts had not led to a decline in offences. Consequently transportation to the American and Caribbean colonies for seven years could be ordered by the courts for non-hanging (non-capital) offences while anyone pardoned for a capital offence would be punished by transportation for fourteen years. Any convict returning to

Britain before serving the full period of transportation would be hanged.

Within a few years of the 1718 Act, transportation had become a popular punishment for people convicted of non-capital property offences. In the Surrey Courts, roughly 60% of the men and 45% of the women found guilty of such offences were sentenced to exile in America. Before the Act, more than half of both male and female offenders had been branded and discharged.

The other big change was that now both petty larceny and grand larceny (small and large theft) were transportable offences. Many offenders who prior to 1718 would have been merely whipped and discharged for petty theft could now be transported instead. Before 1718 grand larceny was a capital crime and the juries could significantly mitigate the punishment by deciding whether to reduce the charge from grand larceny to petty larceny by stating a lower value to the goods stolen. After 1718 the punishment was entirely at the judge's discretion. Neither of these changes worked to the advantage of the accused.

When transportation to the American colonies suddenly ceased in 1776 due to the American rebellion and then independence, no decision was made as to how to handle the emergency. Instead, England's tradition of judicial hairsplitting and pettifogging took on a decidedly ridiculous and farcical nature, humorous only if you weren't one of the poor wretches who received the brunt of its savage punishments. With no transports being sent, Newgate was soon full of prisoners sentenced to be transported but with literally nowhere to go. Initially, many of the men were sent on board ships on the Thames, but there was no legal right to keep them there nor to alter their punishment to a lesser or a different form. It was obvious that the government didn't have a clue as to what to do. Under-secretary of State William Eden wrote that the convicts were to be taken:

immediately aboard some proper vessel … in the usual manner, …after which the matter will, as soon as possible have every proper consideration, and such further steps be taken as may be thought expedient.

What eventually turned out to be the 'expedient' further steps, following 'every proper consideration', was worthy of a Monty Python or a Blackadder comedy. The government had no alternative but to set the convicts free, either by sending them to the army or navy, or merely by giving them an instruction that they were to transport themselves. Historian JM Beattie questions whether either the convicted or the authorities thought they were being serious in this, and it is unclear whether anybody actually did transport themselves although presumably those who didn't were liable to be punished for 'returning from transportation', which was itself a capital offence.

Other convicts, particularly the women but also at least one man convicted of the capital offence of highway robbery, were just granted free pardons and immediately sent back into society. JM Beattie gives the extraordinary case of another man condemned to death who was pardoned providing he took on a fourteen year apprenticeship with a small merchant. One wonders how many of these pardoned convicts attended the hanging holidays at Tyburn and other places of execution to watch other people convicted of the same crimes end their days in the excruciating agony of slow strangulation.

No destination but death

Similar levels of farce attended the reintroduction of transportation in 1783, at the end of the American war. As soon as the war was over the courts reintroduced sentences of transportation and the numbers sentenced rose significantly. However, three years later the Corporation of the City of London protested in a petition that there was a 'rapid and alarming increase of crimes' which they believed were caused by the failure of the government to transport at least four thousand persons still in England but who, in the judgement of the law, were 'proper to have sent out of it', but who instead had either already been released or were about to be released.

The government had reintroduced transportation without having anywhere to send the convicts. Somehow or another they seemed to believe that having finished the war, transportation to America would just automatically start up again. It took a while for it to sink in that the newly independent United States would not be happy to take the refuse from their gaols.

As we can see from the London petition, the backlog of convicts who were serving their sentences in prisons or had already been released back into British society was causing a crisis of confidence in the value of penal sentences. The judges recognised this as well, and death sentences and actual executions rose to a fever pitch. There was no perceived alternative.

This was the orgy of public slaughter that marked the years from the Gordon riots of 1780 to the availability of New South Wales as a convict colony in 1788.

The American war had a two-pronged effect on the punishment of serious offenders. The war had deprived Britain of its traditional dumping ground for transporting convicts while the end of the war had drastically increased the number of offenders that the courts wished to seriously punish, as quantities of young men demobilised from the army and navy turned to crime due to the lack of employment and a post-war economic slump.

Meanwhile, some male convicts were being sentenced to the hulks on the Thames and in Portsmouth harbour, though the judges (in Surrey at least) were not keen on this alternative. Women were being sent to the Houses of Correction, but most of those sentenced to transportation ended up serving limited sentences in the prisons before being released back into their former lives of crime, much to the chagrin of worthy citizens like the mayor and aldermen of London.

A bandage for the Bloody Code

Eventually the British government decided to send its convicts to Botany Bay, New South Wales. Transportation to Botany Bay had a great advantage over the American colonies. It was much further away and consequently people sent there were much less likely to return to Britain before their sentences had been served or, for that matter, even after they were free again.

So like execution, transportation to Botany Bay meant that the recidivism rate in Britain could be effectively curtailed, since most of those sent there could be considered to be exiled forever. On the other hand, transportation, unlike execution, was not likely to raise humanitarian concerns about the excesses of the Bloody Code. And indeed as pointed out by Leon Radzinowicz, historian of English criminal law, though many people criticised various elements of transportation as a punishment, throughout its history there was never any fuss raised as to whether the degree of severity of the sentence fitted the degree of criminality of the offence.

Whereas some voices were raised as to whether particular crimes, especially non-violent property crimes, merited the death sentence, there was no parallel protest that many of the crimes of the convicts were not sufficiently blameworthy to merit three or four years forced labour combined with what, for almost all of them, was effectively a lifetime's exile.

Matching the time to the crime, or not

Whilst transportation was originally designed to provide an alternative for execution, it was never planned to be a replacement for it. However, though it is a very subtle point, there is no doubt that transportation entirely replaced benefit of the clergy and similar forms of automatic release for the guilty and enabled more judicial and royal pardons so that the conditions attached to respite from the gallows were still seen to be very strongly punitive. Though from the bloody 1780s the proportion of pardons increased much more than executions, nevertheless for fifteen years, from the Battle of Waterloo to the end of the 1820s, the number of executions remained high, and still reflected government and judicial attitudes to how best to control crime rates by fear.

What transportation was meant to do was to break up the criminal fraternities that contemporary Britain saw as the cause of most crime. However, the authorities were never quite sure where transportation stood in comparison to other alternatives to the death penalty which had been used hitherto, such as imprisonment and whipping. Imprisonment was considered a harsher punishment than transportation, and the period of imprisonment actually served in place of transportation was significantly less than the period of transportation. For instance, before she was transported in 1825 per the *Midas* as the result of a conviction for larceny, Ann Maloney had previously been sentenced to seven years transportation for shoplifting but had served three years at the Millbank Penitentiary instead. Similarly, on the same ship was Maria Green who had previously been released following five years servitude at Millbank although sentenced to transportation for Life.

New South Wales Governor Gipps wrote to the Secretary of State for the Colonies, Lord Stanley, about this issue in 1843. The female convicts held in prison-like conditions at the Parramatta Female Factory following the cessation of transportation to NSW complained to him that they had been sentenced to transportation, not imprisonment. They argued that sentences for transportation for between seven years and Life had, at the Millbank Penitentiary in London, been typically transmuted into sentences at hard labour for between three to five years, whereas at Parramatta they were expected to serve four to eight years at similar labour and under similar conditions. Furthermore, they argued, the Millbank prisoners gained a free release after their sentence whereas their own release from Parramatta was highly conditional, not allowing them to return home until they could achieve a free pardon. For Lifers this could mean at least 24 years, sometimes never. Unspoken, but no doubt on their minds, was the fact that the Millbank women found themselves immediately back in British society whereas the NSW women had little chance of ever getting back to Britain. Gipps realised that the women had a valid case and arranged that they be assigned to settlers in spite of the fact that the whole of the then dominant probation period ethic was that private unpaid assignment was unconscionable, bearing too much resemblance to slavery. Obviously, in Gipps' mind it was the lesser of the two evils and there was both merit in the women's case and a degree of justice in his decision.

The balancing of a lesser term of imprisonment versus transportation was offset by the fact that convicts were usually able to gain a ticket-of-leave, that they could work for private masters or the government without being held under close confinement, and that exile was designed to be the principal punishment element of their sentence. The tradition of transported convicts receiving a limited freedom such as a ticket-of-leave, after a fixed period and providing they were of good behaviour, went back at least to the mid-seventeenth century when some sentences of transportation for seven years were phrased: 'the last three for their own benefit'.

Another war ends, another crime wave begins

When the inevitable crimewave got underway in 1815, following the end of the Napoleonic Wars and the resulting unemployment of demobilised young men coincided with the post-war economic depression, the numbers of convicts being transported to New South Wales grew substantially. But this was not just because there were more crimes. Other factors contributed.

No longer was there a need for so many male convicts to be kept in the naval dockyards and Thames-side hulk gangs to provide free labour for the war effort. No longer did the armed forces soak up some of those on the run or those who got caught and chose enlistment rather than prosecution. But most of the increase in convict transportations can be attributed to the response from the British legal system which not only increased death sentences leading to increased use of transportation as an alternative to execution (capital respite) but also hugely increased the numbers directly sentenced to transportation. Not only were more people being sentenced to transportation but also a much larger percentage were now actually being transported, and not just to New South Wales. Men were also now being transported directly to Van Diemen's Land and as of 1820 women also would be sent directly to VDL.

And no longer was it the case that transported convicts were nearly all serious offenders, repeat offenders or minor offenders suspected of being members of criminal confraternities. A much higher percentage were clearly first offenders. Transportation, rather than being reserved for the worst ne'er-do-wells, was becoming a standard part of British judicial sentencing policy, and at least in England, Wales and Ireland it was increasingly applied to those who in former times would have been whipped or gaoled for a short period. But those options were less and less available because instead of putting more and more resources into building prisons for the rapidly expanding population, the scarce resources were directed towards the convict colonies. The building of prisons in Britain lagged behind the development of the new prison, Australia.

The old order changes...

The period from 1780 to 1850 was a time of immense changes in Britain: demographic, economic, cultural, social and legal. This was the period of a huge increase in the British and particularly the Irish populations. This was also the period of the greatest impact of the industrial and agricultural revolutions and almost calamitous effects of rapid urbanisation. During this period the laws relating to crime, as well as the Poor Laws, the Corn Laws and the laws relating to the legal rights of Catholics were changed dramatically.

In the middle of the period not only was there the Great Reform Bill but also the creation of such modern institutions as gaols and police forces, registration of births, deaths and marriages and great changes to laws and

---

The 'Black Box'

...This was a box made like a coffin standing on its end - one can neither sit or lie, nor indeed stand comfortably - with little holes at the top to breathe through. It is anything but a pleasant place. It was placed on board for the use of the women - there were some placed in there every day. [As punishment Smith was locked in for 14 hours.]

James Montagu Smith, on the *Sir Robert Seppings* in 1852

attitudes relating to slavery. It was also the time of the Napoleonic Wars, Irish rebellions and a long series of civil disturbances in England, Wales and Scotland. There were extraordinary social and economic dislocations from the continuing enclosure and privatisation of English common lands, the Scottish highland clearances, repeated and frequent economic depressions, famines, and the effects on trade and industry of rapid technological progress.

At the same time vast numbers of people were removed from the traditional support of the old parishes that supplied the only form of social security. And in the 1840s came the Great Irish Famine when millions of people starved amongst warehouses stuffed with food which was exported to the urban workers in Britain and Europe who could afford it.

By 1880 laws had been codified or expressed in much the same way as they are today, by a parliament which was recognisable as a modern and to some extent democratic institution. If anything, the laws themselves, with the exception of a few archaic leftovers, were extremely modern and readily recognisable.

Throughout this period of enormous change 160,000 Britons were exiled to the Australian colonies, the vast majority never to see their country again. Of these convicts almost 25,000 were women, of whom slightly more than half served their exile in Van Diemen's Land.

...giving place to new

If Britain changed enormously in this period, the Australian colonies changed even more; from the early tent and bark hut camps in the first years to significant small cities and large towns in the latter period; from small gardens, farms and orchards in the first ten years of each settlement to vast sheep runs, wheat farms and cattle properties of the later years. Every female convict did not come from a similar society and background, and when she arrived she did not find herself in a similar situation to those who had come before or would come after. Convict society was dynamic and it changed and developed considerably from period to period and from place to place.

The First Fleet to Botany Bay meant exile to a place that nobody knew at the furthest end of the earth. The last convict transports to Eastern Australia in the early 1850s, on the other hand, were being sent to one of the most fabulous and most sought-after places to be created in the imagination of nineteenth century Europe. A place where it was thought incredible riches could be just picked up from the ground, and where wealth had no memory, as it did in Europe. A place where if you were used to hard manual work, you had an advantage over the aristocratic and middle classes. A place where Jack was not just as good as his master, but where, with luck, Jack might become better than his master.

The middle period, too was a time when, following the hard early years, many commentators perceived that convicts were going to a situation where they were materially much better off than in Britain and more particularly than in Ireland. It was true that even while they were still assigned servants many, perhaps the majority, ate better, were better clad and had better quarters than the poorest twenty or twenty-five percent of people in Britain from which the vast majority of the convicts came. Physical conditions for the majority of convicts were probably vastly superior to fifty to sixty percent or even more of the Irish peasantry. Social and political commentators were quick to point this out; indeed they often referred to conditions in the English gaols, particularly the Millbank Penitentiary, completed in 1821 and costing over £500,000, in similar terms.

Some contemporary commentators even went so far as to describe transportation as a reward that many honest hardworking folk would love to attain. Some modern Australian historians, particularly in the 1950s and 1960s, were often quick to agree and emphasised how much better off materially the majority of the convicts were. This view was commonplace also in general Australian society, and many triumphalist accounts abound of convict ancestors who deliberately offended in order to get good food and a free voyage to the new country of opportunity.

While there is no doubt that some convicts were deliberate offenders, they appear to have been very few. There is some evidence that some of the Irish during the 1840s may have sought transportation to escape the horrors of the Great Famine.

> **She refused to eat**
>
> One woman and three children [actually five children] died on the voyage …She refused to eat and literally died of starvation.
>
> James Montagu Smith, on the *Sir Robert Seppings*, 1852

There is also a parallel idea that the occasional kindly magistrate in Ireland during the famine used his official position to throw a lifeline to starving peasants. This is a standard Australian story but the offence most likely to have led to this, vagrancy, was if anything a less common reason for transportation from Ireland during this period. Moreover it fails to take into account the peculiarly and particularly high absolute horror that some amongst the Irish female convicts had of being sent out of their country. This was particularly noted by the Surgeon-superintendents who had experience of shiploads of both British and Irish convicts.

There is no doubt that there were convicts who were victims in being unjustly convicted. Similarly, there is no doubt there were political and social rebels who were transported, though there were virtually none amongst the women, just a bare handful. There is no doubt that most convicts were victims of an unduly vicious and unfairly harsh system of criminal punishment. However, it is readily ascertainable from the statistics that the overwhelming majority of female convicts sent to Australia would have faced significant judicial sanctions whatever day, age or place they were sentenced.

The question though is not whether they should have been punished, the question is whether there was any justifiable reason for punishing them so harshly. The answer to our modern minds is of course that they should not have been punished by what to most was a lifetime of exile, and to that extent and in that way there is no doubt that most were more sinned against than sinning.

Divorced by distance

Q: In marrying the Convicts or Emancipated Persons here, what evidence do you require of their single condition?
A: Merely their Declaration, and not on Oath.
Q: Have Instances occurred in which you have detected a former Marriage?
A: It has occurred Three times, I think.

Evidence of Rev. Robert Knopwood, Colonial Chaplain, Hobart Town; to Commissioner Bigge, 3 April 1820

Q: When parties apply to you to be married and you entertain a suspicion of a former marriage, what course do you pursue?
A: I refer them to the Magistrate of the District, who Investigates the Matter, and, if he is satisfied that there is no former marriage, I am governed by his decision.
Q: Have you some reason to believe that many apply who have been formerly and are still married, tho. separated from their wives?
A: A great many, and there is a general belief amongst the convicts that those, who have been Transported to this Country, are released from their matrimonial engagements.
Q: Does this belief do you think extend to those transported for short Terms, or only those whose sentence to Death has been commuted for a sentence of Transportation for Life?
A: I believe that all the Convicts think that a Sentence of Transportation for any Term releases them from their Engagements.

Evidence of Rev. J Youl, Chaplain, Launceston; to Commissioner Bigge, 27 April 1820

Chapter 4. The Women

There is no doubt that women were treated more favourably than men at each step in the British justice process. Some observers have attributed this to an innate form of chivalry, or to embarrassment, but others are not so sure. Historian J.M. Beattie, for one, comments that any society that burned women at the stake for some offences, or flogged them half naked around the streets tied to the back of a cart for being scandal-mongers, was unlikely to be so far burdened by chivalry or gender-based embarrassment so as to have 'a persistent tendency to let women off more lightly than men'. Instead he suggests:

Any chivalrous feelings in the jury box and on the bench were encouraged and allowed expression by the fact that women were less frequently charged with serious offences, that they posed a less serious threat to lives, property and order. It was not necessary that large numbers of women be punished in public. The broader purposes of the law and of the administration of justice could be served by the very occasional example of a woman harshly dealt with.

Beattie's survey of trial jury verdicts in Surrey to 1800 shows that not only were women far more likely to be found innocent, but also that those found guilty were far more likely to receive the benefit of a partial verdict, especially in those property crimes where a full verdict would incur the death sentence.

We can come to a general conclusion that women were treated much more leniently than men in the general run of the law. Certainly this has been a fairly common perception, which was confirmed by Beattie's conclusions about what was happening in Surrey.

This perception continued for most of the transportation period, however once we come to deal with the mid to late 1840s and early 1850s it becomes a lot less clear that women were being treated better than the men. Lord Stanley, Secretary of State for the Colonies, writing to Sir John Franklin in 1842 makes it quite clear that while a lot fewer of the men sentenced to transportation would actually be sent to Van Diemen's Land, the number of women to be transported had to be increased:

Looking to the alarming disproportion... in Van Diemen's Land between the sexes, it would obviously be the policy and the wish to carry into actual execution the sentence of transportation on females as generally as possible...

However Stanley recognised that there would be problems. The women would have even greater opportunities and incentives to "vice and crime", presumably by working as prostitutes in a society so short of women, or by being placed in household situations where they would be tempted to sexual misdemeanours because they possessed: "neither sound principles, nor feelings of self-respect to protect them".

Who were the female convicts and where did they come from?

In 1965 Lloyd Robson published *The convict settlers of Australia*. This was the result of a statistical study of five percent of all the convicts sent to Australia. Using the results of his work we can fairly easily gain some general perspectives of the circumstances of the male and female convicts. Of course, this sort of work has its drawbacks, and what may be able to be fairly truthfully said about the aggregate of the women who were sent to Australia, and Van Diemen's Land in particular, cannot in any sense be transferred to the individual women, or even to small groups of the women. In particular Robson does not separate out those women who served their sentences in Van Diemen's Land, which is our particular interest; and what was true of the women as a whole does not always apply to Van Diemen's Land. For instance, different colonies did not receive equal numbers of women from a particular country, and that in turn meant differences in religious background.

Young and beautiful, pale as death

There were not a great many very bad characters. The greater number were for petty crimes, and a great proportion for only being disorderly, that is, street-walkers.... One a Scottish girl, broke her heart and died in the river. She was buried at Dartford. Four were pardoned on account of His Majesty's recovery. The poor young Scottish girl I have never got out of my mind. She was young and beautiful, even in the convict dress, but pale as death, and her eyes red with weeping.

John Nicol, on the *Lady Juliana* 1790

The lack of Irish in Van Diemen's Land

Of the female convicts transported to New South Wales prior to 1841, roughly forty percent were Irish, a total of about 5,000 women. But no female convict ship was sent direct from Ireland to Van Diemen's Land before the arrival of the *Mary Anne* on 19 March 1841.

Prior to then about 3,500 female convicts had been sent to Van Diemen's Land but of that number only two or three hundred, well under ten percent, had been convicted in Irish courts and transported from Irish ports. Even those had not come directly to VDL. They had first arrived in Sydney on ships direct from Ireland such as the *Catherine* in 1814, *Alexander* in 1815, *Canada* in 1817; or ships such as the *Janus* in 1820, which was one of the rare ships with a combination of Irish and English convicted women on board. There were also Irish born women in every draft of English and Scottish convicts, typically ten to fifteen percent of the total in each. These were women who had earlier migrated to England and Scotland and were convicted there before being sent to VDL.

Of the eventual total of well over 13,000 female convicts who came to Van Diemen's Land, close to one-third had arrived by 1840 and of them less than one in ten were of Irish origin. The lack of Irishness in the first thirty percent of women convicts sent to VDL had important ramifications. Obviously it meant that VDL was to be less Catholic in its general composition than New South Wales. As late as the 1950s New South Wales had a much higher proportion of Catholics than Tasmania.

'Scottish women were the most abandoned'

Scottish courts were notoriously reluctant to transport women with few previous convictions unless it was a particularly serious crime. According to Robson between 72 and 95 percent of Scottish women had one or more previous offences. Women convicted in the Irish courts on the other hand were far less likely to have offended before and only between 26 and 62 percent had a previous conviction.

Robson comments on this outcome:

> Six out of every ten [of the total women transported] had formerly been convicted, but Scottish and English-tried women were more likely than the Irish to have been punished previously. If, then, it were decided to consider the number of previous convictions as a

criterion of criminality, the Scottish women were the most abandoned, followed by the English, and then the Irish. Nearly half of the women who had previously been punished more than four times were Scottish, and those convicted by the Glasgow Court of Justiciary were the worst of a bad lot.

In spite of this, the terms of transportation inflicted on Scottish women are less than would reflect their relative previous criminality, although the punishments of the Irish women do. This represents the difference shown by the legal systems and courts. Scotland was proud of the difference and separation of its legal system from that of England, and the Scots were far less likely to exile a criminal for a minor offence, but instead more often used the gaols and other forms of punishment. It was from Scotland that most of the those convicted of being an habitual criminal (usually termed 'theft, habit and repute') were sent. In order to convict a woman as an habitual criminal, hard evidence of a number of previous convictions was required. Similarly hard evidence was then required by the Scottish courts of the woman's irreclaimable nature before transportation was considered merited.

In England, evidence of previous offences increased the likelihood of a sentence of transportation and, once sentenced, seems to have increased the chances of a woman actually being transported. Nevertheless many women were still transported from England for what we would consider fairly minor first offences.

But it was from Ireland that the overwhelming number of minor first offenders were transported, and for that matter the overwhelming number of rural and economically distressed female convicts. Economically things

---

Sweethearts

The women were a curious lot enough, nearly all short sentences, seven or fourteen years. Every sailor had one or more sweethearts with whom he carried on a correspondence by means of letters. They were allowed on deck during the day and in fine weather had their meals there; but were all sent below and locked up at sunset. The only means of communicating with the 'tween decks being by means of the hospital in the after part.

James Montagu Smith, on the *Sir Robert Seppings* in 1852

were not good in Ireland even well before the Great Famine in the 1840s. The potato harvest failed frequently during the first four decades of the century. This was the reason of course why so many young women found themselves in the English and Scottish cities and industrial areas, often without friends and family, and were transported from there to the Antipodes.

The city girls

Almost ninety percent of the transported women were of childbearing age. The proportion goes up to 94% if we include women to age 44. To further summarise the statistical analysis done by Lloyd Robson in 1965, over seventy percent of the female convicts were of prime childbearing age, being under the age of thirty.

In Ireland as in England and Scotland it was from the cities and industrial areas that most of the convicts were sent to New South Wales and Van Diemen's Land. Six major regions were the places of trial for almost half the women transported to Australia: London, Lancashire, Dublin, Cork, Yorkshire, Glasgow and Edinburgh. But of those women, a quarter who were convicted in the cities, were convicted in Irish cities, which were as prone as the English and Scottish cities to criminal behaviour of much the same kind.

Marital Status: sometimes a matter of opinion

Of the 945 women in Robson's sample for whom we have marriage data, 321 were married or widowed. This is about one-third of them, and the proportion is much the same whichever country they were convicted in, whether England, Scotland or Ireland.

However this is a somewhat slippery figure. Robson had no marriage data at all for 303 women in his sample. Sometimes no reference meant that the woman was single and at other times it meant merely that she had not been asked. Sometimes a woman answered that she was married when she meant she had been cohabiting with someone, and was not legally married. At other times she would lie and claim she was single, knowing that her best chance in the colonies was to get married; or a woman would answer truthfully but confusingly that she was not married, since she and many others considered that a sentence of transportation to the colonies for seven years or more constituted a de facto divorce.

We have similar problems when dealing with those who claimed to be widowed. People convicted in the United Kingdom were well aware of how the convict system worked and were also aware of the authorities' lack of knowledge about their background. They appear to have frequently used the terms widowed and single both to describe their being married and separated in the UK and also their future state of separation caused by the transportation process.

Because the colonial authorities placed a great deal of store by marriage as a reformatory process and were reluctant to sanction de facto relationships, indeed they were often specifically punitive on women and men who were living together but not legally married, they themselves often ignored the evidence of previous marriage. Knopwood, the first colonial chaplain in Van Diemen's Land, made it a point never to enquire too closely about a person's current marital status.

Their Religion

Using Robson's statistics we can calculate that of the female convicts sent to the Australian colonies, about 58% were Protestant and 42% were Catholic. Van Diemen's Land received a much lower percentage of Catholics than this overall average.

Their Crimes

Of Robson's sample of 1248 cases (5% of the 25,000 female convicts sent to the Australian colonies), only 1138 had the offence for which they were transported recorded. Of these the vast majority, 1080 women, or 95%,

---

Love and rivets

...When we were fairly out to sea, every man on board took a wife from among the convict... they nothing loath. The girl with whom I lived, for I was as bad in this point as the others, was named Sarah Whitlam... I courted her for a week and upwards, and would have married her on the spot had there been a clergyman on board .... I had fixed my fancy upon her from the moment I knocked the rivet out of her irons upon my anvil.

John Nicol, on the *Lady Juliana* in 1790

---

were transported for some species of theft without any particular mention of violence either threatened or actual.

Robson lists these crimes under the following categories: larceny (theft), 587; theft of wearing apparel, 199; robbery, 67; receiving, 52; theft of an animal (not poaching), 46; burglary or housebreaking, 40; forgery, 5; stealing by trick or embezzlement, 5; coining or uttering, 23; theft, habit and repute (being an habitual criminal), 39; vagrancy, 17. Another two women were convicted of perjury.

For the remaining 56 women, 27 were convicted of wilful destruction. However, only 29 committed violence against persons: robbery with violence 14; murder or manslaughter 10; assault 4; aiding and abetting rape 1.

This is in considerable contrast to the men where out of a total sample of 6131 the offence for which they were transported is recorded in 5713 cases. Of these 240 (4.2%) were transported for offences for which there were no parallels amongst the women. Eighty-five men were transported for political or social unrest including treason and 155 for military offences. Of the remaining 5473, a total of 5111 (93.4%) were transported for similar theft categories to the women: larceny 2117; theft of wearing apparel 379; robbery 402; receiving 97; theft of an animal (not poaching) 813; burglary or housebreaking 907; forgery 35; stealing by trick or embezzlement 75; coining or uttering 121; theft, habit and repute 94; vagrancy 44, but also poaching 23; and smuggling 4. In additional crimes we have: perjury 14; wilful destruction 49; sacrilege 11; bigamy 10. The 93.4% theft rate amongst the men in itself is not strikingly different to the female 95% theft rate.

But it is in the type and seriousness of violent crimes that the men differed most significantly to the women: robbery with violence 68; murder or manslaughter 81; assault 80; rape 25; to which we can add abduction 9; other sexual offences 3; and threats and menaces 12.

Thus, out of 1138 women only 29 (2.55%) were transported for serious crimes of violence against the person but of 5473 men, 278 (5.08%) were transported for similar offences. In other words, this sample indicates that female convicts were only half as likely as male convicts to have behaved violently.

Time to pay the price

In the United Kingdom, whilst convict men almost invariably had to walk, or rather march in chain-gangs, to either the transhipment or embarkation ports, the women were carried in open carts or on the tops of the public coaches that plied the highways between major towns. Better than walking perhaps, but many of the women were ill-provided for travelling on the outside of the coaches. Sometimes they had insufficient clothing to even properly cover themselves and it was not unknown for women to arrive frost-bitten and suffering from other physical disabilities brought on by the ravages of exposure and hypothermia. Some no doubt were lucky and had family or friends who were able and willing to supply them with proper clothing for the journey. Certainly few of the women were provided with cloaks or other outdoor apparel suited for and essential for travel at any time other than during the best of the summer. Many coaches kept travelling through the night and even in summer the effects of the cold night air on incompletely dressed people would have been quite unbearable.

Some of the county gaols were quite solicitous about the care of their charges during the journey to the ships, and made considerable efforts to see that, though they might hardly be called comfortable, chained as they were to each other and to the coach, at least they had adequate food and clothing for the journey. But far too often the gaols and the local authorities just wanted to get rid of the women in the fastest and most expeditious manner possible. This was a theme that continued throughout the convict period.

The counties and parishes also wanted to get rid of as many undesirables

---

There was no taming her

Under instruction, John Nicol, a seaman on the *Lady Juliana* in 1790, made up an old flour barrel with holes for head and arms which they called a "wooden jacket" and which was used to punish Elizabeth Farrell who was continually troublesome. At first she made light of it. Later she begged to be forgiven but a few days later "was as bad as ever. There was no taming her by gentle means. We were forced to tie her up like a man, and give her one dozen with the cat-o'-nine-tails."

John Nicol on the *Lady Juliana*, 1790

34

as possible in ways that made them a charge on the central government rather than on their own funds. As long as a woman, particularly a woman with children, remained in Britain there was always a potential threat that they might become a charge on their home parish. This of course was particularly so with those of feeble mind or with signs of mental illness, but it was also true of those whose reputation as a thief or a prostitute reduced the chances of them ever getting gainful and ongoing employment.

A similar situation happened with those women who, either constitutionally or through illness, were unlikely to survive the journey to the colonies. As much as the government insisted that all the female convicts being transported should be fit and well before undertaking the voyage, the county, parish and gaol authorities flouted the guidelines and continued to send inappropriate choices. There was often an element of collusion between the local authorities and the convicts themselves, not all of whom were averse to going to Australia, with the women falsifying their situation to the Surgeon-superintendent, sometimes successfully. This way quite serious underlying conditions were only discovered after the ship had sailed. Surgeon-superintendents sometimes found themselves overwhelmed by the sheer number of arrivals, particularly at the last moment. They found themselves with insufficient time or background information to enable them to make a reasonable decision, particularly since the majority of their charges would have been more than happy to have been refused to be taken on board and returned to the gaol.

A great deal of crying and yelling

…the women were sent on board …two hundred and fifty of them [actually 220], besides children. Their appearance was anything but promising; that greatest ornament of women, hair, had been cut pretty close, and there was a great deal of crying and yelling together with considerable sea-sickness. When one reads of thieves and other bad characters one thinks of them with disgust and abhorrence. But if you see them every day, this feeling gradually wears off and you find there is not so much difference between them and the world after all… The sailors soon became intimately acquainted with them, and I was frequently employed to write love letters for the old salts.

All the fiends of hell and Bedlam

The system of government was founded on the old proverb 'Set a thief to catch a thief'. Several of them were promoted and promised rewards to watch over the rest - thus, one not being able to trust the other, they were all kept under. These constables were far more tyrannical to their fellow prisoners than free ones would have been. They had several fights among themselves, and once there was a general melee caused by the tyranny of the constables. This made more noise than all the fiends of hell and Bedlam let loose, but did very little damage. The hatches were put on and some of them were informed that the sailors would leave in boats and scuttle the ship if they were not quiet. On this lie getting wind, they raised such awful yells that it was truly horrible to hear them. Fancy the lungs of two hundred and fifty well-conditioned women, and pretty good lungs some of them had too. They were soon quieted and the officers sent down to apprehend the most violent.

They were taken on the poop and put in irons. The mate was very violent to several of them. One of them gave him such a tongue-whacking that he was trying to gag her, but he was served out for she caught his fingers between her teeth and bit them to the bone. He struck her violently in the face with his disengaged hand. At this unmanly act there was a great shout among the women and enquiry was made into the cause by the Skipper, and the mate was severely reprimanded

James Montagu Smith, on the *Sir Robert Seppings* in 1852

Chapter 5. Perils at Sea

In the English spring of 1820 the *Morley* was preparing for her third voyage as a convict transport to New South Wales. She had been built on the Thames only nine years earlier. The 480 ton *Morley* was, like nearly all the convict transports, a three-masted ship-rigged vessel. If it was fairly standard of its type it would have had an overall length of between 33 and 36 metres and a beam of perhaps a little less than 10 metres.

She had been fitted out at the naval dockyards at Deptford on the Thames on 24 March 1820 almost two months before she was due to sail. The ship remained at Deptford for another eighteen days while the shipyard workers under the instruction of an appointee of the Naval Board fitted out the ship for her special cargo. The *Morley*, like the vast mass of convict transports used on the voyages to Australian colonies, was a normal merchant ship of the period, designed to carry cargo and a few cabin passengers. The shipyard carpenters not only had to create a prison in the between-deck holds, but at the same time they had to convert a cargo carrier into a people carrier. It wasn't just a matter of sealing off the lower decks in such a manner that the prisoners could only come out up through a barred gateway. Firstly, the very lowest deck holds not only had to be sealed off from the prisoners above, they had to have access past the 'tween deck to enable the shifting of substantial cargo. This cargo was the vast quantity of extra water and foodstuffs needed to feed not only the prisoners but also the crew and other passengers for a period of four months. Other cargo, much in the same line of the usual carried on behalf of the shipowners for the colony of New South Wales and its sub-colony Van Diemen's Land, would have been stowed even further down in the holds. Between April 18 and May 20 the convicts arrived.

It was most probably a clear moonlit night at Galleons Reach on the lower Thames in the early morning of 20 May 1820 when the *Morley* weighed anchor at 3am and slipped quietly down the river. Seven o'clock found her at Gravesend still within the estuary of the Thames, and, as the crow flies, just a little over thirty kilometres from the centre of London. On her six voyages between the years 1817 and 1829 the *Morley* altogether successfully carried 1,019 convicts to Australia, six having died en route.

more children

lowever, this trip was to be a voyage with a difference, for this time instead of male prisoners the *Morley* was carrying women and children: 121 female convicts and some of their younger children, 33 girls and 17 boys. Although the majority of this human cargo was heading for Sydney, fifty of the women together with their children were destined to be the first female convicts from Britain to arrive directly at Hobart Town.

Critical to the safety of the convicts and their children was the presence on board of a medical man in a capacity created a bare five years before: that of the Surgeon-superintendent. Thomas Reid was a veteran of a previous voyage to NSW, almost three years earlier in 1817-1818 when he had shepherded 173 male convicts on board the *Neptune* to Sydney. On that voyage three of his charges had died. The *Morley* was to prove to be both a safe and a swift conveyance for the convicts, taking a mere 14 weeks and a day, to travel from England to Van Diemen's Land, and although a number of children died, no female convicts died during the voyage.

Starting with the *Morley*, fourteen ships carrying female convicts arrived in Hobart Town directly from Britain in the ten years between 1820 and 1829. Seven of the first eight left approximately half their human cargo in Van Diemen's Land before continuing on with the remainder to Sydney. On board these fourteen ships, 1499 women left the United Kingdom, 1101 disembarked in Hobart Town, 384 carried on to Sydney and 14 (less than 1%) died on the voyage.

Riot, wickedness and abandonment

...there was infinitely more riot, wickedness and abandonment, amongst the seven [free] women who were permitted to accompany the soldiers that formed the guard in the *Neptune* in 1817, than amongst all the female convicts in the *Morley* put together.

Thomas Reid, on the *Morley*, 1820

Enticed by Sailors

Four women on the *Morley* received the same comment from Surgeon-superintendent Reid regarding their conduct on the voyage:
"Was enticed by the sailors to get out of the prison one night privately: her conduct previously was excellent, and since that her pentitence has been sincere and her behaviour exemplary."

38

The fourteen who died give us some insight into the dangers on board the female convict ships. Two were killed by accidents which were typical of the dangers of shipboard life and which, considering the total numbers, could scarcely be avoided. One fell overboard and another was hit by a falling spar. Another died in childbirth, which once again, considering the total numbers and the unavoidable dangers of early nineteenth century confinements was probably better than average for the times. Only three women died from diseases or due to the conditions on board, which again is an extraordinarily low mortality rate for voyages of an average of four months duration. However, a further eight women died of the effects of pre-existing conditions which had most likely been exacerbated by the sea voyage.

However, the voyage to Australia had not always been as safe for the convicts, nor would it continue to be as safe, particularly for female convicts.

From First Fleet to last voyage: the women's experience

The First Fleet (arrived Sydney Cove 1788) was a model of planning. Governor Arthur Phillip was an extremely experienced seaman and he was lucky to have subordinates who were able to carry out his instructions efficiently. There was a high percentage of people with medical training or experience on the fleet and Phillip used them effectively. The provisions he took on board were first class, but also he had experience of the subterfuges used by the suppliers and by the individual captains to make excessive profits at the expense of their passengers. Above all he was a wise and humane man who was determined that the voyage would reflect the way that he meant to go on as leader of the new colony.

Although the women on the First Fleet were scattered across four ships, the majority were on board the *Lady Penrhyn* and at the conclusion of the voyage the Assistant Surgeon Boyes commented in his diary how remarkably well the health of the women had been maintained in spite of overcrowding. Of the two who had died on board the ship during the voyage, one was an invalid aged 82 and the other had been in an advanced stage of tuberculosis at the beginning of the voyage. Another of the women embarked on the *Lady Penrhyn* had died of fever during the four months between embarkation and the fleet putting to sea.

The Second and Third Fleets which arrived in 1790 and 1791 were both catastrophes. Day after day the ships arrived in Sydney Cove loaded to the gunwales with dead, dying and violently sick male and female convicts. The lack of a strong leader, good medical direction and proper planning combined with poor quality ships, gross overcrowding, fear of mutiny which had kept the prisoners chained up below, sometimes for weeks on end up to their waists in water, and the rapaciousness and callousness of the ships' officers in stealing the convicts' provisions and medicinal supplies had led to disaster on a huge scale.

On the Second Fleet slightly over a quarter of the convicts died. The worst ship was the *Neptune*, at 820 tons one of the larger ships to carry convicts to Australia but it was grossly overcrowded with 511 convicts being the most ever carried on one ship. The only other ship to carry nearly so many, the *Anson* with 500 convicts in 1844, was over twice the tonnage. Of the 424 male and 78 female convicts on board the *Neptune*, 147 men and eleven women died on the voyage. Overall the women suffered much less than the men on the voyage: 35% of the men had died, but only 14% of the women. As if this was not bad enough, 269 of the 353 survivors were sick. All were indescribably filthy, covered with sores, human waste and

---

Mutiny

The *Lady Shore* left England in 1797 with 66 female and either one or two male convicts on board, bound for Sydney. Ridiculously the guard on board were mainly French deserters, French prisoners of war, Irish deserters from the British Army or soldiers condemned by military courts to serve in the New South Wales Corps. They were clearly mutinous and threatening and had been brought to the ship under guard themselves. Even more ridiculously there was no need for a military guard on board a female convict ship anyway, and they behaved mutinously even before the ship sailed. Four days from Rio they mutinied again and took over the ship accidentally killing the Captain in the confusion but then deliberately murdering the First Mate. The officers and some of soldiers were set afloat in sight of shore, and the mutineers sailed for Montevideo. Upon their arrival the ship was condemned as a prize of war and sold, and the female convicts were distributed as servants in the town. We know no more of their fate. The Frenchmen were treated as prisoners of war by the Spanish, though at least one of them was executed in London two years later for the murder of the Captain.

lice, many could not walk, and those who were not ill were painfully "emaciated".

The Third Fleet was not quite as bad but it was still shocking with an overall death rate approaching 10% and once again the survivors were either very ill or extremely emaciated. Overcrowding and the plundering of the food supplies by the ships' officers and crew were considered to be the principal causes of the deaths. The main reasons for the lower death rate amongst the women seems to have been that they were not kept in chains below decks for most of the voyage. Being seen to be less likely to foment mutiny, they often had more access to the decks and the open air, and they often had the opportunity to trade either their charms or their bodies with the officers and crew for more food and better conditions.

Following the Third Fleet, three independent ships arrived in 1792, the *Pitt*, *Royal Admiral*, and *Kitty*; each had a mixed cargo of male and female convicts, and for the first time the death rates of the female convicts exceeded that of the males. Taking the three ships together, a little under 5% of the males died as compared to a little over 10% of the women. The *Pitt* was the worst ship with nine out of 58 women dying (15.52%) compared with 5.76% of the men. For the first time, there were good reasons for the death rates, although the ship was tremendously overcrowded. Smallpox broke out soon after the ship left England, and calling at the Cape Verde Islands introduced a fever to the ship though principally among the crew, guards and passengers, more of whom died on the voyage than prisoners. Nevertheless, there can be no doubt that the high death rate amongst the female convicts on the ship was at least exacerbated by the quite extraordinary overcrowding which could only help to spread both smallpox and the fever.

During the next twenty-two years the death toll on the transports rose and fell, though a much smaller percentage of women died than men, and then in 1814 disaster struck again. A number of ships arrived in quick succession in Sydney with so many dead and dying that Governor Macquarie immediately instigated an inquiry by Assistant Surgeon Redfern. His report and its implementation completely changed the way that the authorities looked at organising the shipping of convicts. The most important recommendation was that surgeons, preferably naval surgeons, be employed not only as medical men but also with complete charge and full responsibility for discipline, care, supplies and morality of the convicts.

This had previously happened on some ships but more through accident than design. The system was implemented after the end of the Napoleonic Wars in 1815 made very large numbers of ex-naval surgeons on half-pay available for these duties.

Death rates for free emigrants and convicts

We can get some idea of how successful the authorities were in reducing the death toll amongst the female convicts on the ships out to the Eastern Australian colonies by comparing the death rates on convict ships with those on free emigrant ships.

There were a lot of parallels between the two systems and indeed quite often the same ships were employed for both purposes. After the authorities instituted the Surgeon-superintendent system in 1815 the average death

---

Enemy Action

The first shipload of convict women destined solely for Van Diemen's Land departed England in November 1812. The *Emu* had been bought for service in the colonies and was carrying a cargo of 49 female convicts and amongst other things most of Colonel Davey's luggage so that he would be well equipped as the Lieutenant-Governor of Van Diemen's Land. However, much to the Governor's chagrin, his luggage did not arrive and neither did the female convicts.

They were victims of the only case of a convict transport being lost to enemy action. The US privateer *Holkar,* an 18 gun purpose-built private warship carrying a crew of 150, overhauled the *Emu* in the Eastern Atlantic. The *Emu* was both heavily out-manned and out-gunned and in spite of being under the command of the Royal Navy, the crew abandoned the skipper and she surrendered to the American. Six weeks later the captain and the women convicts were landed at the Cape Verde Islands, and nothing more is known of the ship or the women.

It is presumed that the ship was sold as a prize of war in New York and that the women were repatriated to England. If so, perhaps they were sent out to NSW on a subsequent convict transport. Maybe some even ended up in Van Diemen's Land. What is known for sure is that Governor Davey's luggage was never seen again, nor did he get any compensation for its loss.

---

rate per month of voyage for all convicts, male and female, improved from about 11.3 per thousand per month to about 2.4 per thousand per month in the late 1840s and early 1850s. This latter rate is the same as the average death rate for each month of voyage for assisted emigrant adults travelling to the Australian colonies during the period 1838 to 1853. After this period the statistics for both assisted emigrants and male convicts being sent to Western Australia improved to one death per thousand for each month at sea, very much the same as the adult death rate in Britain. This reflected the much better conditions on shipboard, larger ships, swifter passages, better hygiene, improved food technology and storage facilities, and better planning from greater experience.

However, the improvement in the death rates for all convicts from the 1820s onwards was largely due to improvements in the death rates for men and it's not at all clear that as the decades wore on that conditions on the female convict transports were improving much at all. Be that as it may, when we bear in mind that there were bound to be significant differences between the situation on board for free emigrant women and the situation for the female convicts, differences that are often imponderable, the mere fact that the death rates are similar suggests that in general the authorities were probably doing their best for the prisoners.

The imponderables are that emigrants were more likely to be healthy but on the other hand more likely to be pregnant, more likely to have relatively free run of the deck, more likely to have a store of extra clothing or food; and were less likely to be pining for home, husband, or children left behind.

Surprisingly, the death rates for the free emigrants to Australia were in general far better than on the much shorter voyage across the Atlantic to Canada and the USA. Robin Haines proposes that the reason for this was the fact that the authorities had learned from the experience with the convicts and already had the experience, infrastructure and administrative organisation in place to make the voyages of the immigrants extremely safe. The single most effective expedient was the Surgeon-superintendent system, so the authorities continued it and indeed extended and supplemented it later with matrons to oversee young single women amongst free emigrants in much the same way as occurred on some of the later convict transports.

The 1820s and 1830s were the period of optimum conditions for women transported to Van Diemen's Land. Survival rates for the voyages were much better than in the early days, and would never be quite as good ever again. That the majority of the deaths could be attributed to illnesses contracted before going on board tends to reinforce the idea that the women in general were better off on the ships than remaining in the appalling conditions of the majority of English prisons. Certainly the appointment of Surgeon-superintendents on each of the ships had reduced the death toll tremendously. The food improved in quantity and particularly in quality, and specific food and other extras to be dispensed by the surgeon meant that he could quickly intervene, with wine, extra food or fruits and anti-scorbutics, when dietary deficiency became noticeable. Exercise and access

Her child still locked in her arms

The female convict transport *Amphitrite* was barely at sea in the straits of Dover when an appalling storm drove her ashore at Boulogne in northern France on the last day of August 1833. The French pilots risked their lives to reach the ship from the shore and begged the Captain to abandon ship but could not make themselves understood. When the captain later decided he would have to abandon the ship the Surgeon-superintendent's wife refused to get into the boats with the female convicts. Surgeon-superintendent Forrester then ordered the attempt to be discontinued until next morning. During the night the ship broke up and all but three seamen died. Altogether there were 133 deaths including 101 women convicts, possibly five wives of male convicts, going out to join their husbands, and 12 prisoners' children. Eighty-two bodies were recovered, including a female convict mother with her child still locked in her arms. All were buried together in a mass grave, which would be ironic if Mrs Forrester, the Surgeon-superintendent's wife, was buried amongst those she so despised. The English community in Boulogne later erected a grave-side memorial to all who had died in the wreck. The British government paid substantial rewards to the French pilots for their repeated but vain rescue attempts.

Although the deaths on board the *Amphitrite* can be partially attributed to Mrs Forrester's disdain for the convicts and the captain's failure to abandon ship in the face of repeated French entreaties, the actual wreck itself probably could not have been avoided. The four day storm caused 59 separate English Channel claims on Lloyd's, with most being total wrecks. Numerous crews were lost entirely and there were at least fifty other deaths.

to fresh air were also encouraged and, in good conditions, the women could spend a large portion of every day on deck.

Shipwrecks

There were six shipwrecks connected with Transportation, four involving male convicts and two involving females. Two of the male convict shipwrecks were the *HMS Guardian* in 1790 with the loss of five convict men and the *Hive* near Jervis Bay in NSW in December 1835 with no loss of life.

With the exception of the *Guardian*, which was being used primarily as a storeship and only incidentally to carry convicts, there were no shipwrecks of convict transports until 1833. When one considers that an average of between one and two percent of Lloyd's Registry was shipwrecked every year, this record speaks well of the efforts to make Transportation safe. However, in a period of less than twenty-eight months between 31 August 1833 and 10 December 1835, four ships were lost: the *Amphitrite* carrying women, the *George III* carrying men, the *Neva* carrying women and the *Hive*. Then in 1842 the *Waterloo* carrying men was also lost.

In all, 288 male convicts died on board the four male convict transport shipwrecks though this includes a number who had previously died through illness, particularly those on board the *George III*. This is roughly one person for every 440 who sailed and made up approximately 12% of all male convict deaths on voyages.

The women were far more unlucky. On board the *Amphitrite* all 101 women and all 12 of their children were lost and on the *Neva* 145 out of 151 women and all 33 children were lost. Female convicts were four and a half times more likely to have died in a shipwreck than the men: one in every 103 who sailed died in this manner and over 42% of all female convict deaths at sea were attributable to shipwreck.

The women who did not arrive and the men who did the counting

Two Australian historians have researched and written most significant books on the subject of the totality of numbers of convicts sent from the British Isles to the Australian colonies between the years 1787 and 1868. They were Charles Bateson who first published his results in 1959, 1969 and finally with significant additions in 1974, and AGL Shaw, one of

Australia's most distinguished academic historians, who published his results in 1966. Bateson and Shaw had each done a huge amount of work in arriving at their final figures and yet on the surface they seem to have come up with significantly different figures

My interest was in those who arrived, or those who actually died on the voyage through the minor accidents and vicissitudes of travelling, and only incidentally with all those who embarked from Britain. To serve my purposes I adjusted Bateson's figures to take into account some factors such as losses of women by shipwreck as distinct from on-board illness and found that his and Shaw's figures were not substantially different after all. Once allowance has been made for their different purposes, the figures are extraordinarily close, and considering the confusion of the early years of Transportation, it is clear that each has succeeded in a remarkable achievement.

Bass Strait should not be entered at night

On 12 May 1835 the *Neva* was approaching the western entrance to Bass Strait and by the captain's reckoning would pass safely to the north of King Island. On board were either 150 or 151 female convicts with 33 children and nine wives of male convicts with 22 children coming out to join their husbands and fathers in Sydney. Altogether there were 241 persons on board.

Convinced that he was clear of King Island the captain ignored the standard advice that Bass strait should not be entered at night. At two o'clock in the morning in a heavy sea and increasing wind, land was sighted in the wrong quarter and the ship found herself on a lee shore, the terror of all sailing masters. Careful seamanship enabled the ship to escape King Island itself but at 5am breakers were sighted ahead and the ship crashed onto what was probably part of Harbinger's Reefs. There were not enough boats for all on board and the ship began to break up. Panic and the heavy seas caused the boats to founder and by nightfall only a few survivors clinging to wreckage were washed ashore on King Island. Eight seamen and twelve convicts made it to shore alive. In the next few days the men managed to bury 95 bodies. Some of the survivors died before rescue. In all only six female convicts made it to Sydney.

According to my calculations from their figures, at least 576 women died on their voyages to Australia, roughly 2.28% of the 25,266 who set sail. Of these 246, or 0.97% (almost one in a hundred) of those who sailed died in a shipwreck. This was far higher than the equivalent rate of male convict deaths. Using Bateson's figures, only 283, or 0.22% out of 127,172 of the convict men who sailed to the Eastern Australian colonies died as a result of shipwreck.

Why the male convicts had it worse

Looking at just the rates of death on the voyages, the fact that men suffered considerably more due to the conditions on board the ships is not at all apparent. The overall death rates for men and women (1.87% and 2.28% respectively) suggest exactly the opposite. However, when the deaths by shipwreck are excluded, it is clear that the on-board experience of the female transports may have been considerably better than for the men. The adjusted figures for deaths on voyages other than by shipwreck show that 1.65% of men died on board as compared to 1.31% of women.

Two reasons for the greater death rate amongst the men was fear of mutiny by their supervisors, and worse overcrowding on their transports. The fear of mutiny or of the convicts seizing the ship led to the men sometimes being barricaded below for almost the whole voyage, and being accused (often on the most specious grounds) of plotting to seize the ship. Men were cruelly flogged or even, on quite a few occasions, summarily executed. Lack of exercise and access to the decks for health reasons were major contributors to the death rate.

Throughout the ensuing period of transportation there were not only bad ships on the voyage to Australia, there were also bad years. However, there were also good ships and good years. In some years and series of years the death rates were remarkably low. A majority of ships in every period had either no deaths or only one death to report.

The odds on survival

During the early days of Transportation the death rates amongst the male convicts was consistently much higher than amongst the female convicts. However towards the end of the convict period the male death rate for reasons other than shipwreck dropped dramatically from the 1.65% for the whole of the convict period, firstly in the 1830s to 1.04% which was close to the death rate of the women. Then even more dramatically in the 1840s and early 1850s it dropped to a rate almost half that of the women. This coincides with the higher numbers of women being transported on each voyage but also with their poor state of health when they left Great Britain. So, for a female convict sentenced to transportation, what was the chance of surviving the voyage?

Two hundred ships carried 25,266 female convicts from the British Isles to the eastern Australian colonies. If we look at the twenty-six ships with the worst death rates (only 13% of the two hundred) we see that two were lost by shipwreck, accounting for almost 43% of those who women who never arrived in Australia. The other 24 of the 'worst ships' accounted for 146 deaths, over 25% of all the female convicts who never arrived. This means that 68% percent of the women who died at sea were on the 26 ships that embarked with less than eleven percent of all the women sent out from Great Britain. The other 174 ships, carrying 22,526 women or 89% of all who ever sailed, had a total of only 184 deaths, a very reasonable death rate of 0.82%.

When home was far behind

Most of the female convict transports to Australia either had no deaths or only one death on the voyage. Considering the dangers of late eighteenth and early nineteenth century sea voyages, and the length of the trips (usually three to five months but sometimes longer) this was a remarkable achievement. The vast preponderance of voyages had a much better mortality rate than many of the late nineteenth century free immigrant ships to Australia or for that matter on the immigrant ships on the much shorter voyage to the North American countries. That the female convict voyages were so safe was a victory for good planning, a determination to hire good ships, though the quality of the crews was sometimes suspect; a

---

She got herself pregnant

They were all extremely good when they imagined they were nearing their destination. The doctor had sole charge of the women. He was, I believe, a good doctor, but at the same time an infernal old scoundrel. He had two very pretty girls to make his berth and to clean his berth …one of these women got in the family way and threatened to ruin his reputation…

James Montagu Smith, on the *Sir Robert Seppings* in 1852

---

high degree of vigilance over the conditions and cleanliness of the quarters on board and the quality of the provisions; good medical superintendence; and possibly, though this was not true of all periods and ships, the selection criteria used to judge which women should undertake the voyage. It was usually when one or more of these elements was neglected that disaster struck.

Whether we take the overall numbers of female convicts arriving (or rather, not arriving) or the figures for the worst ships or even the remainder of the ships, what emerges is that the worst period for deaths on board was the earliest period. Conditions got steadily better until the 1830s but then started to deteriorate again, though never to the same degree as during the earlier period.

The improvement in conditions from the early days was directly attributable to the increased care taken with both the ships and their human cargoes. Contractors for the supply both of the ships and of the food and other supplies were increasingly liable to penalties if they failed to meet their contractual obligations.

After 1815 every ship was required to have a Surgeon-superintendent on board, responsible in the first instance to the Governor of the colony for the safe delivery of the convicts. This requirement had an inestimable effect in ensuring safe delivery. The death of every single convict had to be answered for. But the Surgeon-superintendents were also responsible to the British Admiralty, and the overall health of every shipload had to be minutely reported. As the convict transportation system increased in experience, so too did the responsibilities and power of the Surgeon-superintendent. No longer could the captain of a ship over-ride the Surgeon-superintendent on matters of health, hygiene and punishment. In the end it was the increasing qualifications and experience of the surgeons that solved the problems and enabled safer voyages for the convicts.

Over the whole period there was a level of technological development which tended to make the voyages safer. The ships grew bigger, the voyages tended to be shorter, and there were considerable improvements in the storage of food and water. The reason for the rise in death rates in the last two decades of transportation can be partially explained by deteriorating conditions in Europe. There was an extraordinary growth in the cities with parallel growth in pollution and the accompanying communicable diseases, and of course the incredible worsening of conditions in Ireland culminating in the Great Famine in the mid to late 1840s. But even with the terrible death toll of the early period and the worsening of the health situation in the 1840s the overall experience of the female convicts on board the ships was never as bad as has often been painted. The British government by introducing the Surgeon-superintendent system had successfully avoided what might easily have become a terrible blot on their reputation.

They almost got away

On 7 February 1816 three Irish women who had been transported on the *Francis & Eliza* arrived at the Derwent from Sydney. They had had a particularly exciting time when they had fallen foul of an American privateer in Long Island Sound on 4 January 1815. Neither participant was aware that a peace treaty had been signed almost two weeks before. The *Francis & Eliza* lost her guns and despatches and a few of her crew who deserted to the Americans. She was relatively lucky; four days later Andrew Jackson led his American troops in the Battle of New Orleans, absolutely routing the British in a battle that cost over two thousand lives, both sides oblivious that the war had already ended. The *Francis & Eliza* was allowed to continue with her female convict cargo intact, but the crew was shorthanded and mutinous and the captain could only command the ship with the help of the male convicts on board (the ship was the last to carry both male and female convicts, the practice having almost entirely ceased four years before). Apparently the convict discipline system aboard ceased, at least until the ship eventually reached the Cape of Good Hope, but we know few details. Still it must all have been very exciting, and for a period, no doubt, the women may have had expectations of being carried off in triumph to freedom in America as a spoil of war, but the Americans weren't interested in someone else's convicts.

Chapter 6.   Entering Exile

The arrival of the *Morley* at the end of August 1820 marked the halfway point between the arrival of the First Fleet in Australia and the arrival in Hobart in May 1853 of the last female convicts sent directly from Britain. Although the arrival of the *Morley* marked the halfway point for the actual years of transportation, only around 4,500 female convicts had arrived up until that time, approximately 18% of all women transported to Australia. The second half of the Transportation period was to see another 20,000 women arrive; more than 60% or over 12,000 of them to Van Diemen's Land.

As has been pointed out by Lyndall Ryan and confirmed and extended by other historians, most notably and most recently Kay Daniels, there were three distinct phases of the systematisation of the female convict experience in the Australian colonies. These to some extent paralleled the male convict systems, but typically they were less rigorous as directions to the officials in the colonies, and hence the female experience, often lagged in time behind the implementation of new systems for the men. The three phases were exile, assignment and probation.

Exile

Exile was a general system where the focus of the punishment was to remove the convict from Britain for seven years, fourteen years, or for Life. Return during the period of banishment was on pain of death. During exile the convict was to be at the mercy of the convict system. They were directed to work for a particular master, directed to live in a particular place and were subject to a different level and form of law enforcement, with more arbitrary, comprehensive and severe mechanisms and punishments than was usual under British law. The convict disciplinary systems, more than anything else, resembled the naval and military discipline of the 1800s.

The essential punishment was exile itself. Although assignment to free masters was part of the system, it was not the focus of punishment and so it was flexible, particularly when people had highly desirable skills and were able to support themselves. Then they were often free to go their own way provided they kept clear of, and did not fall foul of, the authorities. After a specified period of keeping their nose clean or when they had provided particular services to the authorities, or society in general, they were typically rewarded with a ticket-of-leave, a limited pardon or a full pardon. Receiving a full pardon or reaching the expiration of their sentence restored them to free society and they could, if they wished, return to Britain at their own expense.

While there were fixed periods for the gradual rise toward freedom through the intermediate levels of tickets-of-leave and limited pardon, in these early years the system was rigidly enforced only for those who kept getting into trouble. Even then, three or four visits to the magistrate for minor infringements of the regulations did not stop many from gaining their ticket or pardon in the minimum time. At times even major infringements were overlooked. The authorities seemed to acknowledge that just being in the system was a problem, and people released from it were highly unlikely to re-offend.

In this period convicts were typically off-loaded at Sydney or Hobart Town and had to find their own lodgings and employment. A few hand-picked individuals who had valuable skills and employment possibilities would be reserved for government work and paid an allowance for their lodgings. More typically they were only employed for part of the day and then were free to earn what they could working around the town, out of which they were expected to pay for their lodgings. With the construction of the male convict barracks in Sydney in the late 1810s and in Hobart in the early 1820s this all changed though less so than many modern observers think.

Even in the late 1820s the male prisoners' barracks still functioned largely as a central lodging house. Typically the door would be flung open about 4:30am and for the next couple of hours individuals, pairs and small groups

---

"Lost in the Woods"

The *Catherine* disembarked 97 female convicts at Sydney in 1814, but 58 were sent on to Hobart Town. Later two more of them would be moved to Van Diemen's Land. Margaret Quinn, 20 years old, died within four months of her arrival. Another four died in the first few years in the colony. One of them was Ann McDermott, who wandered off into the bush one day in 1818. Her body was not found for three days.

---

would emerge unaccompanied by soldiers or guards to go about their business. The earliest would be the bakers and perhaps a few fishermen or boatmen who would wander off bleary-eyed to their place of work. Later, after their breakfast, there might emerge a dishevelled group of men accompanied by a guard or overseer off for a day's work at the lumber yard. Then perhaps a few more individuals off to work on building sites or small factories around the town. Then might come a large group, perhaps half of whom were in chains, with two or three overseers and a guard or two, off to work for the day at the Government Garden. Their guard might typically consist of either javelin men (convict prison guards) or convict constables or even soldiers. Sometimes the guard would be a mixture of all three. Then with a clomp, clomp, clomp would come a chain-gang off to work in the quarries or on the roads. More typically this gang's guard would consist of at least two or three armed soldiers. All the while single men, pairs and small groups, sometimes with an overseer, sometimes in the charge of a convict constable, but most often unsupervised, would slip off through the gates to attend their place of work.

The women, married women in particular, also experienced this relative freedom, until the construction of the new Parramatta Female Factory in 1821 and in Hobart somewhat later.

Assignment

The implementation of the assignment system for women was not achieved merely because of the construction of better designed and equipped female factories, though these were essential to its success. The focus of the system was that all female convicts would be assigned to private individuals and be completely under their control and direction when they were on their premises, providing their work or behaviour was not subject to complaint. Their masters and mistresses had to house, clothe and feed them, and ensure that they went to church on Sunday. They also had to make sure the convicts were not out after curfew, and were not spending time in taverns, brothels, or in the male convicts' quarters. With the exception of a very few extremely troublesome characters, the vast mass of the female convicts spent most of their time either in assignment or awaiting assignment. Even amongst the very difficult convicts few would have spent the majority of their colonial time being punished in institutions. Overall it was rare for more than between a fifth and a quarter of assignable female convicts to be under punishment at any one time. This meant that the system was very cheap compared to keeping them in institutions with the need for constant supervision together with the cost of feeding and clothing them. As Jane Franklin was to later say in a letter to Mrs Fry: "the assignment system had its origin in economy".

Every other part of the assigned convict's life in the colony was subject to the oversight of the convict department including any complaints by their master or mistress. In Van Diemen's Land Governor Arthur reorganised the magistracy and the police force in new police districts, each with a set of cells, court facilities and effective records. Centrally and most notoriously he created an efficient and largely incorruptible records system, the 'Black Books', under the Principal Superintendent of Convicts. He then set about building the new female factories that relied on drab surroundings, uncomfortable conditions, boring poor quality clothing and food and hard unremitting labour from dawn to dusk six days a week, to encourage the female convicts to make the best of their assignment. Very much in keeping with the new age that was dawning in the late 1820s and early 1830s Arthur was bent on creating a system that was cheap and economical backed up by punishments that less and less relied on the abuse of the body through flogging or wearing an iron collar, or on public humiliation through the use of stocks or head shaving. Instead, the new system relied more and more on the private hidden punishments, designed to affect the mind and crush the spirit, of solitary confinement and the monotonous regime of the factories.

Comparatively free

They all went ashore at Hobart Town and were instantly taken to a factory called the Brickfields where they were detained until they were hired out, which is never very long. It is too handy to get a servant for a mere nominal charge. But on the event of a complaint of bad conduct being made by the master or mistress they are sent to the Cascades and placed at the wash tub for a time; and what they bewail more, their hair is cut short. I believe this punishment is feared next to death by the young ones, but they get used to it after a little colonial experience. The dread of transportation is far worse than the reality. It is the best thing that ever happened to many of them. Directly they arrive in the Colony they are comparatively free, and in a short time completely so... Any free man or ticket-of-leave can, by applying to the Governor, marry any of the newly-arrived convicts...

James Montagu Smith, of the *Sir Robert Seppings*, 1852

The probation period was supposed to introduce new concepts into the punishment, control and coercion of all convicts. At least part of the reason for its introduction was to answer the charge that assignment was a form of legalised slavery. Another, perhaps more salient reason was that assignment to private masters meant that the individual convict's day to day experience of Transportation was arbitrary and largely determined by the whim and nature of the master or mistress. Some masters provided comfortable quarters, good bedding, privacy, excellent rations and luxuries including tea, coffee, tobacco, sometimes pocket money. The work they required in return was safe, not unduly onerous and confined to reasonable hours. Other masters were harsh and tyrannical, provided minimal quarters and food, using the constant threat of magisterial intervention with the cells, chain gang and the lash as a bargaining counter to extract unusual effort and hours from their servants. In between was the usual master, from the government's perspective sometimes far too lax in their supervision, maintenance and provision of work and encouragement for reform of the convicts in their care.

One woman described being with a young settler couple and their baby where she was treated like one of the family. Not only did she get on well with her master and mistress, but she was only required to help with some of the housework and some babysitting. Unfortunately they were so poor they could barely feed and clothe her and so she went back to the Factory for assignment.

Probation

The probation system for men began in 1841 but it didn't get fully under way until towards the end of 1842. The idea was that each convict had to earn their way through progressive stages of punishment under the government, and then through progressive stages of control as paid servants of free settlers. Rather than rewarding good behaviour by decreasing punishment or early release from the scheme, the idea was to punish bad behaviour by withholding entry to the next level or sending the convict to punishment stations of greater and greater degrees of punishment. The first stage was for the convict to be held in a penitentiary in England, or for lifers and 14 and 15 year men two to four years on Norfolk Island. The second stage was to work in an isolated probation gang at hard labour in Van Diemen's Land. Within the gangs three different levels of hard labour would enable minor infractions to be punished and control exercised on a day-to-day basis. When the period of government punishment was completed (its duration could be lengthened but not shortened by the colonial authorities), the convict became a pass-holder and was made available for hire for wages.

Being paid wages, of course, meant the authorities could not now be accused of enslaving the convicts. Three different levels or stages of pass-holding allowed the convict both to get an increasing measure of choice about work and employer and to retain different and increasing proportions of their wages, the remainder to be paid into a savings account. If they obtained a ticket-of-leave at the end of their pass periods they got to keep the money in the bank, but if they were returned to the government for misbehaviour not only were they sentenced to punishment in the Houses of Correction, they also forfeited any savings they had accumulated.

For women the probation system started later and mainly consisted of spending six months on board the hulk *Anson* and then being hired out at £8 to £10 as a servant. The system worked fully for only three or four years and partially for a few more. Except for receiving a pittance as pay for their services the experience of female convicts in the late 1840s and early 1850s was hardly any different to the assignment system.

The origin of the 'Female Factory'

The name originated because, at least in the earliest years, these establishments were factories where the female convicts produced goods

---

Flagitious lives

[The Female Factory] is a scene of feasting, complete idleness and vicious indulgence. The women are occasionally let into the town, and have free communication with their associates. When they bring forth illegitimate children they are received into a nursery, where they live on the same abundant fare, with nothing to do but to nurse their infants... the common practise of the convict women is to get into service, in order to obtain money by theft or prostitution... they are utterly insubordinate and lead most flagitious lives plainly telling their masters that they infinitely prefer the depot - the scene of jollity and every evil communication.

Reverend HP Fry, Rector of St George's Church, 1850

---

to help the growing colonies. But although they were first designed to be used exclusively as manufactories, they soon became used also as a lodging house for women unable or unwilling to find lodgings in the nearby towns.

This slowly began to change because the early governors also needed a place to send women to work as a form of punishment. Consequently there developed a need for other facilities: cells, constant supervision, nurseries for children, hospital yards for the sick, punishment yards for the refractory, sections devoted to housing those convicts who had either just arrived in the colony or those returned to the hands of the government from masters and mistresses who no longer had need of their services.

So, the female factories were much more than places of punishment. They were extremely multi-purpose. After the first years in Parramatta, they rarely if ever operated as prisoners' barracks, that is, as a place where the inmates were confined for the purposes of accommodation during the non-working part of the day, but from which they went to their daily work whether for the government or private masters. By the early 1820s the authorities were reluctant to allow women to lodge other than with their employers. The circumstances were too fraught with possibilities.

Convict women employed in the factories, either assigned to the government or with a ticket-of-leave, would of course stay in the factory both for accommodation and to work. These were not inmates but wards-women, nurses, overseers and teachers who fulfilled tasks in the factory at a lower level than free women employed in the same or similar tasks. Typically they made up two-thirds to three-quarters of the staff. They were paid a standard ticket-of-leave wage and they were also given leave to go into town shopping and for limited social purposes. It was probably women in these circumstances noisily returning from town after a day out who so distressed the Reverend HP Fry at his home in Macquarie Street, halfway on the direct route back to the Cascades Female Factory.

Marriage market?

The female factories in general, unlike the pictures often painted of the early days at the Parramatta Female Factory, did not operate as quasi-formal marriage markets with bachelor settlers eagerly picking out the prettiest prospects from a line-up and plighting their troth there and then. Such situations may have occurred in the earliest days at Parramatta but by the time the other female factories were established the system had been formalised to restrict female convict assignment to only either the very respectable, to married couples and occasionally to a husband or other relative. Meeting a potential husband occurred in the normal course of being an assigned servant, meeting guests, meeting fellow assigned servants, perhaps in the course of shopping or other duties.

As the regimes of punishment and control changed so too did the institutions. Eventually the concept of the female factories as a place for the manufacture of goods declined into the background, almost but never quite forgotten. By then the idea of work as a form of punishment had overtaken the idea that certain forms of work could best be done and most efficiently done in buildings designed for the purpose, ie. a factory. But as far as the institutions departed from the original concept of a manufactory, the name was never lost. Throughout the history of the convict system, and for that matter, as we shall see, even beyond the convict period, institutions for the women were usually labelled: the Female Factory.

Reassignment

Female factories also provided lodgings for those who for one reason or another were between assignments. Generally the magistrates had an eye out for women who were ill-treated, who were assigned to notoriously difficult masters or mistresses or who were at risk of sexual harassment. As bad as the conditions in the factories could be, there is no doubt that at times they operated as shelters from abuse and mistreatment.

In spite of the fact that for masters to give up a convict servant for no reason often precluded getting a replacement, and wanting to change masters or mistresses could earn a convict substantial punishment, the most common single reason for magistrates returning a woman to the Factory for reassignment was a simple request by either the settler or the convict.

Marriage and freedom

Marriages are continually taking place between men and women whose wives and husbands are living in England... this breach of law is punishable at home by transportation... [it] occurs also very often for the purpose of getting a woman out of the Factory.

Surgeon-superintendant Thomas Reid of the *Morley*, 1820

The hospital, lying-in facilities and nursery

The factories also provided hospital facilities for those convicts too ill to work, though these services were also available at the Colonial Hospitals. Permanently disabled and long-term invalids seem to have been few in number but found a permanent home in the factories, doing light duties where possible. Towards the end of the convict period, after the cessation of Transportation, special and separate institutions called female pauper asylums were set up to cater for these women but as we shall see, they were still within the physical confines of the old female factories.

When a woman became pregnant and was no longer able to work she was sent to the factory and put to light duties on a full diet. Those who had married but were still assigned to work for someone other than their husband would be assigned to their husband and not go to the factory unless they had been subsequently found guilty of an offence.

When the baby was due the mother was transferred to the lying-in part of the factory or Nursery. Typically in the late 1820s, the 1830s and early 1840s she stayed in the Nursery until the baby was compulsorily weaned at six months. In the late 1840s and 1850s the babies were usually weaned at nine months unless medical circumstances warranted further breast feeding. Then those newly arrived in the colony who had become pregnant since conviction or those who had become pregnant in the colony as assigned servants were punished with six months hard labour in the Second Class and then sent to a new assignment. Women who were considered well-behaved were allowed access to their babies once a week during their period of hard labour. Some who were considered particularly good mothers might be kept on at the Nursery as nurses and assistants. There is quite a lot of apocryphal evidence that some women were assigned as wet-nurses to free settler families, particularly to the gentry, and avoided serving their six months hard labour, though there is no mention of this in the official regulations. Jane Franklin, the Governor's wife considered it common or at least frequent enough to warrant mention in her letters home.

Children under three were kept at the Nursery until the mother could support them, sometimes through marriage, sometimes through the support of a kindly master or mistress, sometimes through earning her living as a ticket-of-leave servant. When children reached the age of three, or if they were over three when they arrived in the colony, they were sent to the

Orphan Schools until the mother claimed the child and could prove she was able to support it. Quite a few of the children were never claimed by the mother. Well-behaved assigned servants could get written permission from the magistrates to visit their children at the Orphan Schools on Sundays.

Punishment

The early female factories were factories designed for work and not specifically for punishment. But they became so more and more, especially as the focus of punishment shifted from punishing or ridiculing the body to punishing the mind through control, separation, work and discipline of the body.

In the early days punishment for female convicts was through the gallows, extension of transportation, exile to another colony or a penal station,

---

A husband's provocation

Ann Pink arrived in Hobart Town in late 1819 and in the nine months before her marriage to Joseph Clark had twice served sentences for being drunk and abusive. In 1829 she was murdered by her husband. On 8 May 1830 the *Hobart Town Courier* reported:

> It certainly appeared that the poor woman who was killed, was a habitual drunkard, and some allowance must be made for the provocation which a husband might be supposed to feel on coming home after the labours of the day, and finding the companion of his life in a beastly state of inebriety, and his house a scene of riot and desolation. Yet Clark should have borne in mind that the unfortunate creature was still his wife, and the cruel and unmerciful manner in which he had beaten her…

Joseph Clark was relatively lucky and avoided the gallows by having a number of gentlemen to speak for him including the Chief Police Magistrate. He was found guilty of manslaughter and sentenced to 7 years transportation. However it is quite clear that beating to death a drunken and dissolute wife was considered to be somewhat less of a serious offence at least as far as the newspapers were concerned, and these examples give us some insight into the lesser value and status and standing in the community in which ex-convict women were held.

---

flogging, wearing an iron collar, sitting in the stocks for hours, having her hair cut off, or spending a number of days in a gaol cell on bread and water. Fines were also used as a punishment, though their use was necessarily restricted to those known to be earning money, and in practice were usually used as a sanction against ticket-of-leave holders. Admonition and reprimand (a darn good telling off, with a threat of harsher punishment in the future) were also used surprisingly often.

By the 1820s the idea behind the factories was to separate the inmates into different classifications and to use hard labour as a punishment. However this was impossible in the existing Factories in Hobart Town and George Town as they were ill-designed, cramped and vastly overcrowded and with the exception of flogging which had been abandoned for women, the old punishments continued.

Freedom through marriage

For female convicts the free early days were at the one time much freer than the experience of the men but on the other hand the period was restricted sooner. And as soon as the authorities had constructed female factories their much easier regime was curtailed.

In the exile period almost any woman with a good record on the ship could obtain a ticket-of-leave to marry and be assigned to her husband. Provided it was a love match, the marriage lasted and they enjoyed a modicum of economic success, she was in effect free of the convict system providing she never again offended. Few men ever escaped the system so lightly. A substantial proportion of the early female convicts availed themselves of these opportunities.

On 3 April 1820, Reverend Robert Knopwood, who had been the Van Diemen's Land chaplain since 1804, gave an overall picture of the way the system had worked in regard to marriage. The moment they married, the women were largely relieved of the need to work for the Government. Few among the locally born men were attracted to marrying the female convicts and, according to Knopwood, the settlers from Norfolk Island, many of whom had in an earlier generation been convicts themselves, tended to intermarry rather than marry newly arrived female convicts. Although there was a 'good deal' of 'concubinage' (de facto relationships) many of the women had married.

Knopwood accommodated this desire for formal marriage by only requiring a declaration and not a solemn oath that those getting married were in fact single. On at least three occasion he had later discovered the declaration to be false. Many of the ex-convicts wanted their children educated at school and if they were poor, schooling was provided free. He felt that most of the married female convicts stayed true to their wedding vows.

This picture of connubial bliss as a quick escape from the convict system must be viewed with a number of reservations. In the first place, it presumes that the woman landed without any lingering attachments from her earlier life. Many of the women were still officially married, or had children from their previous life accompanying them, though as we will see neither problem was to prove to be an insuperable barrier to future marriage. Secondly, there appears to have been a very high rate of colonial marital physical abuse, domestic violence even to the point of murder. In this vein, the story of Elizabeth Perkins is salutary.

Elizabeth Perkins was convicted of larceny at Bristol in 1816 and sentenced to 7 years transportation. She arrived in Hobart Town in early 1818 and, except for one offence, a few months after her arrival, of being absent without leave for which she received a week in the cells on bread and water, she seems to have kept her nose clean. By 1820 she was living with John Leach, a boat builder, and they had at least one child, a girl.

By February 1829 the Leachs were notorious with their neighbours for their quarrelling:
> stimulated …by a justly founded feeling of jealousy, and the frequent intoxication of his wife ….He had frequently of late been heard to lament his miserable condition, for after the closest industry and long days of labour, he had no comfort in returning home, which he found heartless and desolate through the drunkenness and dissipation of his wife.

One Friday night in 1829, Elizabeth's cries were heard as usual by the neighbours as her husband beat her with a stick, but they suddenly cut off, and the neighbours were investigating when the daughter came out:
> saying her mother's face was cold and she thought she was dead. On entering, Leach was found lying by the side of the corpse of his wife, with his head laid upon hers. The work of death appears to have been [caused] … by a violent beating with a stick.

The daughter was soon to become an orphan. Three weeks after he had murdered his wife, John Leach was executed on 9 March 1829.

The death of Elizabeth Perkins was, of course, the sort of thing that could happen anywhere. By the time she died she was no longer a convict but was free by servitude, but nevertheless, the system which encouraged marriages so as to escape the system had a number of possible outcomes which could unnecessarily restrict life choices to the detriment of all.

Punishment at Hobart Town and George Town in 1820, the year the *Morley* arrived:

Q: What punishment do you Inflict upon the women who behave ill?

A: Confining them to the Gaols and Hard Labour there such as washing for the Prisoners and cleaning the Gaol.

AWH Humphrey, Police Magistrate
to Commissioner Bigge, 13 March 1820

A badge of Infamy

Q: What punishment is awarded to the female Prisoners at George Town?

A: They are put into solitary confinement in a hut near the Barracks, and for very incorrigible women, an Iron collar is used as a badge of Infamy.

Q: How long are they made to wear it?

A: A Day or Two, or according to their Promises of amendment.

Q: Do almost all the female Prisoners cohabit with the Male Prisoners?

A: They do excepting Two, who I believe are married.

Q: Are the female Prisoners from this part of the country sent down to George Town by way of Punishment?

A: They are.

J Lenahan to Commissioner Bigge, 21 April 1820

Q: Is not the Iron Collar the usual Instrument, thro' out the Colonies, to punish women of bad character?

A: I have often seen it made use of, for that purpose, at Hobart Town.

Q: Do you know its weight?

A: It weighs about Six Pounds and a quarter [about 2.8 kilograms]; my Cause of knowledge is I weighed it.

John Boothman, Superintendent,
to Lt. Colonel Cimitiere, Commandant of Port Dalrymple
at George Town, 18 May 1820

Chapter 7. Colonial Crime and Punishment

When the *Morley* disembarked fifty female convicts at Hobart Town in August 1820, Van Diemen's Land was hardly in a ready state to receive them, nor would it be for some years. Indeed, on the next leg of her journey conveying the remaining 71 female convicts to Sydney, Governor Sorell instructed the captain of the *Morley* to also carry seven women from Van Diemen's Land for punishment at the Parramatta Female Factory. There was nowhere to put them in Hobart. It wasn't a matter of numbers. The number of women received directly from Britain over the three years 1820 to 1822 was roughly the same as had been being sent down from Sydney before that. But as yet there was no female factory in Hobart Town.

In the absence of anywhere adequate to imprison women who broke the law, which mostly meant they had breached convict discipline, alternative punishments were used. During the exile period and particularly before Van Diemen's Land had a female factory, the main methods of punishment were very traditional, some going back to medieval days. Other times the authorities had to resort to shifting women from one colony to another, each colony serving as a gaol for the others.

Even before the opening of the Cascades and Launceston Female Factories in 1829 and 1834 respectively, the sending of women to penal stations for punishment had been stopped, the use of the iron collar became infrequent and was soon abandoned, and use of the stocks was also largely abandoned, although the stocks continued for a while in small towns. Small towns also continued the use of a few days in the Gaol cells as a local minor salutary punishment. The practice continued within the factories both for the local magistrates' sentences in Hobart and Launceston on both free and convict women, but also internally as a punishment for disciplinary offences within the factory.

The cutting off of the women's hair continued in the factories. Even when at various times it was abandoned as a official punishment it often continued as an unofficial punishment under the guise of 'hygiene'. Serious crimes were sometimes punished by an extension of transportation, most usually seven years but sometimes less, and invariably twelve months or more in the Crime Class as well. In spite of claims by a number of historians a treadmill was never used as a punishment for women in any of the factories.

Exile within exile: more transportation

Having been exiled already, further exile was used as an extra punishment. For serious colonial crimes women convicts would be sentenced to further periods of transportation, usually another seven years.

Eliza Dowling was fairly typical of a small percentage of constant re-offenders and her record in the colonies stretched over 38 years. Eliza was sentenced to transportation for Life in the summer of 1801 in her native county of Kildare, Ireland. She was almost five foot four inches in height, with brown hair, brown eyes and was highly freckled. She had been a servant. Arriving in Sydney aboard the *Atlas* in July 1802 following a seven and a half months voyage she soon married Lawrence May and appeared to have lived with him until 1816. She received her Free Pardon in January 1815. She was at Port Dalrymple in April 1826 and was immediately in trouble with the authorities for being disorderly. At first she was reprimanded, but when she was in trouble for drunkenness and disorderly conduct in August she was fined five shillings. When she re-offended within a fortnight she was sent to gaol for 14 days and bound over to keep the peace.

In 1828 Eliza followed the same pattern except that this time she was first fined and then given a month in gaol. However in December 1828 she was found guilty of receiving stolen goods and was re-transported for seven years. There were further charges of drunkenness over the next 3 years but then she appeared in the Campbell Town Quarter Sessions on 29 February 1832 for stealing a quart of wine from her master and was again re-transported for seven years. During this next seven years she appeared before the magistrates eleven times, usually for being absent without leave or being drunk, and received various sentences ranging from 14 days in the cells to three months hard labour. Her last offence was on 29 October 1836 when she received three months in the Crime Class at the Female Factory for 'going about gossipping and begging'. She became free by servitude on the 29 February 1839 [sic] which, besides confusing us and presumably the authorities as there was no leap day that year, indicates that at least sometimes re-transportation was not considered to be cumulative but was dated from the last sentence. She received her Free

Certificate the following year by which time she had been involved with the system over a period of 39 years.

Occasionally a woman in New South Wales, already serving time as a transported convict, would be sentenced to a lesser term of transportation to be served in Van Diemen's Land or vice versa.

On 20 February 1818 Sarah Lascelles who had been serving a life sentence in Sydney arrived in Hobart having been sentenced to serve two years in Van Diemen's Land. In 1816 Isabella Noble who was serving her sentence in VDL was sent to Newcastle NSW for three years for breaking, entering and stealing.

The threat of Macquarie Harbour

In the early 1820s Macquarie Harbour on the west coast of Van Diemen's Land was made into a penal settlement for the worst of the male convicts and those re-transported within the colony. It was also planned to be a penal destination for female convicts but only a handful were ever sent there. Historian Irene Schaffer could identify only fifteen, most of whom had left by 1824.

One woman, Rachel Chamberlain was unfortunate enough to be sent there immediately upon arrival in Hobart Town, apparently on the word of her British Gaol Report and the report of the Surgeon-superintendent on board the transport *Mary Anne* which arrived on 2 May 1822. The gaoler's report said she had been in 13 different gaols. When, upon arrival, she was asked what her offence had been, instead of saying theft, she merely said that her husband Abraham Chamberlain was in the colony, possibly intimating that she had deliberately got herself transported. The Surgeon's comments were most interesting:

A most infamous character, a confirmed thief and vile prostitute, a sly woman, hypocrite, blasphemer, drunkard, revengeful, reprobate, refractory, insolent. Her husband at Sydney and her brother at VDL.

Obviously the thought of having such a person free to get her own lodging on the streets of Hobart or linking up with her brother or husband was just too much for the authorities. Two days after she arrived in Hobart Town she was on her way to Macquarie Harbour though she was back in town at the end of the following year, 1823, when she was working as a washerwoman at the hospital. She was found guilty of cohabiting with

George Harris and sent to the Hobart Town Factory. In March the following year she was on assignment when she absconded and was again sent to the Factory. Six weeks later she was one of a group at the Factory charged with singing obscene songs and making false accusations that Superintendent Drabble had stolen prisoners' rations.

Mary Furze on 18 August 1821, for absconding into the 'woods' for several months, was sentenced: 'to be transported to such parts of the Territory as His Honor the Lieutenant Governor may deem proper for the remainder of her sentence'. The proper place was obviously Macquarie Harbour. In 1824 she got into trouble three times for neglect of duty at the settlement and for each offence received a few days in the solitary cells, but these offences were the only blot on her record while still a convict. When free by servitude she had three minor fines and a good behaviour order for being drunk. In her case it was obviously the perceived seriousness of her absconding offence rather than her reputation or general behaviour that had caused her to be sent to Macquarie Harbour.

In February 1825 the government planned to employ the Macquarie Harbour women in making trousers and frocks from the cloth made at George Town.

The Old Treasury on Macquarie Street in Hobart, c1833.
The stocks used to punish minor offenders are visible in the foreground near the centre of the picture.

Collection: Tasmanian Museum and Art Gallery

The lash

Flogging was a very standard minor to medium level punishment for men until the early 1850s, and thereafter for serious offences, but it was rarely used for women. By the time Van Diemen's Land was settled its use was significantly declining and ceased altogether in the mid-1810s. However the lash was used on a very small number of women in VDL. On 15 March 1806, Elizabeth Murphy was brought before Lt Governor Collins on a charge of 'writing or causing to be wrote a letter directed at Francis Dring containing the most infamous language and accusing him of a most heinous crime.' She was sentenced 'to be tied by her hands to the cart drawn by the Gaol Gang, stripped, and to receive 25 lashes, and sent to the settlement at Risdon.'

Abolition of whipping for women

As we have seen above a small percentage of convicted offenders during the six years 1805-1810 were sentenced to either a fine or to whipping. By 1817 the law regarding whipping of women changed. At least part of the concept of flogging was the public disgrace and degradation it entailed. It seems however that the public humiliation of a woman being stripped to the waist and flogged, with all its lewd connotations, preyed on the minds of an increasingly puritanical public spirit. Much as the lower class mob might enjoy the sight and sound of the spectacle, the legislators were persuaded otherwise. A British Act of Parliament (57 George 3, c75) abolished the public whipping of women in 1817, and three years later the Parliament abolished whipping for women in private (presumably in the gaol yard or cells) under 1 George 4, c57. The dispatch of copies of these laws as a matter of course to each of the British colonies would have immediately ended the practices of flogging or carting in New South Wales and Van Diemen's Land. The 1820 law replaced whipping of women with six months or less imprisonment with hard labour, or seven days or less solitary confinement.

The stocks

A relatively common punishment dating back to medieval times was to send a woman to the stocks for an hour or a few hours, often combined with a period, usually three days, a week or fourteen days in the cells on bread and water. A sentence to the stocks meant that the woman sat on a log or low stool in a public place, with her feet sticking out in front of her,

Fatigued but not ill

Assistant Surgeon Owen gave evidence that he had seen Alice Blackstone who was suckling her baby when she had walked to George Town from Launceston and she was fatigued but not ill and believed that it was alright for her to return 35 miles to Launceston the next day wearing the iron collar.

Assistant Surgeon RW Owen, George Town;
to Commissioner Bigge, 8 July 1820

This profligate adultress

…In April 1819, Alice Blackstone was ordered by me into Hospital until her confinement should be over, and orders were also issued by me, that every care should be taken of her. She was confined some time after, and, on her recovery, sent up by water to Launceston.

In the month of September following, not much more than two months after she was confined, she then walked down again to Mr Leith by land for her own pleasure, notwithstanding my repeated orders to the contrary. It was then …that I fully determined to point out to this profligate adultress that I would not allow her or her seducer (who had whilst Superintendent of Crown Servants [convicts] cruelly treated her husband to effect his purpose) to trifle with my Orders, and deemed it my duty to make an example, by sending her up to Launceston, with a small Iron Collar the usual punishment thro' the Colonies for women of Infamous character.

The Proceedings will prove, by the evidence of Assistant Surgeon Owen, that the said woman was well able to walk to Launceston… the punishment itself (not having any other mode of punishing women of that character) was trifling, particularly towards the woman in question who by the proceedings is proved to be a thief and an adultress, and was the cause that her Husband was treated in a tyrannical manner by Mr Leith and such punishment was trifling compared to the profligacy which I am sorry to say exists in this Settlement…

Lt. Colonel Gilbert Cimitiere, Commandant of Port Dalrymple
at George Town to Commissioner Bigge, 8 June 1820

her ankles locked in a timber frame. The purpose was humiliation, and unlike the pillory where head and hands were imprisoned, the stocks were not usually considered an opportunity for the hurling of refuse by the public.

Use of the stocks was a particularly common punishment in the period before the establishment of the original female factories, but was rarer than sending a women to the cells in the Gaol. Punishment by the stocks declined particularly after the establishment of the Cascades and Launceston Female Factories in 1829 and 1834 respectively, with their more stringent classification systems, though they continued in occasional use until the probation period. The stocks were particularly favoured for offences such as disorderly behaviour, drunkenness, or disturbing the peace.

Rachel Wright is a good example of the later use of the stocks. Assigned to her husband, she was sentenced to the stocks seven times between 1827 and 1837 for drunken behaviour. For similar behaviour during the same period she was just as likely to receive a fine of five shillings (eight times), a reprimand (four times), seven days in the cells (once), 28 days in the cells (once) or being bound over to keep the peace (once).

Sometimes a sentence to the stocks was combined with other punishments as with Eleanor Doyle who for being drunk was sentenced in 1816 to three days in the cells on bread and water and to be put in the stocks for an hour each day. In the same year Margaret Hughes, assigned to her husband, was convicted by the magistrates for disorderly behaviour, received one week in the cells on bread and water together with three one-hour periods in the stocks.

Often there was an ascending level of punishment for second offences within a short period. On 17 June 1822 Mary Hart for absconding was sentenced to one week in the Gaol on bread and water with two periods of stocks for two hours. When she was found guilty of pilfering some tea and sugar on 2 July 1822, barely two weeks later, she was sentenced to six months gaol, including 14 days in the cells on bread and water and to three periods in the stocks each of three hours.

Though many of the sentences for the stocks were for a salutary hour or two on public display, sometimes the sentence was much longer. In 1830 Sarah Wilson, Free by Servitude, who was a particularly problematic drunkard received three separate sentences of four hours in the stocks in

71

less than two months. In the two year period she received many fines and was frequently bound over to keep the peace. In 1816 and 1817, Mary Curley and Jane Quinn each received 6 hours in the stocks for being drunk and disorderly and being out after curfew respectively. It was Mary's only offence on record.

The iron collar

The iron collar, or 'joug' as it was known in Scotland, was a traditional punishment dating from medieval times which was used on both male and female convicts in the Australian colonies. It was used on women for the first forty-five years of Transportation but it was dispensed with as the female factories became more effective as places of coercion, control and punishment.

Minor offenders

Mary Boylan and Jane Wheeler were charged on 22 December 1814 with 'quitting Hobart Town without a pass' and were sentenced to 14 days in the cells on bread and water. We are not told where they were headed but it might have only been to New Town or Queenborough which were only a couple of miles out of town. Possibly they were off together to seek out James Brown, Jane's intended husband. They were married less than a week after she had served her 14 days. Mary's only other offences were four drunk and disorderly charges between 1817 and 1819 by which time she also was married and had a ticket-of-leave. She was fined five shillings on each occasion. Jane Wheeler's career was even more chequered and she later faced some serious charges.

Jane Murray only had one colonial offence on her record, but it is an intriguing one. On 6 November 1816, Jane married James Walthorn (Free), at Hobart Town. The next day she was before the magistrates for 'insulting her master and refusing to return to his employ'. She had obviously expected to be immediately assigned to her husband. Found guilty, she was sent 'to work in the Brickfields during the Lieutenant Governor's pleasure'.

Ann Carroll had been married 14 years and free by servitude for nine years in 1828 when she finally fell foul of the magistrates for being drunk and disorderly and raising a false hue and cry for which she had to find sureties to be of good behaviour for six months.

Serious offenders

A year after her arrival Isabella Noble married Boyle Thomas, Free, at Hobart Town. A year later in August 1816 she was fined five shillings for being disorderly and abusing the constables. Six weeks later she was found guilty of breaking into a house and stealing and for this she was sentenced to 3 years at Newcastle, NSW. She was back in Hobart Town in 1820 and was twice fined five shillings for drunkenness within a week in late 1829.

Anne Fraine married William Baker, a convict, on Boxing Day 1814, six months after her arrival at the Derwent. In addition to a few drunkenness convictions between 1817 and 1832 she got herself into a lot of serious trouble. Sentenced to seven years transportation in March 1812, her convict career was to persist to June 1834, a total of 22 years. In 1816 she had to find sureties for threatening Ann Rook (who was probably Ann Rorke, the oldest woman on board the *Catherine* and who was an invalid in the Factory in 1833: 'an old and infirm lady', and who died at the New Norfolk Colonial Hospital in 1839 reputedly at the age of 90. Ann was one of those who had no offences recorded against her.). The following year 1817 Anne was found guilty of receiving stolen sugar and 'aiding and assisting William Mason to rob His Majesty's Stores' for which she received a month at hard labour in the Gaol. Just to make sure they made their point, and perhaps also suggesting the circumstances of the crime, the magistrates also fined her five shillings for being drunk and disorderly. On 30 May 1827, now free by servitude she appeared before the magistrates and was committed for trial at the Supreme Court for: 'stealing on the 19th May one cotton handkerchief, value 1 shilling and three shirts, value 21 shillings, the property of James Kemp'.

On 2 June she was acquitted, but reflecting the situation of being an ex-convict in a convict colony she was brought up again a fortnight later on a charge of 'simple grand larceny', found guilty and sentenced to another 7 years transportation. A convict once again she now was to be assigned and had work as a servant, a situation she obviously found difficult. Fifteen months later she was before the magistrates for 'disobedience of orders in refusing to go to the service of Mrs Dark' for which she got two weeks in Gaol, one week on bread and water. That quietened her down for four months but on 3 February 1829 she was in trouble for 'drunkenness, disobedience of orders and insolence' for which she received 14 days on bread and water in the brand new cells at the Cascades Female Factory. On the day she was due out she assaulted Donald McDonald (possibly a

,table) and was immediately sent back to the Factory for 6 months. ar of any offence for almost two years after her release, and assigned once again to her husband, Ann Fraine committed her last recorded offence when she was found drunk, and was sent to the cells for 6 days.

Capital punishment

The ultimate punishment was used a number of times on female convicts. The first woman executed in Van Diemen's Land was Mary McLaughlan. Sent to the Factory in 1830, Mary was delivered of a son whom she killed by stuffing down the lavatory. It seems likely that the reason she did this was either shame or disgust. She had a husband and family in Britain and it was rumoured that the father of the child was a gentleman. When the time came to approach the scaffold a clergyman persuaded her not to denounce the father to the huge crowd who flocked to see a woman hang.

The old woman and the executioner

Margaret Ball had arrived in Hobart Town in 1818, transported for seven years. She was forty years of age when she arrived, worked for Captain James Kelly, the whaler and entrepreneur, for many years and never got into any trouble with the authorities. She received her free certificate in the minimum time.

One Saturday evening in April 1826 she was in the Elizabeth Street Watch House when Constable Blundell ducked out to buy some candles. While he was gone, Margaret, by this stage 48 years old and described in the press as "an elderly inoffensive woman" was stabbed over twenty times by a man named Thomson, who then cut her throat. He could give no reason for the murder except for his "miserable condition and satiety of life". He had formerly been the executioner at Launceston. Thomson was described by the paper to have "long held human life at a cheap rate" and to have been before the police a number of times with "charges of cutting and maiming".

As an executioner, Thomson would have received a salary and conditions only to be dreamed of by his fellow convicts, but at the price of remaining friendless, shunned by free and convict alike. Margaret's murder was a direct outcome of living in a convict society where numerous persons who held life cheaply, as did Thomson, existed in a nether-world of exhausted ennui at the futility of their life.

Another convict, Eliza Benwell, was hanged for murder in 1845 and Richard Davis, the historian of capital punishment in Tasmania, feels that in this case a miscarriage of justice probably occurred.

Ticket-of-Leave and Free women

When women were given their ticket-of-leave, they were generally free to choose their employer, could move district having notified the local magistrate's office and were partially free of the disciplinary regime imposed on assigned women. They also appear to have been largely free of the evening curfew except when found in undesirable or shady circumstances. The magistrates may have taken that into account particularly when issuing an admonition or reprimand. There was usually a gradation of punishments for similar offences according to the status of the offender. For drunkenness, say, a free person would be admonished, a ticket-of-leave holder would be fined five shillings and an assigned servant would get three or four days in the cells.

Where sexual offences were concerned the difference between having a ticket-of-leave or being an assigned convict might not have been quite so clear-cut. On 10 November 1837 Ann Pirie, 14 years transportation, who had arrived seven years before on the *Mellish*, appeared in the local magistrate's court in New Norfolk. She had a ticket-of-leave and had worked for two months for Mrs Baker and Mrs Holt but lived at Mr Knight's. The magistrates found:

> This woman being pregnant and not knowing by whom she is with child it is recommended that she be kept to hard labor in the Second Class Female Factory for 6 months and to be deprived of her Ticket-of-Leave.

Similarly, on 27 February 1839, Sarah Talbot, 7 years transportation, who had arrived on the *New Grove* in 1835 and who now had a Ticket-of-Leave, appeared in the court.

> Upon the complaint of Mr Smith with being absent from her place of residence last night and found in the house of Mr Chilton. Having been forbidden only a few days before to enter the house of Chilton where she had formed an improper connection she is to be kept to hard labor for 3 Calendar Months in the female House of Correction Hobart and recommended to be deprived of her Ticket-of-Leave.

With these two cases we see how difficult it is to assess just how much more freedom ticket-of-leave women had over their assigned counterparts. Ann Pirie's offence seems to have been not just that she was pregnant but that there was no acknowledged father.

Of course even free persons could get caught up in elements of the convict discipline system, though with significantly lesser punishments than for the assigned convicts or ticket-of-leave holders. Just the day after Sarah Talbot appeared in the New Norfolk court, Media Ludgater, a widow with a young family, and licensee of *The Bee Hive Tavern* in Goulburn Street (the most notorious street for bars and brothels in Hobart) appeared before the magistrates in Hobart. She was charged with being in 'breach of the Quarter Sessions Act in permitting a female servant who was absent from her service without leave to be in her house [pub].' She was fined £10 and in spite of a petition by a dozen leading and worthy citizens of the town for a remission of the fine on the grounds that the *Bee Hive* was well-conducted and the widow 'industrious and deserving of any indulgence', the magistrates found otherwise: 'we cannot recommend a remission of fine... Mrs Ludgater's House is far from being well conducted.'

There was no suggestion in the charge that the *Bee Hive* was a brothel or even that the female convict was drinking or misbehaving in any way other than merely being on the premises. The *Bee Hive* closed in the same year, but whether from the effects of the offence and fine or whether to the detriment of Mrs Ludgater and her children is speculation but this incident certainly shows how the convict discipline system constantly impinged on the lives of the free as well as the bond.

The life-long punishment

Exile as a punishment was chosen by the British authorities not only because it got rid of criminals but because it was greatly feared and caused immense psychic pain particularly to those who had a settled life at home in Britain.

So dreadful was the prospect that five women who had been spared from death sentences in 1789 and were eventually transported per the *Lady Juliana*, tried to refuse their pardons. Mary Burgess, whose term of transportation was to be seven years, said in court, "I would rather die than leave my child and my husband behind me." Sarah Cowden said, "No... I am innocent... I will not accept it, I will die first."

As much as some commentators have portrayed the economic benefits for many who found themselves in the antipodean colonies, such benefits are really only appropriate when discussing free emigrants: those who freely choose to uproot themselves from their background, often people of few or limited ties and of an adventurous disposition. Such views are not only predicated on Australia as an immigrant country in the 1950s and 1960s, but also they tend to be viewed from an economically rationalist perspective that esteems economic improvement above all or most other aspects of the human condition.

Many of the female convicts were in personal situations very different from those of free emigrants. A large proportion were already married and an unknown proportion had significant permanent and ongoing defacto relationships in Britain. Quite a few had children whom they had left behind, some to be looked after by husbands and partners, others by their parents and siblings, and yet others to be looked after by the uncertain institutions for foundlings and orphans in Britain.

The pain of banishment: the despair of exile, the agony of loss

The simple fact is that some people are relatively happy to travel, to emigrate, to leave behind hearth, home and country, family and friends, and go elsewhere and make a new life. Others look on such transmigration with horror and despair.

Most writers on the convict question have accentuated the positive aspects of material considerations upon the lives of convicts and emancipists. In the Australian colonies the average convict ate better and had more opportunities than would have been the case in Britain. But this is to ignore the huge disadvantages. Male convicts for instance had relatively few opportunities to find a mate. Most were condemned to live solitary, sexless lives deprived of that most ordinary and normal condition of marrying and having children.

In Britain in the 1700s and 1800s, and in similar societies, one of the strongest social and moral obligations for a son or daughter was that of looking after aged parents by providing for them financially, emotionally and by giving them a home when they were ill, infirm or no longer able to work. The commandment 'Honour thy mother and thy father' meant far more than mere obedience as a child and respectful treatment when you became an adult. Of the letters that have survived from convicts to their parents, it is clear from many that the convicts felt intense sorrow and sometimes despair at not being the solace and support of their parents in their declining years. Similarly, parents were often unable to emotionally reconnect with the children they had left behind, even when they were able to correspond regularly.

But for most convicts and their families, relationships were cut forever in the last sight of loved ones as they were shuffled out of the courtroom, or when they were loaded onto coaches or wagons or, in the case of Londoners, when the gaolers permitted a last meeting before embarkation. A last meeting that might be cancelled arbitrarily, with no redress, at the very last moment. As happened with women from Newgate who lost their last chance to see their relatives before boarding the *Morley*.

Their departure in 1820 coincided with the trial of the Cato Street conspirators who had planned to blow up the Prime Minister and Cabinet. The heightened security measures at Newgate meant that the usual farewell meeting with mothers, sisters and daughters was cancelled. The London press made much of the resulting riot which left furniture, windows and bedding smashed, broken and torn beyond repair.

Chapter 8. A New World

When Surgeon-superintendent Reid of the *Morley* started looking closely at the way morals and behaviour interacted in New South Wales and Van Diemen's Land he was scandalised to realise that bigamy between the convicts was an everyday occurrence.

> Marriages are continually taking place between men and women whose wives and husbands are living in England …this breach of law is punishable at home by transportation ….[it] occurs also very often for the purpose of getting a woman out of the Factory.

The irony that bigamy was a transportable offence had not escaped the eagle eye of Commissioner Bigge who in the same year had closely questioned both the Reverends Knopwood and Youl in Van Diemen's Land regarding the issue. Knopwood's attitude was quite clear from his reply, that if he did not question them closely or directly the convicts would not have to lie too seriously about their already married state: they only had to make a declaration, and did not have to swear an oath.

David Collins who had been the first Van Diemen's Land Lieutenant Governor in 1804 had in that same year published a book on the foundation of New South Wales sixteen years before. Collins noticed that 'the general sentiment on the subject by the convicts' was that most believed that marriages celebrated in the new colony were not binding and that in the early days the government 'wished that matrimonial connections should be promoted … [and] none who applied were ever rejected' except when everybody knew that one of the betrothed was definitely married in Britain.

The belief that the very act of being sentenced to transportation created grounds for a voluntary divorce seems to have been part of the folk tradition of much of Britain. Some held that you had to have been sentenced to death, and thus could be considered by the other spouse to be legally dead. Others believed that the minimum sentence of transportation being seven years, meant that the convict would be missing for seven years and thus a remarriage could be contracted. Reverend Youl, Chaplain of Port Dalrymple stated to Commissioner Bigge at Launceston in 1820: '…all the convicts think that a sentence of Transportation for any term releases them from their engagements'.

Convicts and concubinage

Q: Do you find that there is a Disposition to marry amongst the People of this Settlement?

A: At present I do not, they have so long been without the presence of a Clergyman, that adultery and prostitution are common. [but not among the native born].

Evidence of Rev. J Youl, Chaplain, Launceston;
to Commissioner Bigge, 27 April 1820

Q: Are the women [convicts] very profligate?

A: They are.

Q: Do they change the men that they cohabit with?

A: They do. I impute this to their fondness for liquor, and they will leave a person with whom they have lived for a short time in order to obtain Liquor from another.

Evidence of Assistant Surgeon RW Owen, George Town;
to Commissioner Bigge, 15 April & 8 July 1820

[There are] Female convicts living with officers in Launceston including District Assistant Commissary General Walker and Captain Barclay, the magistrate.

Rev. J Youl, Chaplain, Launceston;
to Commissioner Bigge, 27 April 1820

…. Governor Phillip …proclaimed that permission to leave the colony would be denied to any freed convict with a dependent wife or children. According to Collins this measure had been prompted by William Bryant and others frequently stating that they did not consider colonial marriages to be binding.

The problem was that from the earliest period both the colonial authorities and the clergymen had encouraged the convicts to marry. By the 1820s the authorities wanted to control the convicts by punishing those living together while not married and especially those who were causing social turmoil and moral scandal by living with someone other than their spouse. Bigge's recommendations were merely that better records should be obtained in Britain and sent out so that fewer convicts would be able to hoodwink the authorities.

Bigge was mainly voicing the concerns of Reverend Marsden at Parramatta and twelve years later Marsden was still worried about the issue and writing to Elizabeth Fry. Fry's reply was strange to say the least. According to her the government thought:

> the best plan to adopt is not to have any account taken of whether the women are married or not …those who make it clear they are married certainly should be treated as such, but it appears almost impossible [to be sure]. Our Under Secretary of State also says that it is a law of the country, that any woman who has not heard of her husband for seven years may marry again.

Clearly Fry agreed with this plan which rather ingenuously combined the circumstance of a spouse missing and presumed dead with that of a person who had a pretty good idea of where the absent partner could be found. Perhaps Fry believed that a form of divorce should be available to the convicts who most certainly would not have been able either financially or through connections to obtain a divorce through a private members bill in parliament.

Strumpets and whores?

The female convicts had an extremely bad reputation, largely undeserved, at the time they were alive and, thanks to many modern historians who have written about them, the bad reputation has continued.

One of the most extraordinary debates that has taken place in the second half of the twentieth century has been about the behaviour and sexual proclivities of the female convicts. This has to some extent taken place in isolation from the enormous changes that have happened in our own century, as though when discussing the female convicts there is a collective amnesia regarding our current acceptance of the individual woman's right to have a full, complete and satisfying sexual life as a normal part of living.

But women didn't just achieve this right, they have been asserting it and living it throughout history. After all, people don't change that much.

What has changed is a woman's right, and for that matter a man's right as well, to discuss the issues involved in an open and forthright manner. Yet when debate turns to the matter of how the female convicts behaved, the tendency has been to judge them according to the standards, however hypocritical, of the middle classes and the officialdom of their own century.

Much of their reputation was ill-founded at the time, based principally on a non-understanding of different class morals, and an insistence that by merely demanding that the female convicts change their attitudes, language and behaviour they would immediately do so and become well-spoken, compliant household drudges for the middle classes. The remarkable thing is not that quite a few were unwilling or unable to undergo this immediate and extraordinary transformation, but that so many, probably a majority, did undergo such a change.

Language itself was a problem, or rather the lack of a language that could be used in public discourse about private matters so as to convey the truth without being salacious or offensive and without being seen as somehow justifying immorality by merely speaking of practical realities.

The simple situation was that although people in the late eighteenth and early nineteenth century were aware of the hypocrisy and double speak around the question of sexuality they simply didn't have the language or acceptable words and concepts to deal with it on a formal basis. It wasn't possible, for instance, for a colonial governor to write back to England saying something like: 'Many of the convicts have paired off, have successful sex lives, and their family life and family responsibilities are helping them become responsible and honest members of society'. It was equally impossible for him to write: 'It's a good thing that there are a proportion of women convicts who are happy to make their living through prostitution, otherwise because of the lack of available partners all the men would be buggering each other all the time, just like they do in the

> "She is a notorious strumpet and a most dangerous girl...
> Repeatedly I have been obliged to put her into irons and confined her in the Coal-Hold."
>
> Matthew Burnside, Surgeon-superintendent re Julia Mullins, 1826

Navy'. There was no language to deal formally with these issues, and there was no place for recognising realities of sexual drives.

This lack of formal language or contexts to deal with the sexual nature of individuals was reflected in other ways. Bigamy was a major ecclesiastical sin as well as an extremely serious civil crime. It could get you hanged or transported for Life. But in the absence of formal divorce, clergymen of the eighteenth century mould, such as Reverent Knopwood of Hobart Town, obviously thought it much better to remain ignorant of people's marital status than to look into the question too closely. No doubt his justification was that the state would gain more by colonial couples living formally married rather than merely cohabiting or as the more technical would have it 'in a state of concubinage'. By doing this of course colonial society could be seen as working in an acceptable manner, convicts could be seen as having become successfully integrated back into a normal form of society.

The culture gap

Openly 'brazen' and flirtatious behaviour is notoriously hard to interpret across cultures. We must not forget that there was a huge cultural divide between the poorer classes and the middle classes in British and Australian colonial societies.

To get a notion of the cultural divide in colonial Australia, try taking any cross section of society (let alone a section that has already shown that they are prepared to break laws which may lead to a death sentence). Pluck them from their society and loved ones, having assured them they will never see them again. Send them on a potentially dangerous voyage half-way around the world, put them in a totally foreign landscape, forbid them love and affection, and assure them if they have babies that the children will be taken from them for a number of years. Do all this with the belief that you can bend them to your arbitrary will and use them as household drudges with a high degree of unsupervised time but no degree of autonomy. Forbid them association with their natural and freely chosen associates. Then expect them not to rebel or take opportunities to skimp on their work or to talk to the men they came across. Did the authorities really believe that the female convicts would not take every opportunity to rebel and to subvert the system?

One of the major problems was in the upper middle class attitudes of the people who ran the system. For them, the convicts were workers and servants, and female convicts were all suited to be household servants. However, few of the female convicts had a proven and satisfactory history of being successful live-in household servants, positions that required not only training in their daily tasks but a natural aptitude and an ability to fit in, a demureness of spirit, an ability to hold your tongue and, most importantly, to keep secrets

What was a servant?

The generic, broader, earlier term was very generally used in forms such as *assigned servant*, *crown servant* and even in the most common way of concluding a letter or note as *your most obedient servant*. In Britain the term had been embodied in such concepts as *the masters and servants acts*: Acts of Parliament which controlled many if not most aspects of employer and employee relationships. Historian Barrie Dyster tells us that during the 1820s doubt was cast on whether the English legislation could be applied in New South Wales and that consequently 'the local authorities in 1828 promulgated *An Act for the better regulation of Servants, Labourers and Work People*. This legislation [was] usually known as the Masters and Servants Act…' In Van Diemen's Land the first master and servant legislation had to wait until 1840 to be promulgated, not the least because an 1837 Act which was scarcely different had been refused the Royal

---

Truth and consequences

In 1831 Bridget Nolan charged Captain Bamber, her master, with having an incestuous relationship with his daughter and, upon his finding out her knowledge of the affair, threatening to have her sent to the Factory. The magistrate, instead of facing Captain Bamber with the allegation, charged Bridget with '...having laid scandalous and malicious charges against her master'. The magistrate refused to hear evidence from the other convict servants in the house who, Bridget claimed, all knew of the affair, and he refused to hear from Mary Brown, an eyewitness. Neither Bamber nor his daughter were asked to refute the charges in court. Bridget Nolan was found guilty and sent to the Factory. The magistrate recommended that she be kept there 'for the remainder of her sentence and never be assigned again'. However someone in the government must have had a sense of justice for, although she served a number of years in the Factory, she was on assignment to another master in 1834.

Assent ostensibly because of inequities unfavourable to employees. Both legally and in common conversation, to refer to someone as a servant during the colonial period could mean quite a number of things we would not ordinarily think of.

Terms such as indoor servants, domestic servants, house or household servants are often necessary for us to be able to fully identify the main position or job description. Even here we can be misled. For instance indoor servant usually meant that the servant was employed indoors but might refer to someone who worked close to the house and hence was part of the domestic economy, rather than the farm or business economy. Similarly domestic servant might refer to someone who worked mainly out of doors like the family carriage groom, or a milk maid. Here once again the reference is to whether they were seen to make up part of the domestic as opposed to the farm economy. It seems that most male assigned servants wherever their actual job was, indoors or out of doors, tended to live outside of the main house, though on the larger establishments their quarters would be separated from those of the farm workers.

Female convict servants nearly all lived inside the main house or, if it were a very large household, sometimes in immediately adjacent or nearby quarters. Almost invariably they were involved with, and almost all of their work was carried out as part of, the domestic economy of the household. Cooking, kitchen work, cleaning, acting as maid, childminder, charwoman, laundry worker, household sewing and mending of clothes were probably the most common tasks for those who worked largely indoors. Dairymaid, feeding farmyard animals, collecting eggs, milking cows, tending the kitchen garden, shopping, running messages, supervising and taking children for outings or walks would have been the main outdoor tasks.

Most assignments would have required a mixture of many of these tasks but sometimes women were employed specifically as cooks, wetnurses, or nursery maids or governesses and were able to insist that they only perform the one task. Good cooks and educated women were difficult to get and retain, and wetnurses were in high and immediate demand.

The luck of the draw, except...

Assignment was usually by lot, with the next approved master receiving the next available female convict. However there are a number of examples of highly qualified and experienced cooks being passed from senior government officer to senior government officer or from the gentry to the gentry. We only get to know about these women if and when they became a particular problem or were always getting into trouble. Otherwise they didn't make it into the records. If you can imagine an excellent cook being given the opportunity to live in relatively luxurious surroundings, eating the best food, perhaps with the assistance of a scullery maid, and with numerous other minor perks, the advantages of not getting into trouble far outweighed the inconvenience of being a servant. In such circumstances most would not have been heard of again. They would serve their time, get a ticket-of-leave, and go about their lives.

However, from some cases it is apparent that even when female convict behaviour was at times problematical, nevertheless the more skilled of them were in high demand and the gentry and officers got the first pick.

Mary Revlet had received a Life sentence for larceny and was 38 and a widowed servant when she was transported in 1821. Amongst others she worked for were Jocelyn Thomas, Lieutenant Miller, Chapman, Hone, Captain Wood, John Burnett and James Kelly. All were senior officers or gentry. Typically she stayed out of trouble for between a year and two years until her temper, alcohol or her penchant for sharing a bed with a

---

A liar, a thief and a wench, but...

In a letter to his wife, written in 1824, GTWB Boyes tells of a 'Lady of a worthy Law Officer who received an early visit from an acquaintance whose husband was 'not far removed from the Head of the Branch'. The visitor was not happy with a female servant for whom the Lady had written a reference: "In the first place she steals everything that comes her way — then there is no believing a single word she says— and she has twice staid out the whole night, and I discovered by accident that she had passed each night with a different soldier in the Barracks!"

Her friend replied, "...she was undoubtedly the best servant I had met with during the six years of my residence in this place. I must admit that she is a liar, a thief and a wench, but she is also clean, sober, cleanly and industrious and I will take it upon me to say that there are not five girls in her situation in the Colony with half so many good qualities."

man would get her into trouble. Mrs Kelly, for instance, received a bottle in her face which had been aimed at her husband. Also typically, the charges related to a number or sequence of incidents and it was not unusual for her masters or mistresses to want her back after she had been punished. It is clear from the records that Mary was a highly prized servant, and that most of the charges resulted from a 'final straw' situation, where previous incidents had been overlooked. It is equally obvious that when her nuisance value overwhelmed her servant value and the masters finally got sick of her, her skills were sufficient to get her another job with the gentry who, from dining out at their friends' homes, were well aware of her talents, and were prepared at least for a time to overlook her faults.

Phoebe Allen was also in high demand for her skills. Forty-three years old, and married with a seventeen year old child when she was transported for fourteen years for stealing a silk dress, she had been a cook, housemaid and highly skilled laundress for twenty years back in Britain. In Phoebe's case, in spite of a huge number of charges and frequent incarceration she was more often than not returned to her master's house after serving her time. This would have been at either his or his wife's instigation.

While most assigned female convicts worked both within the traditional constraints of being within the household economy and within the intimacy of the house and household overseen by the mistress of the house, a significant segment were employed at tasks more related to a business run by either the master or mistress of the house. Pubs, laundries, sewing and tailoring shops and similar ventures all would have had female convicts working there.

Whether as domestic or business servants, the female convicts were part of the lives and the households of the free settlers. As people, as human beings from different backgrounds and with different ways of life, they had to live with each other on a daily basis.

The master class

For a number of reasons, British society was traditionally one that allowed more upward and downward social mobility than many of its continental contemporaries. There was room at the top, though the vast majority of roles were held by aristocrats, for outstanding men of political, social, martial, religious or economic success and women of outstanding families, beauty, social grace or economic means.

The entrenched attitudes to upward and downward mobility were to have a huge effect on the ways that the Australian convict colonies operated in dealing with all levels of society. In the absence of a significant presence of genuine aristocracy, the top element of society was comprised of appointed officials: governors and their families and entourages, senior government officials, army and navy officers, churchmen, large landholders and substantial merchants. This was not too different from the British experience, but it was in the construction of the lower classes and middle classes that the experiences of early Australian colonial society differed substantially from its British origins.

The lower class, and the lowest of the low

Since early New South Wales and Van Diemen's Land were convict colonies, it is no surprise that they immediately placed convicts at the bottom of society. Within the society of convicts themselves there was a hierarchy which had at the bottom those under sentence, then ascended to those assigned to masters, those assigned to the government, educated convicts working for the government in barracks, those in lodgings, ticket-of-leave holders and lastly government employed ticket-of-leave holders such as convict constables, penitentiary or female factory workers. Ex-convicts generally fitted into this lower class, though some were able through economic success to escape to the middle classes. To these we might add a number of categories of very poor people who had come to the colonies free but who were considered by society at large to be pretty hopeless: the frequently drunk and incapable, those who consorted with convicts, brothel keepers and the like. These people too could find themselves consigned to the lowest of the low, the mainly convict class within which they intermingled.

Middle class and moving up

It was the middle class in the colonies that differed most surprisingly from the British model. Some of the early convict arrivals who had married well, or had done particularly well at farming or as merchants were definitely allowed into this group, but as time went on it became increasingly difficult for ex-convicts to escape their origins. Although female convicts who married well and were considered respectable were always able to move up the social scale, they might have to face the occasional insult or veiled reminder of their origins when in *polite* society.

The prodigiously wealthy Mary Reibey was an object of scorn becaus her convict origins as far as Jane Franklin was concerned, even mor because her sons were boring.

The convict based society in Australia turned a number of points of social etiquette on their heads. A gentleman could no longer refer to a drunken, useless carter or ferryman of free estate merely by his surname. 'Smith' became 'Mr Smith', and 'Jones' became 'Mr Jones'. This protocol may well have accelerated the Australian penchant for informality in calling people by their first name, though it should be realised that the taking of unwarranted liberties with first names was to some extent paralleled in New Zealand, Canada and the United States, as was generally noted by middle-class English southerners unaware that such a tradition was unremarkable in at least Lancashire and Yorkshire and probably in many other regional areas of Britain.

With the occasional exception of those ne'er do wells mentioned above, all those who came free to the colonies were considered to be within the middle or upper classes. This could be taken to absurd lengths as when an ex-convict who had served a sentence in one colony was considered to have arrived free in another. All men in this class were referred to by the title Mr, thus immediately differentiating them from the convicts and ex-convicts who were almost invariably referred to by their surname, though occasionally by their first name. In formal situations, just the bare surname would be used for a convict.

Female convicts assigned to their husbands would still be referred to by their maiden name and as wife of their husband's name, but upon receiving her pardon or ticket-of-leave she would quickly come under the title of Mrs and her husband's name. That is, 'Jane Smith, wife of Mr Jones' was a convict but as soon as she was free she became simply 'Mrs Jones'.

The convicts themselves were able to assert a certain measure of social control by refusing to acknowledge the term *convict*; instead they were *servants* or *crown servants* or *government men or women*. Furthermore, government officials and magistrates were known to get very tetchy and impatient with masters or mistresses of assigned servants who had initiated trouble by ignoring this essential element of colonial etiquette.

A city sparrow, not a bush bird

Rebecca Kerr was 16 years old, four foot eleven inches tall and late of Fleet Street, London when she was transported for 10 years. She arrived on the *Nautilus* on Monday 29 August 1838 and barely three months after arriving in Hobart Town she was facing the magistrates at the New Norfolk court accused of insolence by her master, Mr Lightfoot. In spite of Mr Lightfoot's sworn evidence she was found not guilty but admonished by the magistrates anyway. The next morning, Tuesday, District Constable Smith hauled her before the court on a charge of "disorderly conduct in refusing to return to her service" and she was sentenced to three days in the cells on bread and water.

Friday morning found her obstinate in her refusal to return to Mr Lightfoot's service and Smith charged her with misconduct in "refusing to return to her service without sufficient cause", the *sufficient cause* presumably referring to Smith having questioned her as to whether her master had improperly used or abused her. The sentence was a further three days, but this time the magistrates emphasised three days and *nights* in a *solitary* cell. This was finally too much for Rebecca and she returned to her master's service.

We hear no more of her for seven weeks, but then on Saturday 19 January 1839, her master Mr Lightfoot brought her before the magistrates again, this time for insolence and neglect of duty. Lightfoot claimed she wished to be assigned in Hobart. The magistrates officially reprimanded her and sentenced her to 3 months in the 2nd Class at the Cascades Female Factory and recommended she not be assigned in Hobart upon her release.

Interestingly, and almost uniquely, we know no more of Rebecca. Somewhere along the line she either found a protector or husband who had sufficient reason, connections or bribe money to remove her youthful records from the Black Books or she arranged it herself. Whichever, almost the only record we have of her in Van Diemen's Land are those of the New Norfolk Court.

As for Mr Lightfoot, Rebecca was not the first female convict who had been assigned to him in 1838. She was the sixth in a row.

The Servant Problem

Into the houses of the colonial elite and the middle classes of the tiny colonial proto-cities of Sydney, Hobart and Launceston, were poured the sweepings of the streets of London, Manchester, Dublin and the other great British cities as well as a leavening of women from the fields and small villages of England, Wales, Scotland and Ireland. Some of the female convicts, of course, were also sent to work in small manufactories, as garden and outside servants and as charwomen and housemaids in pubs. But it is largely from those who were household servants that we hear.

These women were not the self-selected household servants of British experience, those who had some experience at home and in the households in their own neighbourhood, and who fancied working in someone else's house either as a waged live-out servant or a salaried live-in servant. Nor were they the successful applicants for an advertised position who had previous experience and 'characters' (references from previous employers). Neither was there the opportunity of a week or two of trial employment where either the mistress or master or indeed the servant herself could discover that they just didn't get along together.

Despite many of the women having claimed to have been servants (and we must remember that the term did not necessarily refer to household servants) this can not be taken by any stretch of the imagination to mean that they had been successful servants or that their experience as servants in Britain would overcome other equally important background elements which might make them very unsatisfactory employees. However it is clear that more than a few became very satisfactory servants indeed, and with the exception of the occasional lapse that brought them before a magistrate, their lives as servants are almost entirely hidden from us.

It is the others, the ones who did not fit, that come to our attention. The colonial officials are the people who brought the failure of the system to our notice. More than any other group, they are the ones that categorise the female convicts. Throughout the convict period we see no attempt to segregate or separate those women who could be expected to be good household servants from others, or to find more congenial work for the others, except for the work provided in the female factories. There appear to have been two exceptions to this, one at the Eagle Farm Female Factory, near Brisbane in Queensland, where all the women did fieldwork and at Emu Plains, in New South Wales, where a small detachment of women

91

were sent to do fieldwork but more particularly to enhance their marriage prospects with the large numbers of male convicts and settlers in the area. But in those cases, there is no record that these women were chosen because they wouldn't make good house-servants.

It is actually quite difficult to be a good house-servant. One needs to guard one's tongue, do things according to the way you are told rather than the way you like, work to another's timetable, fit into the background, and become part of the household but not part of the family. You also have to fit into a different family's culture, and treat the children the way someone else expects you to and not they way you naturally would. Most importantly you have little privacy or time to yourself. This is, after all, someone else's family and not your own; you have no stake in it; and you are treated differently to everybody else. Your person-hood, sexuality, mode of life, your hopes and wishes, your clothes and food and most especially your time are entirely within someone else's control. You may have to prepare food, drink and luxuries of which you are not allowed to partake. No form of external discipline, only self discipline, can enable you to succeed at your tasks and under these controls. But even worse, no matter how successful you are at controlling your own circumstances, you are still at the whim and command of your mistress and master, who may well be neither understanding nor as well acquainted with the pitfalls of having servants and with the limitations of control and discipline as you are.

Irresistible force meets immovable object

Many mistresses of female convicts were of course trained and experienced in dealing with house servants, but whereas normally they would have had limited control over their servants, they were now able to evince almost total power over their servants' personal and private lives. They could forbid all sorts of behaviour that would usually be entirely beyond their control, particularly as far as interpersonal inter-gender relations were concerned. Middle-class morality was changing rapidly from the freer eighteenth century model to the beginnings of what was to be called the Victorian age, with its particularly strict oversight of all human sexuality, but particularly female sexuality. There can be little doubt that British lower class morality was neither moving as fast, nor necessarily in the same direction as that of the middle-class. It was becoming very obvious that the sexual morés of the groups from which most of the female convicts came were almost entirely at odds with the developing Victorian model.

At the same time the growth and respectability of new sects and, within the established churches of Britain, the growth of a Calvinist Evangelical Anglicanism of which Governor Arthur was an exemplar, meant that a larger portion of the community who had power, also wanted to intervene in others' lives in a manner and in matters which had previously been ignored. People with this new view, regardless of their own level of hypocrisy, were no longer prepared to turn a blind eye to public elements or even, if they had direct power over the people involved, the private elements of what they saw as sexual misbehaviour. Combined with this was possible ignorance about people's true sexuality. When they saw women openly displaying sexual desire or openly flaunting their sexual availability, they deemed them to be extraordinarily strange and unnatural creatures. However much the authorities recognised that the men were equally immoral, they attributed this to the naturally base natures of the men. This was the age which pictured women as either the most exalted creatures of pure and kind intentions or as whorish manipulators of the worst elements of men's natures.

Pregnancy as a crime

Reverend H.P. Fry described the comvict women as leading 'most flagitious lives'. The Concise Oxford Dictionary defines flagitious as: 'deeply criminal, atrocious, heinous, villainous'. Fry was hardly alone in this opinion. Almost all 19th Century writers on the female convicts felt that they were the most depraved, degraded and vicious group amongst all of the convicts and certainly far worse than the men. Widespread agreement was that the women were not reformed in the House of Correction but quite the reverse. The only possibility of reformation came through assigning the women to respectable homes as household servants and marrying them off as soon as possible to settlers, whether free or emancipist. This gives a clear indication of what was deemed to be their major depravity - not criminal viciousness but sexual licentiousness. The authorities, and the society they represented, only wanted the women legally married. To them the sight of a ticket-of-leave woman leading an honest quiet life in a de facto relationship (which they termed 'concubinage') with a good man was a horrible offence while a convict woman legally married but just one step ahead of the hangman was quite respectable. That many of the women were already married with families in England whom they could not expect to see again was no excuse in the officals' eyes. They were evidently expected to be chaste for the rest of their lives.

A study by H.S. Payne (of 7,000 female convicts who arrived in VDL 1843-1853) came up with some remarkable facts. Over a third of them never served a sentence in a female factory, a truly amazing achievement considering the trifling offences that resulted in such a punishment. The strangest result of the survey was that although 86% of the women had been transported for theft, only 5% of their offences in VDL were concerned with this crime. Sexual offences, which included misdemeanours such as having an intended husband in her bedroom, amount to only 5% of all offences, and only 3% of the women were charged with prostitution.

Cascades Female House of Correction dealt only with those women who were convicted of offences in the colony or who were pregnant. Out of 150 women, twenty-five gave birth to twenty-eight children at Cascades. The average age of the women was about 26 and they served an average of between four and five years before becoming eligible for a Ticket-of-Leave, so the number of unsanctioned pregnancies by female convicts seems not particularly exceptional. Quite the reverse.

As Payne's study showed, many of the convict women were sent to the Factory merely because of pregnancy. A number of people at the time, including Coroner Moore, commented on the unfairness in incarcerating the pregnant convicts while the men remained unpunished. The law expressed the twin maxims of Victorian hypocrisy: one law for the rich and one for the poor, one morality for the male and one for the female.

The women in the Factory were both poor and female. Commenting on this double damnation, the Committee inquiring into Female Convict Discipline in 1841 said:
...Society ...fixed the standard of the average moral excellence required of women much higher than that which it had erected for men, and that crime was regarded with less allowance when committed by a woman ...because the offender was deemed to have receded further from the average proprieties of her sex... a higher degree of reformation is required in the case of a female, before society will concede to her that she has reformed at all.

Perhaps the worst crime committed against women in history has been to degrade those who fall pregnant while not married or who eked out a living through prostitution due to their poverty. A convict woman was almost wholly at the mercy of her master and even if she was not threatened into sexual relations, the pressure of knowing that her future was largely at the whim of one man would have been sufficient that threats were not required.

Some recognition of this plight seems to have occurred. Many times the allegations made by masters were not upheld by the magistrates. Instead the women were sent to the Factory, not for punishment but to await reassignment, hopefully to a better master or mistress, or at least to one they could get along with. The 1837 Molesworth Committee recognised that while a convict could seek legal redress for harsh or illegal conduct from a master, it was '...rarely sought for, and still more rarely obtained by the injured convict'.

An unfortunate year for Mr Lightfoot

Before his troubles with Rebecca Kerr, Mr Lightfoot of New Norfolk had been assigned five other female convicts as servants. None of them seemed to suit his household.

On 23 February 1838 he charged his servant Rebecca Mace with being absent without leave. Three days later Ellen Fielding who had been in the colony four months was returned to the government as unfit for assigned service. Barely a month later, 28 March, Margaret Tough was sentenced to 2 days cells on bread and water and returned to the government for reassignment. On 5 May Mary Gillespie was officially admonished for refusing to work, then only a fortnight later on 21 May she was in court for insolence and neglect of duty.

Things then went quiet in the Lightfoot household for a while when Margaret Lacey arrived. She could only have been with Lightfoot for four weeks when on 15 August 1838 he charged her with disobedience. She only lasted another four weeks with Lightfoot before being returned to the government.

Interestingly she offended again only once when she received a month at the wash tub for being out after curfew in November 1839, virtually the seventh anniversary of her original sentence.

A drunk and disorderly character

Mary Carter didn't marry until 1824 when she had been in the Colony ten years and she had been married another two years before she had her first brush with authority.

She was fined almost £2 for selling underweight loaves of bread. Twelve months later, something in her life had turned sour and she was reprimanded for "disorderly conduct leaving her house and breaking the windows of her husband's house Sunday night". From this it is possible to assume that she was no longer living with her husband. A month later a charge of breaking the peace was dismissed. A month later again a charge of being drunk and disorderly was also dismissed. When she came before the magistrates five weeks later, once again drunk and disorderly, they were obviously losing their patience and remembering the previous occasions they called it a second offence. This time she was found guilty and had to find sureties for good behaviour. Seven months later she was admonished for again being drunk and disorderly. Five months later, on 1 October 1828, she was up on a more serious charge of being a "drunk and disorderly character and found drunk and disorderly in a disorderly house [brothel or low pub] kept by one John Goundry in Melville Street [Hobart] last night at two o'clock", for which she was sentenced to 14 days hard labour in the Gaol.

Two years later to the month Mary Carter started a real decline: "Drunk last night, being a drunken and disorderly character and having no visible honest means of obtaining a livelihood". For this offence she spent what was probably her first time in the Cascades Female Factory: 28 days hard labour. In all during 1829-32 she faced 13 charges related to drunk and disorderly behaviour for which she was reprimanded once, fined five shillings nine times (once default four hours in the stocks), sent to Gaol in default of fines once, and twice ended up in the Factory. After 1832 we hear of her no more. Did she finally get off the grog? Did she merely find a home and become more discreet? Perhaps she died, but she was still only in her early forties, so the chances are that she cleaned up her act in some form or another. Even more intriguing is what caused her decline in the first place. It seems to be a reasonable guess that her marriage had broken down in 1827 and it was this that led to her decline in the first place, having not offended at all in her first 12 years in the colony.

Chapter 9. The Female Factories

The aim of the female factories was to reform the mind of the female convict through hard unremitting toil, a bland diet, plain clothing, forbidding any luxuries including alcohol and tobacco, constant surveillance, silence and instant obedience. Approval of behaviour meant gradually moving up the classifications, gaining lighter work, companionship, better food and perhaps luxuries in the diet such as tea, sugar and milk until once again they were considered fit to be assigned. Disapproval of behaviour meant poorer diet, removal of luxuries, and being transferred to the "separate apartments" where work and sleep were all carried out in the same separate cell. Severe disapproval meant punishment by the magistrates, perhaps days in the cells on bread and water, removal to the Crime Class, work at the wash-tub or even removal for days or weeks to the triple-doored cell with total deprivation of companionship, sound and light.

Where were the Female Factories?

There were six major institutions for the reception and punishment of female convicts in New South Wales during the convict era between 1801 and the closure of the female part of the system in the late 1840s. They were: Parramatta Female Factory, Newcastle Female Factory, Bathurst Female Factory, Port Macquarie Female Factory, Brisbane Female Factory (in the Moreton Bay District later to be Queensland), and Eagle Farm Female Factory (outer Brisbane). There was also an Orphan School at Parramatta for their children, and for a short period an out-station at Emu Plains, as well as colonial hospitals and short-term gaol accommodation in small town gaols in New South Wales.

There were eight major institutions for the reception of female convicts in Van Diemen's Land starting in the early 1820s. They were: George Town Female Factory; the original Hobart Town Female Factory (in the middle of the town); its successor, the Hobart Town Female House of Correction at Cascades known generally as the Cascades Female Factory (3 kilometres out of town); Launceston Female Factory (successor to the George Town institution); the separate Cascades Female Factory Nursery; Brickfields Female Factory, also known as the Brickfields Hiring Depot, later the

Brickfields Nursery and a branch of the Cascades Female Factory at Brickfields (North Hobart); the probation station hulk *Anson*, moored for most of the time either in or near Prince of Wales Bay on the River Derwent; and the Ross Female Factory, located in a country village roughly halfway between Hobart and Launceston.

There were also a number of other minor or short term institutions which were used to hold or punish female convicts. Examples include nurseries at Liverpool Street and New Town Farm near Hobart, town gaols with short-term cells such as those that can still be seen in the general gaol at Richmond, a small village a few kilometres outside the extent of the modern city of greater Hobart. The other major institution was the Queen's Orphan Schools at New Town, a little less than five kilometres from the centre of Hobart.

Parramatta Female Factory: the original 'factory'

There had always been gaols that were used for both males and females, so too in the new colony of New South Wales. But these gaols were created in the old image of the English town and county gaols and not in the form of the new gaols that would become so commonplace in Britain, the USA and the Australian colonies as the 19th Century progressed.

Thus in October 1796, eight and a half years after Sydney was founded, a log gaol was built at the growing agricultural centre of Parramatta west of Sydney. The purpose of the gaol was to detain male and female convicts who had broken the law or breached the convict regulations. It burnt down at the end of 1799.

However, from the days of the First Fleet there had been an idea that the female convicts would help the new colony to produce some of its own needs in the form of linen and woollen cloth. And it was at the same time as the small log gaol at Parramatta was operating that linen-making equipment was embarked in England on the *Minerva* together with master weaver Edward Wise in 1798. With the arrival of Wise and the equipment a number of men and 'all available women' were put to work making linen. By 1801-2 a manufacturing process was under way employing 20 men and 40 women successfully making blanket material and linen cloth.

In 1804, an upper floor of the rebuilt Parramatta gaol was set aside as both a refuge and as a workplace for women working at producing the woollen and linen cloth. Male convicts working on cloth production were housed on the lower floor. The upper floor was one large room 18 metres by six metres. Initially it had no bedding and the women and children slept amongst the bales of wool and partially manufactured goods. In the early days many of the women just worked in the factory during the day and took lodgings in the town at night, or dossed down in a number of outbuildings that grew up around the main buildings. Laurel Heath notes that, whilst the upper floor worked well as a factory, it was far less successful as a refuge or as living quarters for the women convicts and their children. However, it was to serve as the principal institution for female convicts in NSW until 1821.

That the first substantial institution in the colonies designed to house and control female convicts was a manufacturing establishment, combined with the partial purpose of all the future female houses of correction being to provide disciplinary activity through work and in particular through spinning, weaving, tailoring and cloth and blanket making, makes it seem almost inevitable that all future female convict institutions would be called 'female factories'. And that is what happened.

New Parramatta Female Factory

The new factory at Parramatta was contracted to be built in May 1818 to a design by Francis Greenway the legendary New South Wales colonial architect. Macquarie's new factory was too grandiose for Commissioner Bigge who instructed that all minor architectural embellishments were not to be completed on the grounds of their cost. Designed to hold 300 women, the Parramatta institution was, like the later Cascades Factory, frequently extended and overcrowded. When Cascades opened in 1829 there were 531 women and 61 children at Parramatta. By 1840 and the cessation of Transportation to New South Wales it held 887 women and 405 children. Two years later there were 1203 women in the institution and it was not until the end of that year that the numbers started to decline.

Francis Oakes who had been the Superintendent of the old factory since 1815 was also to be in charge of the new factory. His daughter Mary (wife of Rev. Hutchinson) was later to be the Matron of both the Cascades Factory and the Launceston Factory. However, Oakes resigned in July 1822 after numerous clashes with the visiting magistrate. Personality and professional clashes were to be a serious problem in the running of the Parramatta institution. The worst clash occurred between Superintendent

Clapham and Matron Leach both of whom had been appointed in England and then sent out to run the Factory. Eventually Governor Gipps sacked both of them.

There was an unbelievable riot and mass escape in 1827 when about a hundred and forty women charged into the town and scooped up food as they went. They had been unhappy with their rations being reduced. Eventually the local soldiers got most of them back into the factory where they declared their solidarity with each other and demanded they should all, those who had escaped and those who hadn't, be punished in exactly the same way. Some had even got away into the bush and were not returned for a few days. A few years before a coroner's jury had found that Mary Ann Hamilton had died in the factory as a result of hunger and bad treatment and it was alleged that the staff were stealing the rations of the women. It is quite clear that whether at Cascades or at Parramatta the women were not getting enough to eat.

During the early 1840s the women from the other New South Wales female factories were transferred to Parramatta as the system started to run down and in 1848 the Factory closed.

Newcastle Female Factory

Not all the female institutions started out as manufactories and a few of the smaller ones in New South Wales and the later hiring depots in Van

The new Parramatta Female Factory, visited by Thomas Reid of the *Morley* while it was being built in 1820. Unlike Cascades, the site was 'dry, healthy and cheerful'.

'Female penitentiary, or factory, at Parramata, NSW', by August Earle; Rex Nan Kivell Collection. By permission of National Library of Australia

Diemen's Land appear never to have served this function. In 1804, the same year that new settlements were started at Hobart Town and at Port Dalrymple near George Town, a small penal station was founded at Newcastle. One room was provided for women at the convict barracks, though most were expected to find lodgings. This was still very much the exile as punishment period, and being sent to Newcastle was seen as exile and isolation within the larger exile of NSW. By 1820 there were 51 female convicts at Newcastle and a total of 86 in the district, roughly 9% of the female convict population of NSW. In this year an expansion to the barracks extended the building so that it might house 50 of them. At some stage it became a complete female factory, though it was quite small by comparison to others in the colonies. In 1836 it held only 23 women and five children.

Bathurst Female Factory

In 1817 the institution that was to evolve into the Bathurst Female Factory was founded as 'a staging depot' for the female convicts being sent across the Blue Mountains to work as assigned servants on the properties of the rapidly developing western plains. It was still a staging depot in 1833 when it was decided that the local magistrates should arrange to organise it into place of extended punishment for women rather than sending them on to the Parramatta Factory. If its story is much like the other holding institutions, up until this time it had probably functioned as a place where the women could be sentenced to a few days in the cells or the stocks or kept for a few days until an escorted cart could be arranged to take pregnant women, those sentenced to extended periods or those due to be reassigned out of the district to Parramatta. The factory closed in April 1846 and the women who were being held there at that time were sent to Parramatta.

Port Macquarie Female Factory

This factory, on the east coast of Australia about halfway between Sydney and Brisbane, was formed in 1821 as part of a penal out-station in rather the same manner as at Newcastle, but it remained after the penal station was closed in 1830. It continued to function until 1842.

Moreton Bay and Eagle Farm Female Factories

The Moreton Bay (Brisbane) Female Factory was established in 1824 and the later main building was erected around 1829. In 1836 there were thirty women in the establishment employed at washing, needlework, nursing and picking oakum. There were also forty women at Eagle Farm employed as field workers. There was an interesting scandal at Moreton Bay when the doctor and some sailors got into the building at night and had a party with some of the women. This led to the surrounding fence being replaced by a more substantial wall. The establishment closed in 1839 at about the time the area was opened to free settlers. The remaining 57 women were transferred to Parramatta.

George Town Female Factory

Until 1820 a small wooden hut at Launceston was used to confine or provide quarters for women convicts. This was always seen as unsatisfactory but the growth in the female convict population in northern Van Diemen's Land made the circumstance even more obvious. The visit of Commissioner Bigge to Port Dalrymple exposed a number of problems regarding female convicts there.

Need for a women's refuge in Port Dalrymple

In May 1820 Commissioner Bigge, sent from Britain to investigate conditions in the colonies, took a deposition from John Simmonds regarding the rape of Mary Nesbitt by at least two soldiers next to his property at Launceston ten days earlier.

Simmonds and his pregnant wife had intervened on behalf of Mary but both were badly beaten by the soldiers. Because of the assault the baby was born dead with a broken neck, dented head and multiple bruising. A group of soldiers had stood nearby and watched both the rape and the assaults. Simmonds himself was badly injured with broken ribs and badly cut head which kept him in bed for eight days. But perhaps the most telling thing about the incident was the statement by one of the rapists when attacking his wife (formerly Catherine Tobin, per *Canada*, 7 years). John Simmonds said:

> I ran up and seized him by the collar and pulled him away from my wife, telling him that she was not in a state to be ill used [because of her advanced pregnancy]; and he made use of horrid language, saying he would serve every convict bitch in the place in the same way. Mary Nesbitt knows who the soldier was that ill used her and beat my wife.

Part of the male population of Van Diemen's Land seemed to feel that the female convicts were fair game for attack, ill-usage in general, and were to some extent suitable prey for sexual abuse and even rape.

As well as a rape incident, there was evidence of a scandal involving senior officials in May 1819 at Launceston. Lt. Colonel Cimitiere complained that Assistant Commissary General Walker (they were respectively the Commandant and the senior military supply officer) had not only being scandalously improper in cohabiting openly with a convict woman but had driven her in a carriage through the town and 'in view of Lt. Colonel Cimitiere's house'.

Original research on the George Town Factory was reported by Laurel Heath (1978) and Diane Phillips (1997) but neither was able to determine exactly when it was established. It was definitely underway in 1822, though Phillips is uncertain whether this was on the same site where artefacts were later found. Certainly by 1825 the Factory was housed in a building originally designed as a parsonage where it continued until it was closed in late 1834. Bigge had reported that in 1820 the women from the *Janus* had either been placed in the hospital if necessary, or in a house 'nearly opposite that of Chief District Constable Boothman'. In spite of what Phillips describes as an exhaustive search and the existence of 'a substantial number of records' regarding George Town's development in this period, she says 'there appears to be no instructions to build a specific building to house the women …'

The first record of the existence of the Factory seems to be a Hobart newspaper reference in March 1822 referring to a statement by Magistrate Thomas Bell based on information from Governor Sorell's visit to the northern settlements earlier that month: 'In the Factory at George Town, cloth from the coarse wool of the Colony, of very good fabric, is made; as are leather and shoes of excellent quality'. In this same year Mark Wilson, the Chief District Constable is listed in the records as being also the Factory Overseer.

Governor Arthur obviously regularised the positions at the Factory from that of the District Constable having a part-time responsibility for the women, to appointment of Robert and Sophia Graves as a husband and wife team of Superintendent and Matron. They held the position from 1825 to August 1829 when Graves was dismissed for drunkenness.

The positions were advertised and Samuel and Mary Ann Sherlock were appointed 9 October 1829, having been recommended by one of the police magistrates, They held the positions until they resigned in January 1831.

In the period between Graves' dismissal and the appointment of the Sherlocks, Principal Superintendent Spode had received the new rules and regulations for the running of the female factories and had forwarded them on to the northern settlements. Launceston magistrate John Sinclair replied that the building precluded separation of the women into suitable Classification as required by the new rules.

In January 1827, Robert Graves had written to the Colonial Secretary informing the government that there was a lack of wool and that the women were consequently unemployed. With the opening of the Cascades Female Factory at the end of 1828 it had been planned that the women in the George Town Factory would be transferred there. Phillips notes that apparently the women were not sent down to Hobart, but that the spinning and weaving equipment was, leaving the women with no means of work. Arthur suggested a number of remedies for the situation including sending up spare equipment from Cascades and the production of machines copied from those in use by the men at the penal settlement on Maria Island.

Phillips believes that it is unlikely that any of the ideas for providing work were carried out and points out that as late as January 1832, Principal Superintendent of Convicts Ronald Gunn at Launceston was asking for information about the type of needlework carried out at Cascades, as at George Town there were 29 female convicts without work.

Neglect of the women and children

In June 1829 the chaplain at Launceston, William Browne wrote to the Colonial Secretary, for Governor Arthur's attention, complaining about the conditions in the George Town Factory and the 'neglect' of the 31 women and eight children. The women were completely unemployed and were:

> unfortunate creatures too far removed from any person interested in their reformation … [and living in conditions of] cold and damp from the want of repairs to the windows which are all broken.

This led to a new Factory being planned for Launceston. The plans were drawn up and the process went as far as tenders being called on 11 December 1829, but then the intention was abandoned, and as we shall see the women were left to their fate 'too far removed from any person interested'. Twelve months later conditions at the Factory had not improved.

On 4 December 1830, Gunn wrote a report on the current state of the George Town Factory, which showed that if anything it was in an even worse state than the Hobart Town Factory had been prior to the establishment of Cascades in 1829:

... [the] Female House of Correction for the County of Cornwall is situated at George Town, about 40 miles from Launceston, it is two stories high and contains seven rooms - 2 occupied by the Superintendent, one as a hospital for the Females and the other four as the Factory. The whole building is in a very dilapidated state, there are no windows, or at least the apertures for windows are without glass ... and are now boarded up [with] ... holes made through the boards to admit the light. The fencing round the Yard is very insecure, and any of the women could easily get over... its general ruinous state is beyond what I can describe....The internal regulations are equally bad, there is no labour whatever performed except washing the few articles soiled in the hospital, and no punishment inflicted, as there is no classification and consequently the greatest punishment of cutting the hair is never done, not even in cases where the women are sentenced to the Crime Class.... The women being sent down [from Launceston] by monthly conveyance, a considerable portion of their sentence expires before they can be confined in the Factory, and as there is no labour performed when they are there, they generally [perceive time in the Factory] ...without any dread, and more a time of rest.

The hospital would have served all of the assigned female convicts and ticket-of-leave women in the area and possibly also some of the poor free women. Repairs to the fabric of the building were impossible at the time due to the shortage of skilled labour in the town.

During the next four years numbers of women and children housed in the Factory increased steadily and overcrowding was a constant and ever worsening problem. In July 1832 the *Launceston Advertiser* a local newspaper attacked the appalling condition of the building:

...as a place of punishment, the Factory is useless. The dilapidated state of the building, and the want of employment [prevents discipline and control] ...the doors are without sufficient means of security, and the walls... would give way before the least force... [the main door] without hinges even.

Launceston Female Factory

The Launceston Female Factory, designed to look like it incorporated all the latest ideas of the penal reformers but internally merely a very pedestrian and old fashioned example of the female factory design, was opened in 1834. It was situated just a few blocks from the centre of the town on the corner of Bathurst and Margaret Street on the site that later became the Launceston High School in the early twentieth century and later Launceston College. The octagonal design was quite striking and the building allowed significant classification and segregation of the various classes. It was originally designed to hold 100 women.

By the early 1840s the twelve solitary cells in the building were considered by the superintendent to be only half as many as were regularly needed. He felt it was necessary on occasion to carry pistols and related to the 1841 Inquiry that he could only move some of the women around the institution by using force. By the middle of 1842 the building was not only grossly overcrowded with 250 women but the factory authorities were expecting more to arrive. Every possible room was used for accommodation and classification was impossible. Aside from the picking of oakum, washing for the hospital and some sewing there was little opportunity of employing the women.

The 'ferocity' of the women

In 1841 there was a riot in the factory that lasted through the night. The superintendent was entirely overwhelmed by what historian Kay Daniels referred to as the 'ferocity' of the actions of the women. Eventually the riot was put down by deputising fifty male convicts from the prisoners' barracks next door and using them as temporary special constables. Even so the men needed sledgehammers and crowbars to force their way past the barricades.

During the Probation period there was a house rented in the town as a Female Hiring Depot. The depot was closed in 1848 and the Factory started to operate in much the same way as it had before the Probation system was introduced, with women arriving directly from the ships and being assigned to those who agreed to pay their wages. The Factory continued until the end of 1855 the last few years under the superintendence of Mary Hutchinson when it became part of the Launceston Gaol and the women were transferred to Cascades.

The anomaly of the *Anson*

The *HMS Anson* was originally a battleship, converted at enormous cost to transport male convicts to Hobart and then to serve as an accommodation hulk for convicts. Moored on the River Derwent at various sites but mainly off Dowsings Point up-river and north of Hobart, near where the Bowen Bridge now crosses the Derwent opposite Risdon Cove, it had arrived in 1844, and was modified for the imprisonment of women convicts at a time when, with introduction of the Probation System, it was hoped that usage of the female factories would drop as the women who passed through the *Anson* would be more aware of the pitfalls of bad behaviour, would be better trained for domestic service and be more likely to find a permanent job. It was expected that passholders' levels of offences and punishment would come to resemble former levels amongst ticket-of-leave holders rather than those traditionally associated with assigned servants. In the event, as the Comptroller of Convicts reported in October 1847, women who had served their six months on the *Anson* were not notably less likely to offend as those who hadn't.

The Probation System was introduced for women in the mid 1840s to remove some of the more blatant inequities of the old assignment system. On arrival in the colony the convicts were not allowed to mix with convicts who were already on the island and were placed in an institution of primary probation. For the women this meant that the initial six months in the colony were to be spent on board the *Anson*. Here they were required to work at sewing, spinning and dressmaking and were taught the rudiments of reading and writing. There was also quite a heavy dose of religious instruction. Exercise was obtained by perambulating the decks in file twice a day for an hour each time. Quiet conversation was allowed. The heavy discipline seemed to work; punishment was relatively rare and although it could be a few days or weeks in solitary cells on bread and water, most usually it consisted in being demoted a class within the internal classification of the institution.

After the initial six months the women were sent to hiring depots to be assigned to settlers much as under the assignment system except that they now had to be paid for their services. As they progressed through the three levels of being a pass-holder they were allowed to retain a higher proportion of their wages, the remainder having been banked for them to access when they eventually left the system. Hiring depots were established at Brickfields in North Hobart, Liverpool Street in the centre of Hobart, in a rented house in the centre of Launceston, at Ross and, after the closure of the *Anson*, at the New Town Farm just north of Hobart near the Orphan Schools. The hiring depot at Ross was an exception because it was housed within the Female Factory; generally the authorities wanted the depots to be quite separate.

The *Anson* had relieved the pressure on the female factories by becoming the institution of first call upon the arrival of the transports from Britain. The creation under the Probation System of separate Female Hiring Depots in Hobart and Launceston for the convicts who had either served their time on the *Anson* or were between jobs also relieved the female factories from their previous responsibility of caring for the newly arrived women awaiting assignment.

Having been hired, the women were still under the strict discipline of the convict system, and a host of petty regulations could send them to the local cells for a few days or to a sentence at one of the Female Factories. Oddly enough, the potentially strongest form of discipline, consistent fines levied on their pay and savings, was rarely utilised as a control mechanism.

As it happened no improvement in behaviour was achieved by use of the extremely expensive *Anson*. By October 1847, after less than four years, the experiment was considered to be a failure and the Convict Department wanted to close it down. Following the death of the superintendent Dr Bowden in 1847 the pressure for closure accelerated. However, the hulk continued in use for another three years.

Ross Female Factory

The Ross Female Factory was opened in March 1848, five years before the end of the transportation to Eastern Australia, but it was also the period of the highest proportion of female convicts to male convicts arriving in Van Diemen's Land. Figures derived from Charles Bateson (1974) show that in just five years, 1847 to 1851, twenty-eight percent (3778 women) of the estimated 13,500 female convicts who spent part of their convict experience in VDL arrived at Hobart Town. For the last six and a half years of arrivals (1847-1853) 4957 female convicts arrived and the parallel percentage of total arrivals to VDL rises to almost thirty-seven percent. By 1846 and 1847 Van Diemen's Land had to absorb a greater number of female convicts each year than had formerly been sent to the whole of the

Australian colonies. This put enormous stresses on the system and on the institutions. With the arrival of the *Anson* in 1844 and the introduction of the Probation System with separate hiring depots it was hoped that these stresses would be relieved, but the steadily increasing numbers of new arrivals and the failure of the *Anson* to notably increase good behaviour or employability meant that the system was being continually placed under further demands.

Moreover the sheer pressure of increased numbers of female convicts and the tightening up of the system under the Probation System meant there were corresponding pressures on the female factories as places of punishment, as lying-in, maternity and nursery institutions. Before 1850 Cascades mainly served for punishment, the Nursery being in separate quarters at Dynnyrne House, though the close proximity and the sharing of administrative responsibilities often meant that Dynnyrne House was no more than an immediate extension of the Factory with the distance between them just an added problem.

The problem of female solidarity

Throughout the history of transportation to Van Diemen's Land the authorities had used various devices for separating the women from each other either to break up 'bad' friendships and problematic groups or to remove the women from the temptations of the fleshpots of Hobart and Launceston. The most common device was for a magistrate to order that an individual was to be 'assigned to the interior'. More frequently being assigned to the country or a small village would merely have been part of a general rather than a specific administrative action.

Groups of women who showed any form of solidarity with each other, or who had banded together on a friendship basis on board ships, at the factories or even amongst the larger employers of assigned labour, were routinely broken up at the first sign of trouble and in many cases just on principle. Some would be assigned in Hobart, others in outlying areas nearby, others to country villages like Richmond, New Norfolk, Oatlands, Campbell Town, Norfolk Plains (Longford), yet others to Launceston and the remainder rather amorphously 'to the interior'. At other times the *interior* referred to anywhere outside of Hobart, though more commonly outside of Hobart or Launceston. Such breaking up of friends, soul-mates and sometimes lovers, tended to create some sense of joyous return to the two large towns, even if it meant serving time in the factories.

But the exile of problematic women to the interior was a form of theoretical control at the expense of actual control. Isolated farms and small villages meant that the women were to some extent out of sight and out of mind of the magistrates and at a distance from both courts and potential punishment. Travelling to and from the isolated districts (as did travel between Hobart and Launceston) exposed the women to opportunities for creating problems and misbehaviour. Women often travelled singly or in small groups under the supervision of a convict constable and the constables were notorious for taking advantage of the situation, as indeed were the convict women. While the travellers were supposed to lay up at settlements with a magistrate and cells, it was inevitable that many would find themselves out in the bush overnight. As late as the mid-1840s, suitably spaced overnight accommodation was often lacking even on the 200km highway between Hobart and Launceston.

In order to solve these two long-standing problems of an overnight station for female convicts and a place of punishment for recalcitrant female convicts in the centre of the island, it was decided to open a female factory at Ross.

Ross is a small village 122 km from Hobart and 78 km from Launceston tucked under a fold of rising ground on the banks of the Macquarie River. It was one of the substantial villages near the half-way point between Hobart and Launceston and it was near the centre of a flourishing grazing area. It was just twelve kilometres from the much more significant town of Campbell Town (66 km from Launceston) which was the centre of a police district and had a magistrate, police barracks and cells. From Ross thirty-five kilometres to the south was Oatlands which was also the centre for a magistrate and police district.

Until the Ross Factory was established, the Factory at Launceston had met the needs for this whole area and the area south of this. It was the southern limits of the northern midlands and the northern limits of the southern midlands where the need was most pressing to establish a new Female Factory.

The Ross Female Factory was constructed in an old chain-gang station around the hill from the main village area. It was first projected to be merely a combination punishment station and hiring depot with the added attraction of being an overnight stop between Hobart and Launceston for women moving between the two centres. However when the Comptroller-General of Convicts John Hampton put forward the final proposal to Governor Denison in October 1847 it was for a full and complete female factory. He argued that it was difficult to arrange medical attention at Ross and there just happened to be a recently retrenched medical officer on their books. Consequently he recommended that Dr Irvine be employed as joint Superintendent and Medical Officer together with Mrs Irvine, whom he described as well educated, energetic and of active habits, as matron.

Hampton then described the situation in Launceston, though he was very coy about the death rates in the Factory:

> There is no separate Nursery Establishment in Launceston, and the Female House of Correction there is so crowded by lying-in women and young children as to interfere very seriously with both the discipline and the health of the inmates, I … intend to remove a number of these women and children to Ross and… to make Ross a depot for pregnant women…

When the Committee of Officers reviewing Convict Expenditure agreed with Hampton's proposal they saw the combination of the duties of medical officer and superintendent in the one person as a fortunate measure of economy, but it is possible that what can be seen as providing a secure job for a redundant officer may have had a more humanitarian impulse behind it. By this time it was obvious to all except the most obstinate that a medical solution, similar to the more than thirty years success in using Surgeon-superintendents at sea, might solve the problem of the unhealthy and life-threatening conditions in the female factories and nurseries. Hampton had orders from Britain to wield a new broom, to shake things up and amongst other instructions to investigate and stamp out all suggestion of unnatural or homosexual vice. He also had to undertake such reforming tasks as the reduction and eventual abolition of all corporal punishment for men which was to be largely achieved by 1851. Solving the problems of the female factories and nurseries were part of his focus.

The provision of uncrowded quarters, fresh milk and vegetables was to drastically reduce the death rate amongst the children. The relief to the Launceston Female Factory meant that the death toll dropped virtually overnight. This is borne out by a return showing the reduction in the crowding and mortality rate amongst the children in the Launceston establishment. In the twelve months prior to the opening of Ross the Launceston Factory had an average number of forty children of whom seventeen died. In the six months following the opening of the Ross Factory, the Launceston establishment had an average of only twenty-three children and of these only two had died. Further, they had been premature twins who died within a week of birth and for whom little could have been done in any case.

Just two months after the opening of the Ross Factory Comptroller-General Hampton wrote:

> The healthy situation and pure atmosphere at Ross also render this newly-formed establishment peculiarly eligible for lying-in women, a considerable number of whom have already been removed there. Arrangements have been made, by the purchase of cows, and by the cultivation of the large vegetable garden attached to the station, to reduce the cost of the establishment and at the same time provide for the better maintenance of the inmates.

The Ross factory continued until January 1855, eighteen months after the cessation of Transportation. During the whole period it operated, the Superintendent had been a married doctor with his wife acting as Matron. Despite a considerable turnover of staff, it seems that Ross had a much better ratio of free staff to inmates than any other female convict institution with the possible exception of the *Anson*.

After closure the Police Department took over most of the establishment but the Roman Catholics of the town were given the use of the chapel at a nominal rent. Its makes you wonder how many devout parishioners at the church had attended mass in the building when they were inmates at the female factory.

Chapter 10.   Hobart Town Female Factory

By 1817 free settlers were beginning to come to Van Diemen's Land in ever growing numbers and demand for convict servants was growing. At the end of that year Lieutenant Governor Sorell had noticed that some more female convicts were to be expected and he wrote to Macquarie in Sydney:

> The prospect of receiving women convicts in number points out to me the necessity of making some preparation for lodging, employing and keeping them in order. A number in or about this place [Hobart] would be productive of incessant disorders; I therefore propose, if Your Excellency approve, to place them at Pitt-Water, the only district in which a magistrate (Mr Gordon) resides, and to erect a building for them there.

Sorell proposed building a female factory at Pittwater, twenty to thirty kilometres from the capital, accessible by sea for transport purposes and in a rapidly growing rural area. The parallels with Parramatta in New South Wales are obvious. As with Parramatta the purpose of the factory would be lodging and employment in the first instance as well as keeping the female convicts in order by having a local magistrate, restricting access to the capital and housing them in the one building. Five weeks later, 10 January 1818, Macquarie wrote back refusing permission. Whilst approving a significant barracks for the male convicts he thought:

> …it is not my intention that there ever should be more female convicts sent from [Sydney] to Van Diemen's Land than are necessarily required for the use of the settlers on that island, I do not think that it is necessary in the present infant state of your settlements, to have any public buildings erected for the female convicts either at Hobart Town or at the Pitt Water. It being my intention soon to erect a Factory and Barrack on a large scale at Parramatta for the employment and accommodation of all the female convicts victualled at the expense of the government, you will be left at liberty to send up to that seminary such refractory or disorderly ill-behaved female convicts from the settlements in Van Diemen's Land, as you may deem expedient.

Almost exactly three years to the day from when he proposed the building of a factory at Pittwater, Sorell again wrote to Macquarie on 6 December 1820 proposing to build a Factory:

> Having reason to expect that a female convict ship may be destined to this settlement at no distant period, I beg leave to submit to Your Excellency the want of a Factory or place for restraint or labour for female convicts. Without a building for this purpose on a moderate scale be prepared, no alternative will remain here but to allow the mass of females who arrive to go at once at large, and of the females who are in service quitting their places which at present is found nearly impossible to prevent, the sentence to labor in the gaol not being sufficient without more permanent confinement.... A plain building of size to admit 50 or 60 women being kept to labor might be erected by contract, should Your Excellency [agree]....

In the period between the first request to build a factory in 1817 and the second request three years later things had changed considerably in Van Diemen's Land. Firstly there were a lot more settlers and many more were expected. Secondly it was planned that both male and female convicts would be sent to the island direct from Britain and indeed the *Morley* had already arrived.

"A dirty reprobate... a very abandoned depraved girl"

Mary Davis was convicted of larceny in a shop in London in June 1821 and sentenced to 7 years transportation at age 17. Her father was a sheriff's assistant but in spite of her youth and respectable background she was described in her Gaol Report as being a "prostitute and bad character" and in the Ship's Surgeon's Report as "a dirty reprobate, vile prostitute, a very abandoned depraved girl". She arrived in Hobart on board the *Mary Anne* in May 1822 and stayed out of trouble. She was assigned to Henry Rice who had properties at Jericho, in the Midlands, and at Glenorchy, just north of Hobart. Mary became Rice's assigned housekeeper and lover, bearing his child at the end of 1823 or early in 1824. The three of them were in Hobart Town one day in November 1824. The adults had been drinking but were sober when they set off home in a cart drawn by four bullocks. One of the bullocks was untrustworthy, the cart struck a tree and was overturned, and Mary Davis was killed under the cart, her child held safe in her lifeless arms. Henry Rice was utterly inconsolable.

In 1821 Governor Macquarie listed the number of inhabitants based at the various districts in New South Wales and Van Diemen's Land as at November 1819. In New South Wales with a population of 25,818 there were 1066 female convicts (about four percent) while in VDL there were 262 female convicts in a population of 4270 (about six percent).

Obviously the numbers of female convicts in Van Diemen's Land suggested that it was about time the authorities made arrangements on the island for something more than using the local gaols to accommodate refractory female prisoners.

Investigations by Commissioner Bigge, sent from England to report on the state of the colonies, had shown the situation and attitudes of officials and settlers to the female convict question in Van Diemen's Land during the course of 1820. Police Magistrate Humphrey for instance was questioned:

Q. In the case of the arrival of women [convicts] in the settlement, how are they distributed and lodged?

A, They are assigned to such married persons as apply for them and the remainder are sent to find their own lodgings.

Q. Are not women [convicts] very much wanted here?

A. Very much indeed.

Other information gained by Bigge during his 1820 visit to Van Diemen's Land, such as the rape of Mary Nesbitt, would also have alerted Macquarie to the problematical circumstances of the female convicts on the island and the need for a place of refuge as well as incarceration. However, it was not until 30 June 1821 that Macquarie wrote to Sorell ordering that a 'female convict barrack or Factory' be constructed at Hobart 'as soon as possible'. Heath suggests that the steady demand for female convicts had meant that up until this time 'none but the most refractory were withdrawn from service' and that consequently a single room at the Hobart Gaol, measuring just four metres by three metres had been sufficient to hold those sentenced to punishment. Following Macquarie's orders a small building was erected on the corner of Macquarie and Murray Streets next to the Hobart Town Gaol and was used as the Hobart Town Female Factory for the next eight years. It was never big enough, nor entirely suited for the purpose. At the end of his governorship, in May 1824, Sorell was recommending that the gaol should be combined with the existing factory and the whole improved for the reception of the women.

In August 1824, not long after he arrived in Van Diemen's Land, Lt Governor Arthur was writing in similar terms to London in reply to Elizabeth Fry's suggestions and blueprints for a new factory:

> The plan for a new Female Factory appears very judicious, and as the present establishment is exceedingly confined and dilapidated I shall be happy to take advantage of it as far as circumstances will allow. The Jail and Factory at Hobart Town at present stand on the same ground, being separated only by a brick wall - both buildings are in a ruinous state, but more especially the Jail, which is altogether insecure, it appears to me therefore, more desirable to construct a new Jail as soon as possible, and to appropriate such parts of the Old Jail as can be rendered at all habitable to the use of the Factory which I hope will answer every purpose until better accommodation can hereafter be provided.

Arthur was seeking to shift the gaol to the site of what was to become instead the prisoners' barracks in Campbell Street, but in the end this didn't happen for another thirty years, right at the end of the Transportation period. The site of the gaol in Murray Street, diagonally opposite St David's Church, and opposite the government offices, which were later to become the Supreme Court and the Police Office, was just too handy. Meanwhile he focused on what he perceived to be more important priorities. It was

---

Industrial action at the Hobart Town Female Factory

A group of at least fifteen women were involved in a protest activity for which they were punished. On 2 October 1823 at the Hobart Town Female Factory. They were charged with wetting the wool to make it measure more when weighed, in order to fulfil their daily quota of work. Whether it was full blown industrial action, minor sabotage or just an opportunistic lark in thumbing their noses at authority is debatable. My personal view tends towards the latter, though the method of expression shows that the women were well aware of the benefits of combined action taken in an industrial setting. They were all charged formally with the same words: 'Wetting the yarn spun by her with intent to defraud by increasing its weight and thus make her work less.'

more than a year before he again dealt with the existing Factory. But the authorities in England were assuming that the circumstances in the colony had improved, for the number of women they sent to the colony was steadily increasing.

Meanwhile things were not going well at the Factory. On 23 September 1825, the Female Factory Superintendent, JE Drabble was asked to explain why the women's productivity was so low that it failed to pay for their maintenance. Drabble blamed the government's penny-pinching attitude in the building and fitting out of the Factory:

…the defects of the present Factory, combined with the increase in its inmates, especially pregnant women and children, operate not only against productive labour, but lessens… the quantity of work formerly performed.

In January 1826 Arthur finally ordered an investigation into the conditions at the Hobart Town Female Factory. Conditions were very unsatisfactory. Fifty-five people were crammed into two sleeping room which were not only cramped and crowded but were also unventilated. There was only one yard for the use of the Factory, consequently no possibility of classification or keeping some women separate from others. The yard was in full view of executions in the gaol next door. Communication through and over the walls, both to the gaol and to the streets outside, was absurdly easy. The crowded conditions and lack of separate rooms and other areas meant there was no space that could be used for work. The superintendent Mr Drabble and his family lived in an apartment that was not separated from the rest of the factory and were subject to constant abuse from the inmates.

Arthur did nothing for nine months, but in October he was forced to visit the Factory himself. He detailed his findings to the Colonial Secretary on 20 October 1826:

I have visited the Factory within the last week, and have found it in a very bad state… look out for a building, either to be purchased or hired, capable of receiving 40 or 50 women…

This was the first activity by Arthur towards obtaining a new female factory in Hobart Town. The extraordinarily poor conditions in the existing factory pushed the governor into rectifying the situation as rapidly as possible and was to lead to the purchase of Lowes' Distillery at Cascades without him showing his usual foresight and prescience, and was to create a situation where both he and his successors were to be lumbered with a most inappropriate site for a major institution. It is worth noting that at this time he really did have a lot of flexibility. After all, any fairly large house and outbuildings with room to expand would have suited his purposes; he was still only looking for a place to hold fifty women and perhaps a dozen children.

An incident in November 1826 highlights the colonial authorities' problems regarding the Factory at this time. Mary Hamilton per *Alexander II*, convicted of stealing a watch at the Dublin City Courts in February 1815 and sentenced to 7 years transportation, was committed for trial before the Hobart Town Supreme Court. She had arrived at the Derwent on board the *Kangaroo* in April 1816, one of sixty Irish female convicts from the 81 who had arrived in Sydney earlier that month. Three years later she married Joseph Pendle, Free, at Hobart Town. She had a number of convictions for disorderly conduct and being drunk and disorderly but was now free by servitude when on 3 November 1826 she was charged with: '… stealing a child's frock, the property of Mrs Dixon of the Waterloo Inn'. The *Hobart Town Gazette* reported the outcome of the trial:

"Save me!"

Ann Williams arrived in Hobart Town in October 1823, aged 21. She had been sentenced to death for stealing from a dwelling, but the sentence was commuted to transportation for Life. Four and a half months in the colony, she was convicted of theft and received twelve months in the Hobart Town Female Factory. Six weeks into her sentence she stole "a pair of stockings, the property of the Crown" and was sentenced to 14 days in the iron collar and had her hair cut off. She did not re-offend, and in July 1826 married William Turner, convict. In April 1830 her husband was in Gaol and she and her children "had been left almost wholly destitute". They were living in a house in Argyle Street, North Hobart near the Brickfields, when her clothes caught fire and she raced out into the street. A man threw his coat over her but she panicked and "impatiently threw it off, running into the open air and calling out "Save me! Save me!" She died next day.

The punishment of Mary Pendle for stealing in a dwelling house, was necessarily different from that of the other guilty of a like offence, owing to the difficulty at present existing in the Colony of finding punishments suited to female offenders. She was sentenced to 6 months imprisonment and hard labour, and His Honor added, that he really hoped the labour she would undergo would be hard.

The point about the judge hoping the labour would indeed be hard labour was probably a reference to the inability of the old Hobart Female Factory to effectively classify prisoners according to the severity of the punishment or to keep the inmates employed, due to excessive overcrowding. Of course the judge may also have been harking back to the earlier days when Mary might have received a good flogging as well, which he no doubt felt she richly deserved.

The end of the Hobart Town Female Factory

In spite of the newspapers' doubts about the new Factory at Cascades, there seems to have been a certain amount of satisfaction when the *Colonial Times* reported on 2 January 1829:

The Old Female Factory is at last about to be abandoned by the female prisoners, one hundred of them having been removed to the New Factory near Cascade.

In late December 1828 and the first few days of 1829, over a hundred women were transferred from the now unbearable conditions of the old Factory next to the town gaol. Because of the building delays, Arthur had had to order part of the Domain Barracks be fitted up for the temporary reception of the female convicts to tide over the transition period. By the end of February 1829 the old Factory had been converted into a bond store.

'Every species of immorality and vice'

Not long after Cascades was established, it was suggested to
Governor Arthur that the fathers of the children to convict mothers
should be forced to pay maintenance. Perhaps such a course of
action would not only reduce the cost of running the factory but
would also help to reduce immorality.

The details of the fathers of the illegitimate children in the Factory
prove most interesting. In the case of one child, the woman refused
to name the father. Another child was the son of a convict who had
no means to provide maintenance. A third child was the daughter of
a ticket-of-leave man who intended to marry the mother as soon as
possible and was prepared to maintain the child. The remaining five
were all children of free men who refused to take any notice or to
pay maintenance.

One of these five children was the son of Ann Fry and Edward Lord,
who once had aspired to become governor since he was the Acting
Commandant at the time of Governor Collins' death. Lord's wife
from whom he was estranged at this time was the former convict
Maria Risely. She was noted as being a respectable merchant and
entrepreneur by dint of her good marriage and clever business
ability.

So, of these eight children in the Female Factory, the only father
willing to do the right thing was an ex-convict. In the end the
maintenance could not be collected because the Poor Law of
England did not apply in the colony.

In spite of this evidence, Arthur continued to believe that it was the
women 'accustomed to every species of immorality and vice... and
their profligacy, in connection with the assigned convict men' which
was the cause of the pregnant women in the House of Correction.
Not only did he ignore the involvement of free men, he put all blame
on the women for the sexual encounters.

Chapter 11. The Man with the Black Books

Between the earliest years of the convict system and the later years, the Exile-Assignment system shaded into the Assignment System proper. It is impossible to give specific issues or events that marked when and how the change happened, but the changes were very real and the experience of convicts who arrived in the Australian Colonies in the 1830s was a very different experience both qualitatively and quantitatively to those who had arrived ten or fifteen years before.

The female factories provide a way of marking the transition. In the new factories the women could be imprisoned and punished systematically using oversight, classification and separation. In New South Wales the new female factory at Parramatta was ready in 1821. In Van Diemen's Land the new Cascades Female Factory in 1829 replaced the old Hobart Town Factory established in 1821.

During,this period when the experience of female convicts was to change so drastically, the ultimate control of Van Diemen's Land was shifting from Sydney to Hobart. Until December 1825, VDL was administered as a section of New South Wales, directly under the control of the Governor of that colony. But from then onwards it was a separate, self-sufficient colony, under only nominal control of the senior governor and effectively under the sole control of one man, the local governor. For over a decade that man was George Arthur.

A man with a plan

Governor Arthur created a complete system for the convicts in Van Diemen's Land, including the Conduct Registers, a set of big black books in which to record essential official information regarding the convicts in VDL, a permanent record of offences, sentences, punishments, even marriage and death.

Arthur had served as an officer in the British Army from 1804 in the Napoleonic Wars, rising rapidly through the ranks. Between 1814 and 1822 he served as the Lieutenant Governor of Honduras, putting down a slave rebellion during his service there. He was a consummate senior bureaucrat in the British Army mould. Spending endless hours at his desk, often far into the night, overseeing the reports that flowed into his office, he relied to an extraordinary extent on his subordinate officers, although he did on occasion venture out into the field. WD Forsyth quotes a description (by Beattie) of Arthur and his entourage making a surprise visit to the Cascades Female Factory:

> Dashing up to the gate at a smart canter, their approach was only announced by the thud of the horses' hoofs and the rattling of their accoutrements. Throwing the reins to the orderly, the governor and his aide passed hurriedly through the gates, only recognising the superintendents by a stern look and a condescending nod. Leading the way himself he examined and pried into everything. The yards, the cells, the wards, the drains, the spinning lofts, the washing and cooking departments, the hospital and nursery - all received the closest inspection. Returning to the office he so far unbent as to make a few remarks to the superintendent suggested by the inspection, to give expression to his wishes, to write a short minute in the visitors' book, and then departed as cavalierly as he came.

How accurate this description is of an actual event is difficult to know, but it certainly fits with everything else we know about the man. It is surprisingly easy to get into his mind; almost every document produced during the twelve years of his governorship has his detailed comments written on it. Ascerbic, cutting, probing, supercilious but never witty or lightened by humane considerations, Arthur oversaw every single detailed facet of life, and particularly every element of convict life. But almost always at one remove: on paper; through the eyes of his subordinates; rarely ever directly in touch with matters that might demand his resorting to the personal and humane.

From barbaric to methodical

While it is easy to see the transition between the old and the new systems in the construction of new female factories and in the changes they wrought upon existing institutions, it is impossible to say that the construction of female factories at George Town and in Hobart Town next door to the town gaol in the early 1820s were part of the change between systems. They still reflected too much of the old; and their purpose mirrored too closely the early days at Parramatta.

The transition between systems is easy to see in the purposeful design and construction of the Cascades and Launceston Factories opening in 1829 and 1834 respectively. It would seem to be no accident that the use of the iron collar persisted between 1829 and 1833 most often in the north of the colony. This reflected Arthur's attitude and the attitudes of his magistrates that whilst its use was barbaric there was no alternative but to use the old methods until completion of the new institution at Launceston with its new system of methodical imposition of graduated and steadily more forceful punishments.

In the foreword to the 1970 edition of *Governor Arthur's Convict System*, WD Forsyth is largely approving when he quotes JV Barry regarding Arthur's system as having functioned with 'a totalitarian exactitude and relentlessness'. The system's brutalities were not sadistically inspired but 'justified by utility' and Arthur's 'perception of what was unjust was often limited and was frequently subservient to expediency …compassion and humility were not among his virtues.' Forsyth disagreed with Barry's opinion that Arthur lacked compassion and asserted that: 'in a father-figure as Arthur certainly was, [compassion] is not incompatible with severity'. Perhaps not, at least in theory, but I tend to side with Barry on the grounds that Arthur's actions were never father-like nor subject to any compassion he may have held privately.

These were indeed to be the characteristics of the new system, Governor Arthur's system: exactitude on the part of all subsidiary officials; relentlessness in the increasing gradations of punishment; utility, expediency, efficiency and reduction of expense as the watchwords for all aspects of planning and organisation; and a total absence of compassion for fellow suffering.

The Governor himself was to be at the very centre of his new system with all correspondence (and there was an insistence that all communication be in writing) from lower functionaries flowing through to the heads of the various departments, then to the Colonial Secretary. During Arthur's administration there were few details other than purely and solely internal matters within departments that did not end up in his hands. Every sentence by magistrates, every request for an indulgence, every ticket-of-leave, every request to marry, was overseen by Arthur's steely, jaundiced and compassionless stare and either approved or disapproved and returned for appropriate action.

In 1827 Arthur created a new category of stipendiary (salaried) magistrates thus replacing the old system of Justices of the Peace on allowances and allocated one each to new police districts of Hobart Town, Richmond, New Norfolk, Clyde (Bothwell), Oatlands, Campbell Town, Launceston and Norfolk Plains (Longford). The magistrates were given a staff including police constables chosen from the ranks of the better behaved convicts. Each sub-district within the police district had a part-time paid District Constable who was usually a settler of good standing though sometimes an emancipist (ex-convict), who in turn would have a number of convict constables under him. Senior department heads, most notably the Principal Superintendent of Convicts, some serving army officers and visiting magistrates were also given magisterial appointments.

Besides the obvious localisation, professionalisation and standardisation of judgement regarding minor offences, the new system removed the power of punishment and of improper indulgences from local landholders who had formerly served as voluntary justices on cases involving their neighbours' servants. This gave Arthur the opportunity to place his own men in the system, together with the ability to more easily rid himself of any magistrate who failed to live up to his expectations. But there was an added bonus to the creation of police districts: it increased the internal control of movement and residence of the convict population. Potential abuses of power or indulgences by settlers with regard to their assigned servants and ticket-of-leave holders could be better controlled. Henceforth ticket-of-leave holders could be restricted to a particular district, and would have to seek permission to move; troublesome groups of convicts could be split up more effectively without having to bring charges against them; there were now a multitude of places of exile within the larger gaol that Van Diemen's Land had become.

The most important roles of policing the system were in the hands of free persons: the principal superintendents of convicts, the magistrates, the institutional superintendents, the chief district constables etc. But the day to day activities and supervision were in the hands of ex-convicts, ticket-of-leave holders and government assigned servants: the wardsmen and wardswomen, the javelin men (guards so-named because originally in Britain they held spears), the instructors and instructresses, the nurses and in particular the convict constables. These were the people who were the front line in all dealings with the convicts.

One of the more problematical issues in dealing with the female convicts was the movement of women from place to place around the country districts of the island. Sometimes individual female convicts were alone under the control of convict constables for days on end and it was inevitable that the rules would be flouted. If the individuals concerned were discreet, it was highly unlikely that their misdemeanours would ever be discovered. It is the indiscreet who were reported and who give us a human insight into the people and circumstances: In December 1829 Constable John Williams was dismissed from the Field Police for: 'taking female prisoners ...to improper places and for unnecessary delaying on the road...' A month earlier a convict constable was dismissed for 'giving liquor to and beating a female convict whom he was conducting to her service'.

Religious zeal at bargain prices

As for the staffing of the female factories, Governor Arthur showed a preference for the clergy, especially the Methodists. He was staunchly religious and by nature a member of the evangelical wing of the established Church of England. However, in common with most early governors, he was not narrowly sectarian and was highly supportive of all respectable men of the cloth, whatever their sect or religion. Indeed, there was little choice in the matter. By the late eighteenth and early nineteenth centuries England had taken on the mantle of tolerance in religious affairs. Even religious groups that were officially discouraged and legally encumbered, such as Roman Catholics, tended to be treated according to their civil station and personal qualities rather than their religious affiliation. In the colonies the opportunity of enforcing or recreating a narrow sectarianism was in any case almost impossible. The Presbyterians were the first to raise this issue when they pointed out that these were British colonies not English colonies and since they were the established Church of Scotland they should have equal status with the Church of England.

There can be little doubt that Wesleyan Methodists were the perfect people for running government institutions under Governor Arthur. He demanded sobriety, respectability, vigour, impeccable honesty and integrity, combined with high moral and religious zeal as essential to reform or crush the convicts. Moreover, the Methodists had an advantage of being both perfectly respectable and yet being of a substantially lower class than most gentlefolk. Since Arthur required a woman to run the Female Factory together with a husband who was basically an administrator and accountant but who was also able to turn his hand to preaching, what could be more perfect than a missionary?

Certainly an Anglican minister would seem to fit the purpose, but such people were at the top of colonial society and were accordingly extremely expensive to employ. Beyond this, an Anglican minister's wife was not expected to fill any employment and certainly not a position that entailed disciplining and overseeing incarcerated convicts. With Arthur's attitude towards the Methodists and the availability of them for mid-level government work, it is neither surprising nor coincidental that all the staff appointed to the Cascades Female Factory during Arthur's governorship were in fact Methodists, and a number were appointed to the Launceston Female Factory during the same period.

Superintendent Drabble of the old Hobart Female Factory died suddenly on 13 February 1828 less than a year before the completion of the new Factory at Cascades. The Principal Superintendent of Convicts, John Lakeland, wrote to Governor Arthur the following day, pointing out the need for the 'immediate appointment of a respectable married person' to superintend the Factory, and recommended Esh Lovell as Drabble's replacement. He continued:

> the immoral habits and general bad conduct of the female convicts will require all the energy and nerve that any individual may possess to keep them in a proper state of subordination and discipline. The new building intended for their reception being now nearly completed will on their being placed there considerably increase the duties of the Superintendent and require his constant attendance.

Lakeland reminded Arthur that the position held 'great inducements to abuse' and recommended that the salary should be commensurate with such a high position of trust so as to place the superintendent above any corrupting influence.

Arthur instructed the Colonial Secretary to immediately write to Lovell offering the joint positions of Superintendent and Matron to him and his wife at the combined salary of £150 a year plus housing, rations and wood and water for their whole family. The Colonial Secretary was also to state that:

> …a system will be laid down for the government of the Factory and that all I shall require will be a close and rigid attention to that system

which will embrace the general management of the women, their employment and moral improvement ... The main exertion will rest with the 'Matron' of the Establishment... He will be expected to offer Mrs Lovell every assistance in the regulation of the accounts and ...the religious and moral direction of the institution.

Esh and Ann Lovell were officially appointed Superintendent and Matron on 29 February 1828. They moved into the staff apartment as soon as Mrs Drabble was able to be re-housed. They were told that the rules under which they were to organise and conduct the Factory would be made available within a few weeks. However Arthur was busy with other projects and the regulations were not drawn up until the following year.

The Lovells had arrived in Hobart Town in 1823. They were staunch Methodists and they became heavily involved with the Methodist church group in the town with Esh becoming a trustee of the Chapel and both he and his wife teaching Sunday School. They earned their living as shopkeepers until Lovell was appointed to the Launceston Methodist mission as an unordained preacher. His work in Launceston was not successful and he approached the government for a position as a school teacher.

Towards the end of 1828 when the move to the new factory at Cascades was imminent, Jesse Pullen, another Methodist, and his wife were appointed Assistant Superintendent and Assistant Matron. Although the salaries offered by Arthur were enough to attract people like the Lovells and the Pullens at times when they faced difficulty in obtaining employment, it is not at all certain that the salaries were attractive enough to keep people in better times and when they had proven their worth as public servants. Arthur made clear what his perspective of the employees at the Factory was when Pullen applied for an increase in salary two and a half years later because he and his family could not live on it. Arthur commented in a memo to the Colonial Secretary that the salary was quite sufficient for a man in Pullen's station in life.

When Pullen resigned in 1831 ostensibly due to his wife's ill-health but more probably also due to the low salary, it was another Methodist couple, William and Elizabeth Cato who were Lovell's nominees to fill the positions of assistant. Later in 1831 an investigation into the management of the Cascades Factory caused Superintendent Lovell to resign when it heard evidence in his absence and gave him no right of reply. Governor Arthur was extremely unhappy with the outcome of the enquiry so perhaps it was just as well Lovell had resigned. Lovell had not implemented the system rigidly enough, and the women had done some of his wife's sewing. To Arthur these were not minor indiscretions but gross negligence and serious corruption.

Arthur found another Methodist couple for superintendent and matron. Reverend John Hutchinson, an ordained minister, and Mary, his 22 year old wife, were appointed at the beginning of 1832. They had four children, and eight more were to be born at the Factory. Half of them died in childhood, sharing the same fate as the children of the convicts. During the next twenty years while the Hutchinsons were in charge at Cascades about ten thousand female convicts arrived in Van Diemen's Land. It would be reasonable to assume that Hutchinson made some attempts to reclaim the souls of his charges but when an enquirer asked whether time spent at the Factory had any positive moral outcome Hutchinson just "shook his head incredulously".

The George Town, Launceston and Parramatta Factories had a number of serious scandals, but only minor infringements were ever proven against the staff at Cascades.In the end, Arthur's idea of employing Methodist families to run Cascades was highly successful.

The Rules

It was Arthur himself who drew up the new rules for the Cascades factory. The 'Rules and Regulations for the Management of the House of Correction for Females' were sent by the Colonial Secretary to the Principal Superintendent of Convicts on 23 January 1829 with the explicit demand that they be adhered to without 'the slightest deviation or departure'. The rules were proclaimed in the *Hobart Town Gazette* on 3 October 1829. These rules and regulations were the basis for much of the inhumanity that was to occur at the Factory through malnutrition and overly strict discipline over the next twenty-two years until new regulations came into force in 1851.

Governor Arthur's orders regarding the administration of the Female Factory are part of the instructions to the Principal Superintendent of Convicts, who was in overall charge of the convict system, and they stress a sense of overall priority. The first, to do with the close and careful oversight of accounts and requisitions says *"and, most especially, the expense of the Institution"*. The second reads:

> ...the Establishment must necessarily be a heavy charge upon the Government, and the most scrupulous attention to *economy* is therefore expected to pervade the whole system of the establishment.

Economic 'efficiency'

A major factor in the disaster of the Cascades Female Factory is one that is familiar to modern readers. The planning and operational controls placed cost-cutting, financial controls, economic efficiency and the importance of money on an equal or superior footing to moral and humanitarian concerns. Reduced or severely controlled budgets were the basis of reward, rather than healthy well-conducted humanitarian outcomes.

The knowledge of how to ameliorate the conditions at Cascades was there. Such knowledge had even been put into practice in the parallel conditions of shipping convicts to the Australian colonies, and it had succeeded. But it had succeeded at a cost, and it was a cost that successive administrators were not prepared to recommend to their superiors in London.

Stress on reduction of costs and the saving of money even at the price of other important priorities pervades Arthur's instructions with regard to the Cascades Female Factory. His phrases 'most especially, the expense of the Institution' and 'most scrupulous attention to *economy*' are highly typical of him.

Economy influenced his decision to purchase Lowes' Distillery in South Hobart as the site of the factory. Situated in a boggy hollow under the gloomy shadow of Mount Wellington, it was the worst possible site but at first it looked as though it would be cheap.

"…I have … approved of a purchase of a building for a factory for the female prisoners, which will require considerable additions… A more desirable arrangement might have been made… if it had not been urgent at once to place the female prisoners in a better state"

Lt Governor George Arthur, Hobart Town, 24 March 1827
to Earl Bathurst, Secretary of State for the Colonies, London

---

129

Cascades Female Factory. Far left is Yard 4 (the Nursery), then Yard 3 (open space). In the centre is Yard 1 (dating back to the 1828 adaptation of Lowes' Distillery) and further right are Yards 2 and 5.

Above:
the Chapel designed by John Lee Archer and built as part of the original Female Factory. Yard 1 is more open to sun in this photo than when first built with seven internal yards with high walls.

Right: the cells

Photographs courtesy of State Archives Office of Tasmania.

Chapter 12. Cascades Female Factory

In 1827 in a small widening of a valley at the conjunction of two creeks, one of which was the main supply of water for the growing town of Hobart two miles away, a number of factors came together which were to inexorably lead to one of the major tragedies in the history of Tasmania. With the exception of the Black War, which was to reach its peak during the five years or so either side of 1827 and which resulted in the destruction and dispersion and eventual exile of the remnants of the native people, no other scene of greater tragedy was to blight two hundred years of history on the island.

The many factors which came together at the Cascades site to create the tragedy can all be discovered relatively easily in hindsight. Hindsight, of course, has the power to make fools of us all, though in this case most of the factors could have been foreseen by an intelligent, able and careful person at the time. Furthermore, guidelines and specialist knowledge were available at the time which could have prevented disastrous decisions. Even having made the wrong decisions, the authorities could have drawn upon that knowledge, combined it with what they learned from the first five years experience of the Cascade Factory and realised they should abandon their efforts and make new decisions that could yet have forestalled the impending and growing tragedy. They didn't.

Exactly the wrong site

Hobart has an excellent and healthy climate: cool summers with frequently sunny winters, low rainfall spread fairly equally over the year, very few frosts, almost never fog. Dampness or dryness of the soil is related much more to the summer and winter evaporation rates rather than rainfall, though semi-drought conditions can occur in a matter of weeks especially in summer. But the above description can be very misleading, for the environs of Hobart are composed of a mass, dozens perhaps hundreds, of microclimates, each considerably different to the other. The major influences are the broad but, above Hobart, rapidly narrowing and shallowing Derwent estuary and the huge massif of Mount Wellington.

Warmth is provided by sunshine, low altitude and absolute proximity to ιne estuary; coldness is created by shade of the many hills, higher altitude, and distance from the deeper parts of the estuary. Relative coolness in summer is provided by a sea-breeze on hot, clear sunny days or by clouds and rain. Relative warmth in winter is often provided during the day by sunshine or at night by clouds and rain.

But there are other factors and they are crucial to understanding the local microclimates: fog on the Derwent above the city often brings quite cold mornings to the low-lying northern suburbs (northwest of the city); and the drainage of cold air from Mount Wellington or the other surrounding high hills of the city can cause frost and freezing conditions in the narrow creek valley beds where conditions only a few hundred metres away are substantially warmer.

There are a few places where the combination of shade due to foothills to the north and a rapidly narrowing and shallowing valley directly below the mountain cause the cold air falling from the mountain to pool and gather. It was in such a spot that Governor Arthur and his advisers decided to place the Cascades Female Factory.

Flaws in the design

Having decided to use the site at Cascades, all was not lost. The centre courtyard of the new Female Factory could still potentially allow considerable sunshine into the yard. However the construction of two-storey buildings on the inside of the northern wall immediately limited the sunshine and the division of what remained of the courtyard by high internal walls so that there were six yards instead of one, so as to better allow the separation of different classes of inmates, severely reduced the amount of winter sunshine that was allowed to fall within the walls.

Then there was the groundwater problem. The site had originally been a rain forest bog but adequate planning and proper drainage work could have rectified this problem. As it was, rain pooled in the cobbled yards, exacerbated by their use for laundry purposes on a commercial scale. We know that at times the problem was so bad that women were up to their ankles in water. The constant immersion in water was also considered to be one of the reasons that the inmates' footwear didn't last as long as could normally be expected. Often the water was so bad that the contents of the middens and ash-pits used for toilets were washed from the yards across the short intervening space and into the Hobart Rivulet. Here in the creek it ended up in the water races used for powering the mills of the town and supplying drinking and washing water for the townsfolk.

No planning for epidemic diseases

Also contributing to the disaster of the Cascades Female Factory was a problem that was not foreseeable in itself, but which the authorities could have planned for or could have adjusted their plans when it occurred. Somewhere around the very late 1820s and particularly the early 1830s there was an upsurge in the virulence, volatility, spread and mortality of certain communicable diseases in Western Europe followed by flow-on effects elsewhere in the world. The Australian colonies were not immune, and indeed because the cities of Sydney and Hobart had grown so rapidly, they appeared to be suddenly and particularly affected. These diseases were exacerbated by overcrowding, poor sanitation and poor nutrition and historically they are generally seen to be the causes or major contributing factors to the extraordinarily high death rates amongst children in the Victorian industrial cities.

The multi-purpose role of the factories

The very use of one institution to serve a variety of often quite separate purposes proved to be unfortunate. Unlike institutions for male convicts within the overall penal colony that was Governor Arthur's Van Diemen's Land, the female factories had to be all things to all women who came under government control or judicial management. With the exception of local lock-ups attached to local courts in the smaller towns which might be used for short sentences of less than four days or so, the female factories were expected to handle every other case calling for an institutional response for female convicts.

A female factory was a place to put convict women for many different reasons: when they first arrived in the colony while waiting to be assigned; when they were punished for serious offences; when they were punished locally by a few days in the cells and a factory was nearby; while they were pregnant and unable to work; while they were having the baby and breastfeeding; while they were serving their sentence for having got pregnant; while they were ill or otherwise unable to work; if they were mentally ill; while they were on remand facing trial; when they were travelling and needed to stay overnight; when they were between assignments; when they were returned from an assignment in order to protect them, or because the assignment had proven to be unsuitable, or the employer had been deemed unsuitable; when they were assigned to the government nearby and especially if they worked at the factory itself (most staff and particularly nurses were either assigned or ticket-of-leave convicts).

Factories were also used as remand centres and gaols for free women sentenced to gaol terms, and at least on some occasions as a lying-in (maternity) hospital for poor ticket-of-leave and free women who needed the facility. Besides being places of punishment, coercion, correction and discipline for convict women, and the occasional free woman, the factories were the only government institutions able to provide protection, maternity assistance and refuge for any woman in the colony whether convict, ticket-of-leave or free. With the exception of the Colonial hospitals for cases of illness or accident, and later the New Norfolk hospital for the insane, there were no other institutions that were designed to deal with women.

Planning Phase

On 30 August 1823, Secretary of State for the Colonies, Lord Bathurst, sent a dispatch to the then newly appointed Lieutenant Governor Arthur. Enclosed in the dispatch was a letter from Elizabeth Fry, suggesting arrangements for the female convicts in VDL. Fry had spoken personally to Arthur before he left England, and was in communication with Governor and Mrs Darling in New South Wales regarding the female convicts in that colony. Bathurst strongly recommended that Arthur consider Mrs Fry's ideas.

Mrs Fry stressed concern for the establishment of a system most likely to lead to the moral improvement of the women:

> …we deem it expedient, that a building be erected at Hobart Town, for the reception of female convicts - That a respectable and judicious matron be there stationed, to superintend the whole establishment under the direction of the Governor, or some magistrate appointed by him for that service. That part of the build-ing be appropriated to the use of an adult and girls school, and that school-mistresses be selected by the matron from among the reformed prisoners, provided they be sufficiently qualified….We are pleased to understand that the Factory in Parramatta has more than cleared its expenses during the last year, as the interest we feel in the welfare of the colonies induces us, not only to desire the religious

and moral improvement of the population at large, but in all our plans we wish to keep in view such a system, as shall eventually prove the most economical to Government, as well as the most beneficial to the colonial states.

Fry recommended that only those who had already shown reformed habits on the voyage out should be assigned immediately. Those who had not should be instructed and employed at the factory until they had changed their ways. She recommended plain, strong and decent clothing both on the voyage out and in the factories. Throughout the letter she emphasised the use of matrons as supervisors, rather than men.

Lowes' Distillery

TY Lowes arrived in Hobart Town in early 1823 bringing a small but respectable fortune of almost £2,000 in cash and goods including alcohol and distilling equipment. He was granted 20 acres [8 hectares] of land on which to erect a distillery about three kilometres up the Hobart Rivulet at Cascade Grove. Eighteen months later the distillery was in operation, but within a short time it was to prove unsuccessful. By May 1826, Lowes was in business as an importer and was looking for a buyer for his distillery.

A few months later the government advertised for a building suitable to be used as a female factory and the only response was from Lowes, offering his distillery for sale for £2,500. Governor Arthur requested that officers in charge of major departments report on its suitability and potential usefulness.

Colonial Architect David Lambe was asked to assess the building's suitability for reconstruction into a female factory. He replied that the current estimated value was £2,760. His best estimate for the conversion was less than £700. A later investigation showed that Lambe's estimates were wildly inaccurate and that the current valuation should have been less than £2000. The final cost of the alterations was more than £4500, six and a half times Lambe's estimate. In this case, Arthur was poorly served by his subordinate Lambe, but surely even a non-specialist could have deduced that a plan which entailed twice to four times as much construction as already existed could scarcely cost only a quarter as much. Luckily for Arthur, in the following year, 1827, John Lee Archer arrived to take up the post of Colonial Engineer and as such the architect for all colonial government buildings and it was his design and not Lambe's that was used.

Joshua Drabble, Superintendent of the existing Hobart Town Female Factory, wrote to the Colonial Secretary with his own conclusions. He did not explicitly condemn the site but his report suggested that many important issues would not and could not be solved by purchasing Lowes' Distillery:

> … a Female Factory ought to be on an elevated site for the attainment of cleanliness, health and internal privacy; and as near as possible to where the population is most dense for convenience and access to services [especially doctors, magistrates and police] …The proposed building ought to be erected on principles of classification and complete seclusion from external intercourse…

Drabble then stressed the need for good ventilation, isolation, the need for plenty of cells, and that the sleeping rooms should never contain more than four women at a time. He further said that if these ideas were followed:

> … the dread of solitary punishment combined with the love of society would act as a stimulus to good conduct, escape be prevented, external communication cut off, subordination maintained, industry excited, health preserved, the safety of work or other property secured, and religious instruction communicated with a more rational hope of ultimate success…

Drabble was emphasising the absolute need for the new factory to be secure from unwanted intrusions, from damage to equipment and from the possibility of escape. He also emphasised that it must be on an elevated rather than a valley site for health and security purposes; and it must be properly fitted out so that the inmates could be separated for classification, security, reform and health purposes. There was no emphasis in his report that these were the most important aspects for the success of the new institution but nevertheless Arthur and his other chief departmental heads should have been alert to these dangers. Drabble, as Superintendant of the old Female Factory, was the man with the expertise but no-one seemed to be listening. He went on to point out the disadvantages to the distillery site:

> The disadvantages are its being overlooked in all directions …its irregular plan, the expense of the necessary alterations… the difficulty of access… the badness of the road…

Why Arthur didn't listen to Drabble is hard to understand, for he had instinctively identified every major fault of siting the new factory at the

Cascades. In defence of Arthur it should be pointed out that in spite of these obvious problems Colonial Surgeon Scott had no reservations at all about the site, stating that '…the health of those placed there is not likely to suffer any detriment, but on the contrary is likely to improve…'

Scott made this statement in January when the area around the Cascades is at its most pleasant but it is truly remarkable that he was not more perceptive. He should have realised just how bad the place could be in winter or during any prolonged spell of bad weather. Perhaps his statement merely highlights the extremely bad state of the old factory.

Factory Superintendent Drabble had also pointed out some of the advantages of siting the new Factory at Cascades:
> …the principal advantages of Mr Lowes' Distillery are the substantial nature of the buildings, its separation from the gaol, the difference of time necessary for its completion… and the abundance of wood and water.

The poor state of the old factory and the increasing numbers of female convicts arriving in Van Diemen's Land made Arthur think that he must have a new factory as soon as possible. Throughout the period of reconstruction of the distillery Arthur frequently expressed his impatience and the urgency of the work. Drabble had noted that the immediacy of the need as well as the expense precluded the building of an entirely new factory, and Arthur obviously agreed. But in fact, rushing to buy the distillery certainly did not save any time and quite possibly did not save any money over starting from scratch on a more suitable site.

Drabble also suggested other reasons why Arthur possibly felt the Cascades property was a good site. The old Factory was very inefficient and costly for the supply of wood and water for the washing work performed by the female convicts. Carting of water must have been almost continuous. By the end of May 1828 the old Factory was receiving 53 cartloads of water a week. Wood for heating and boiling the washing water was a substantial cost as well. These supplies were not only expensive but also posed a threat to the security, with carts and draymen coming and going all the time. Cascades had a supply of water running through the old distillery and was closer to the forests on the mountain to supply firewood. Furthermore, the new Factory would enable separation and classification of the female prisoners in order to more effectively control them and to reduce the perceived contamination of the less hardened by the more persistent offenders.

The other major worry was security, and the ease with which the female convicts escaped from the old Factory. On Friday night, 2 May 1828, Mary Ann Hagan and Susan Leake had very little trouble in clambering onto the roof of one of the buildings and making good their escape. Colonial Secretary Burnett could only comment wryly that the current situation was unsatisfactory.

None of these aspects were greatly improved by the transfer to the new Factory, but Arthur was being pushed and pulled by the twin needs of keeping the disciplinary situation under control and at the same time being ordered to spend as little as possible. Having made the decision to buy Lowes' Distillery, he had little option but to press ahead and to hope for the best.

Eventually Lambe's drawings were abandoned, John Lee Archer drew up new plans, and tenders were called in June 1827. John Faber was contracted to do the construction of the Factory at a price of £2344 within nine months with the government furnishing much of the materials and labour. Five out of the seven tenderers had offered to do the work for between £2900 and £3350 but each felt it would take twelve months. In the end the government would have found it better to have accepted the more expensive quotes, for Faber ended up taking over twelve months to complete the work and the workmanship was quite unsatisfactory. Some of the work had to be repaired or done again, and it was eighteen months before the project was completed.

Building the Cascades Female Factory

The alterations consisted of raising the outside wall to the equivalent of two storeys high and building a two-storey building, with rooms about 4 metres wide, down the inside of each side wall. A chapel was built in front of and connected to the rear buildings of the old distillery. Inside the front wall a two-storey building for staff quarters 18 by 4.2 metres was added, the upstairs being for the superintendent's family, the downstairs for offices and gatekeeper. The courtyard in the centre of the complex was divided by high walls into seven small courtyards; one each for the office area near the entry, the Nursery, the Hospital, the Kitchen and for each of the three classifications of prisoners: First or Assignable Class, Second Class, and Third or Crime Class. A range of twelve solitary cells were included in a building at the northwest corner of the old distillery. During construction a number of flaws and limitations in the design were discovered and these were rectified as the work progressed. The major improvement was the substantially increased size of the chapel.

A committee of officers was instructed to assess the quality of the workmanship. Their findings were that the overall quality was very poor and the builder had failed to meet the requirements. An extra £775 had been spent on levelling and draining the yards. This sum was more than Colonial Architect Lambe had originally allowed for the total cost of the reconstruction. In the end the overall cost for the purchase and reconstruction was in excess of £6600. This was more than the cost of the Parramatta Female Factory which had been designed to hold twice the number as Cascades and which had been built on a 'dry, healthy and cheerful' site.

The dilapidated condition of the road to the new Factory was a major problem. Arthur ordered the building of a new road three kilometres long which extended Macquarie Street from the edge of the town (at Barrack Street) to the Factory. Work on the new road began after July 1827 and, like most things to do with the Factory, not only took longer but cost a lot more than was expected.

At New Year 1829 over a hundred women were transferred to Cascades from the now unbearable conditions of the old factory. Because of building delays part of the Domain Barracks had to be fitted out for female convicts to tide over the transition period. In spite of Arthur's hopes, the same problems which had dogged the old Factory began to recur immediately. The location and style of the buildings at the new Factory were also to cause trouble.

The Riot

A serious riot broke out in February 1829 barely six weeks after the move to the new Factory. It began when some of the women in the yards started calling out to soldiers of the 40th Regiment who gathered on the steep hill behind and closely overlooking the Factory. According to later evidence the soldiers made a habit of walking the three kilometres from the barracks to the Factory every Sunday in order to visit women they knew. Since visits at the Factory were strictly forbidden, the soldiers gathered on the steep hills surrounding the Factory from where they could look down into the yards. The hills were so steep and close to the walls they had no problem identifying their friends and communicating with them. This, of course was precisely what Drabble had warned about when he had specified that the new Factory should not be capable of being 'overlooked'.

Some of the soldiers moved closer to the walls of the Factory and began throwing parcels of bread, butter and cheese over the walls into the yards. The food was confiscated by Jesse Pullen, the overseer, but the women gathered round him threateningly and hooted him from the yard. Superintendent Lovell restored order by putting the two ringleaders, Sarah Bickley and Elizabeth Davis, into their cells.

The Crime Class women were then confined to their sleeping wards, but continued to catcall obscenities and insults to the staff. After an hour or so, they began to push burning material and clothing through the ventilators of the sleeping rooms. Lovell was able to put out one fire before it took a proper hold, but as he extinguished one blaze, another would erupt and soon it appeared the whole building was alight. Women in other parts of the Factory where there had been no problems began to fear for their lives. Screams for help and pleas to be let out of their wards turned the smoke-filled Factory into a bedlam of panic, confusion and noise. Some of the women fainted.

At this stage a quantity of burning material was pushed down into a stairwell which was constructed entirely of pine. Flame and smoke erupted but with the exertion of the staff the fire was eventually extinguished. At 9pm Lovell sent Pullen to get James Gordon, the Principal Superintendent of Convicts. Because of the distance to town and the difficulties in locating the officers, Pullen was away for three hours and did not return until midnight. Gordon had also brought two constables, and with their help Pullen and Lovell were able to finally get the worst behaved women into solitary cells. What had happened to the soldiers and other onlookers we don't know, but we can suspect that they hadn't alerted the authorities to the riot and fires. The ridiculous length of time it took to obtain help and to finally subdue the women was an outcome of ignoring Drabble's warning that the Factory should be close to the centre of things and near to medical, magisterial and police support.

When Gordon reported to the Colonial Secretary the next day, he requested that a fence be placed around the Factory to prevent a recurrence of the problem. A fence would not have stopped the men going onto the hills each Sunday but it would have alleviated the problem of contraband being thrown over the walls. Arthur, as thrifty as usual, required the Colonial Secretary to investigate the matter, stating that any fence should combine 'security with economy'. Five months later nothing had been done. Arthur, and presumably the Colonial Secretary, were still investigating:

> A fence round the building is, no doubt, very desirable and the engineer had better state it better be carried into effect combining our *Means - Security* and *Expense...*

Arthur accepted that lack of a fence was a significant problem, but his first concern was the potential expense, even if it led to significant delay in securing the site. His insistence on thrift and economy led to extreme delays and in the end it was easier to 'shoot the messenger' instead of listening to the message.

Punish the innocent as well as the guilty

Arthur's comments on the riot indicate that he placed most of the blame on the staff having failed to comply with his rules and regulations. However, and most tellingly, he had only just sent the new regulations to the Principal Superintendent two weeks before the riot. It is more likely that it was the new regulations which themselves created the trouble. After all, the confiscated contraband had not been tobacco or liquor but fairly mundane items of food: bread, butter and cheese. It suggests that the regulations' harsh regime of plain food and never enough of it, particularly fats and greens, was already starting to tell on the inmates.

Gordon suggested that those Crime Class women who had refused to take part in the riot should be rewarded by being placed in the 2nd Class Yard, thus encouraging the women for good behaviour. Arthur, however, was obdurate. The well-behaved women should not receive improper favours. Indeed, on the contrary they should be punished for collective responsibility: 'I fully expected to have found the whole Class under some serious restrictions and subjected to privations with additional labour.'

In other words punish the innocent along with the guilty. Not only was Arthur's answer monstrously unfair and improper to those who had not taken part in the riot, but it also betrays a serious flaw in his perception of human nature and how his system might better mould the convicts to his purpose. Presumably wiser heads prevailed, for Arthur's eventual and more thoughtful decision lay in further dividing up the Crime Class, and he requested that the Colonial Engineer John Lee Archer advise on separate apartments [ie separate cells] and the building of a new yard. When the plans were drawn up and presented to him Arthur decided to wait until

---

A girl on the town

Sentenced to seven years transportation for 'larceny from the person', a charge typical of a girl 'on the town' who had robbed a client, Sarah Simmons was about 17 years old when she arrived in Hobart Town on the *Sovereign* in 1827. Less than a fortnight later she absconded and was sentenced to a week in the cells and a further month in the Crime Class at the Hobart Town (old) Female Factory.

Sarah kept her nose clean for another 11 months but then was found guilty of having been absent without leave "on Saturday night last", for which she was sentenced to 14 days in a solitary cell on bread and water and 12 months in the Crime Class at the Female Factory. For being found guilty of a further charge of "striking one of the witnesses who gave evidence against her and using gross and violent expressions in the presence of the convicting magistrates" she was given a further twelve months in the Factory. Of course this meant that Sarah was sent to the old Factory and was one of those transferred to the new Factory at Cascades at the turn of the year. She appears not to have been one of the offenders at the riot in February.

But on a dark night in October 1829 Sarah climbed onto the roof of the Pullens' apartment and lowered herself to the ground outside with the aid of a clothesline and thus made good her escape from the Cascades Female Factory. On 21 October she was apprehended, charged with absconding and sentenced to solitary on bread and water for fourteen days and to be put back in the Factory Crime Class. This was a fairly light sentence for her escape.

What is different about Sarah is that as she continued to misbehave for the next five years, instead of receiving light sentences that grew progressively heavier, the opposite appears to be the case. She didn't serve all her sentences in full, but it is clear she spent at least half of her sentence of transportation in close confinement, including the final sixteen days. In April 1834 she was free. And what is truly remarkable is that she was never recorded as having offended again.

---

more experience had been gained in handling the women in the new Factory.

No cure for old problems

In spite of Gordon's report and recommendations for an immediate response to particular problems, Arthur had resorted to ignoring the immediate need and instead retreated behind a wall of long term strategy. This in itself was not a bad idea, except it was also a costly idea, and thus Arthur would refuse to implement it until it was too late and other developments had overwhelmed the progressing situation. Gordon's recommendations may have been makeshift, but they were possible and financially feasible. Arthur's view was for the long run, and showed itself to be an early proof of the dictum that in the long run we are all dead. In this case, as we shall see, it was to be some of the women and many of the babies who were to be dead. In any case, more than three years went by before anything was done about building the second yard and separate apartments. Meanwhile sugar, bread, butter and tobacco continued to sail over the walls every Sunday and the men of the town continued to gather on the hills and communicate with their girlfriends.

Just as building the new Factory had not prevented external intercourse and the passage of contraband and food, so too it did not prevent escapes. In the matter of escapes, and in spite of being newly built, the Cascades Factory was almost as unsatisfactory as the old Factory in town. Sarah Simmons, one of the female convicts who had been transfered from the old Factory to the new Cascades Factory made a daring escape in October 1829.

Water and pollution

Superintendent Drabble's recommendation that a factory should be in an elevated position referred not only to the undesirability of being overlooked, but also to the health problems involved in being in a damp valley. The proximity of the new Factory to the Hobart Town Rivulet was not only bad for the health of the inmates, it was bad for the health of the townsfolk of Hobart. Within three months of opening, on 3 March 1829, it was noticed that the sewerage and other unwholesome effluents from the Factory were discharging into the Rivulet which was the source of the town's drinking, washing and industrial water.

By the end of the first winter, the grievous error of ignoring Drabble's recommendations regarding the most suitable situation for the factory was obvious to all, and the situation at the Factory was unhealthy and physically almost unbearable. Assistant Surgeon Bryant, constantly at Cascades, wrote that the solitary cells were:

…extremely damp and unwholesome… the beds being placed on the floors… [in]the water which oozes beneath the walls of the building, so as to be frequently saturated with moisture…

Bryant warned that it was just as unhealthy to be in the damp atmosphere of the cells as it was to be lying in wet clothes and bedding. Arthur's only response was to order the beds to be raised two feet off the floor, which of course did nothing to help the atmospheric conditions.

Overcrowding

Already, within a year of opening, yet another of the Factory's most persistent problems, overcrowding, had become obvious. By mid-October 1829 the new Female Factory was already overcrowded with nearly two hundred women in residence in an institution designed for half that number. The overcrowding was to result in the decision early the following year to increase the size of the Factory.

And no Christmas pudding

For the women in the Factory the year ended much the same way as it passed. When the women (who would have included Sarah Simmons, back inside after her escape) requested an extra half pound of meat and some plums for a Christmas pudding, the Principal Superintendent passed the request to Governor Arthur with his approval because in general the women's conduct had been: 'most orderly and correct … considering they are confined for punishment'. But Arthur, possibly remembering the riot, but more probably thinking of his own regulations, decided to give a frosty negative to such improper indulgence. His demeanour and attitudes were surely as grim and bleak as the new Factory.

Chapter 13. Pity the Children

The first year in the new Cascades Female Factory was to set the scene for the future. By the end of January 1829, the first month of occupation, all the preconditions for the horrors of the next decade were in place, and most tragic of these horrors was the infant mortality rate.

There were six major factors in creating the enormous death toll amongst the infants. We have already discussed five of them: the faulty siting and design of the institution, Arthur's new regulations, the gross overcrowding, Arthur's thrust for efficiency and cost-cutting and the flaring up of highly infectious diseases about the time of the move to the new Factory. It is now time to turn our attention to the sixth factor, the forced early weaning of the babies in order to more quickly have their mothers available for punishment.

Early weaning of babies

In December 1828, almost exactly a year before the move to the new Factory, the nursing mothers at the old Hobart Town Factory had gone on strike and refused to work so long as they had to attend to their infant children. Arthur ordered a board of enquiry consisting of Colonial Surgeon Scott and an assistant surgeon to consider:

> …at what age infants may with safety be separated from their mothers and placed in the nursery which is intended to be formed in the New Factory.

The outcome of the enquiry was the forced early weaning of the babies at six months of age and their separation from the mothers who then had to serve six months hard labour in the 2nd Class for having become pregnant. This policy continued after the transfer to the new Factory. A large percentage of the deaths at the Cascades Factory were directly attributable to this early separation of mother and child.

During the ten years from 1829 to 1838 inclusive, hundreds upon hundreds of children died at the Cascades Factory and the institution reeled from one scandal to the next. Building maintenance meant the entire complex was frequently whitewashed in an attempt to improve the sanitary condition of the buildings, but failed to keep pace with the even more frequent government attempts to whitewash the continuing scandal of the death rates amongst both women and children.

Death rates in the Factories and Nurseries

In the winter of 1829 the first major scandal about infant mortality erupted. In a letter to the *Colonial Times* on 7 August a letter by 'Humanity' claimed the Factory was badly situated and 'always cold and damp; in fact the sun seldom shines upon it', and placed the blame on the penny pinching attitudes of the British government. The *Colonial Times* editorialist then took up the cry and asserted that although the colony had a very low mortality rate, things were very different in the new Factory. In the colony generally, child deaths were a '...rare occurrence... [yet] as many as six or seven children have laid dead there at the same time ...'

This was all true. Both New South Wales and Van Diemen's Land were well known for having a low infant mortality rate and for the general suitability of their climates for growing children. Like Superintendent Drabble, the *Colonial Times* had expressed grave doubts about the location and surrounding environment of the Factory long before the government had been committed to buying the distillery:

Before the government had entered into any expense of purchasing or altering ... we pointed out the insalubrity of the situation and the probable consequences which unfortunately now seem realised ...

The newspaper demanded a public investigation and suggested that the answer might be for the government to build a separate lying-in [maternity] hospital.

Two months later the *Colonial Times* attacked again. There had been no official reply to the charges made in their columns. Meanwhile the situation had substantially worsened. The newspaper emphasised the immediate need for a separate and new lying-in hospital stating that a 'great number' of deaths amongst the children had occurred because of the poor conditions at the Factory and the exacerbating influence of the winter damp. If we consider Surgeon Bryant's report, on the first winter at Cascades, of the unwholesome and foetid conditions in the cells and Arthur's barely interested response, it seems quite likely that the newspapers attacks were not only warranted but probably substantially correct.

Hygiene

When the Hutchinsons first took over the Factory in 1832, Governor Arthur visited and inspected it. As he was to comment in a memorandum to the Colonial Secretary, there were bugs and fleas everywhere throughout the buildings but nowhere was it worse than amongst the children. Their bedding was 'quite black with fleas' to such an extent that they could hardly sleep.

Descriptions of the Factory during the late 1830s and the 1840s usually remark on the extreme cleanliness of the premises, and many attribute this to Mrs Hutchinson's zeal and effectiveness. If this was true then perhaps the Hutchinsons' regime was responsible for cleaning up the Factory, although there was a limit to what could be done so long as there was excessive overcrowding. But the descriptions of conditions in the forties are to some extent at odds with what unexpected visitors found in the thirties, particularly the Coroners and visiting surgeons. In late 1836 two magistrates charged that women servants had been sent to their assignments in a filthy and lice-ridden condition.

Reverend Hutchinson replied that this was because of conditions on the female convict ships and was not the fault of the Factory staff, but this is evidence that the system did break down, whoever was at fault. Hutchinson should have notified the appropriate authorities that women were being landed and taken from the Factory for assignment whilst unclean. The charges still reflect badly on the conditions in the Factory. New arrivals were expected to be sent to the Factory to await assignment, and at that time to be properly bathed and inspected, and not to be sent out until they and their clothing were clean. There was a limit to what any system could do in the circumstance of the overcrowding. It is probable that the staff did their best to ensure cleanliness, nevertheless there are frequent references to the stench emanating from the Factory in summer.

The reputation of the Factory was so bad that in October 1834, Coroner JH Moore reported to the Colonial Secretary that coroner's juries were no longer prepared to take witnesses' evidence for granted and were demanding to visit and inspect the institution to report on actual conditions inside. They reported the prisoners were very clean, but that the overcrowding was unbelievable and unhealthy. Over twenty adults and 42 babies were crammed together in two rooms the combined size equivalent to three modern medium-sized bedrooms (45 by 11 feet, or about 45 square metres). Elizabeth Flint, a prisoner and the overseer of the children, stated that in one room alone, with only seven beds, seven women and 13 children lived. It would be more accurate to say that they died in the room, for in this one room alone, two children had died the day before and on the previous Saturday, as well as Elizabeth Lush upon whose death the Coroner was enquiring.

Altogether ten children had died in the previous six weeks and three more were not expected to live. In 1833 forty children died out of a total of 103. In the following year 1834, thirty-eight out of 90 died. Whilst in themselves the figures are bad enough, they do not represent the true annual statistical percentages. Such figures would have been much worse. Many of the children would not have been in the institution for a full year. Others amongst the 38 children who died in 1834 would have been survivors from 1833. Thus the annual death rate in the Nursery may have been as high as 50% deaths or more. Because children were often in the Nursery from birth to the age of three, they had to live for three years with these horrendous odds against their survival, though of course as they grew older, medically their chances of survival increased.

'Rigid discipline extends to the unborn'

Coroner Moore came up with many suggestions, as had Assistant Surgeon Bedford earlier that year. Both were agreed on the necessity of removing the children from the environs of the Factory. Moore, however, had the perfect method to prevent the public scandals revealed by so many official and open inquests. He suggested that all that had to be done was to place the Nursery by proclamation technically outside of the House of Correction and there would no longer be the legal necessity for having expensive and scandal-causing inquests. This suggestion was entirely unworthy of Coroner Moore, who in all other respects seems to have been a humane and kindly man much grieved by so many unnecessary deaths. But this sort of strategy is indicative of government officialdom's extensive and active attempts to cover up the facts at all costs.

In his report Coroner Moore objected to every facet of the management of the Hospital and Nursery at the Factory especially because the women were punished for getting pregnant by receiving six months sentence to the Crime Class after the baby was weaned, 'whilst the father of the child …is rarely if ever punished.'

Moore also condemned the catastrophic effects of:
the rigid discipline … [which] extends to the unborn infant privations which become too evident when the child is born, and after birth a species of severe imprisonment unsuited to its tender age or free birth.

Here of course Moore was hitting the nail on the head. The children died in such numbers because the priority was to punish the mother at any cost, including the lives of the children. All the best strategies to improve the babies' survival would mean reducing the penalties applying to the women, even though as Moore had pointed out, punishing only or mainly women for having got pregnant, and not at the same time punishing the men, was extremely hypocritical.

The deaths of many more children meant that Arthur, following a negative report by Assistant Surgeon Bedford, was forced to approve the planning of a new hospital, nursery and infirmary. It was proposed that the new buildings should be placed outside of the walls and under the control of the Surgeon and not under the Superintendent's control. Principal Superintendent Spode objected to this as undermining his authority and Arthur upheld Spode.

Meanwhile at the end of 1834 little had been done except planning and arguing including a number of tantrums and similar scenes between Spode and Bedford. A hospital was eventually built in the second yard. Neither plans nor details of exactly when it was built seem to have survived.

More scandals, more reports

Another rash of scandals erupted during 1837 and 1838 and once again the coroners attacked the crowded conditions of the Nursery, the lack of sunlight, the damp rooms, the poor food and the ever soaring infant mortality rate.

There was a coroner's investigation into the death of Barbara Hemmings at the Factory on 26 March 1838. In the report the coroner decided Hemmings had died from the effects of diarrhoea which was currently 'prevalent in the town and gaol'. But the coroner also attacked the conditions in the Factory which he felt had exacerbated the effects of the disease. The nurseries were crowded, the yard was too small, there was no sunlight and the cells were too dark. The coroner's jury reported:

Coroner's Report on the death of Barbara Hemmings, a prisoner in the Cascades Female Factory 1838

Foreman's Statement:

The Jury consider it their duty, respectfully to submit, thro' the Coroner, to His Excellency Sir John Franklin, that having been permitted to inspect the Female Factory House of Correction, they found upon investigation there there is no place, where the children can take exercise of any sort, except in a wet flagged yard, to which (it is in evidence on the oaths of the Assistant Superintendent of the Prison and other witnesses) for four months of the year the Sun's rays never penetrate, and during that period it is never otherwise than in a wet state.

The Jury have further to represent to his Excellency, the close and confined state of the Children's wards - two small rooms each about 26 feet by 12 feet in which there are at present upwards of Seventy human beings confined, and in "the weaning room" Thirty Five; the effluvia from which, even in the day time, the Jury found most offensive, and must be most injurious to the infants confined there, particularly, from obvious causes, during the night.

The Jury further submit to His Excellency that having been permitted to inspect the Prison, altho' the Coroner objected to their going into any evidence not immediately connected with the death of Barbara Hemmings, they have respectfully to submit to His Excellency the extremely offensive condition of the dark cells*, in which the Jury found women closely confined upon bread and water for periods of from Seven days to one month.

The Jury further submit to His Excellency, that no exclusive Register of deaths is regularly kept in the Prison. That it appears by the books of the Medical attendant, that Twenty deaths have taken place since the first of January last, and it is in evidence before the Jury that two have taken place within the last fourteen days, and the Inquests have not been held.

All which the Jury respectfully submit - to the consideration of his Excellency Sir John Franklin.

R.L. Murray, Foreman
March 26th 1838

* The dark cells were triple-doored and allowed some ventilation but no light or sound to enter. The women had two tubs, one with water and one for use as a toilet. They had to tell which was which by touch alone.

… the portion allotted for a nursery was infinitely worse than our imagination had painted it… of two apartments an upstairs and ground floor, into which the suckling nursery is divided, all of the recent deaths have occurred on the lower floor, which is not ventilated in any way and on which the sun never shines. The upper floor is ventilated and has windows on which the sun shines for a few hours during 8 months of the year, nevertheless the general appearance of the children was much more healthy than we expected to have found them...

Seventy mothers and babies were held in two large rooms each a little over eight metres long by three and a half metres wide, the total area equivalent of less than a modern two-bedroom flat. Into one ward alone there were crowded 17 women and 17 children and the poor food took its toll on all.

The Weaning Room held ten nurses and twenty-five babies: 'the effluvia from which, even in the day time the jury found most offensive, and must be most injurious to the infants'. The babies being weaned were fed bread and milk, which was insufficient for good health, and they lacked exercise and appetite. Nursing mothers were given rations that in quality and quantity were significantly less than those available at the Parramatta Female Factory. The coroner cited Assistant Superintendent Cato saying two other children had died in the previous ten days, there was no sun for four months of the year, the flagstones in the yards were constantly wet and cold [this was in March] and in summer the wards smelled badly. Twenty inmates of the Factory, mainly children, had died since the beginning of the year.

This time, finally the Government acted. But the action was too little, too late, and was driven once again by trying to do everything on the cheap, putting efficiency and economy before trying to save lives.

Nursery at Liverpool Street

The Cascades Female Factory Nursery was closed down by 17 October 1838 and the children, nurses, weaning mothers and lying-in facilities transferred to a small house in Liverpool Street in the middle of Hobart. This meant the women and children were far from the environs of the Factory, away from the likelihood of catching diseases from the other women and were close to medical attention and magisterial oversight.

However, the conditions in the new building were hardly better than at Cascades except that there would have been more sunlight. The most critical factor, overcrowding, was if anything worse. The rations and care of the children remained unchanged, and the distance and separation of the weaned babies from their mothers, who previously could visit them regularly when they had been in another section of the Factory, was now impossible until after they had served their six months sentence, and then only possible if their new masters were close enough and caring enough to give them a pass on Sundays. No doubt many of the babies pined for their mothers and died from the effects of the separation. The child mortality rate did not decrease at the Liverpool Street Nursery. The overcrowding grew gradually worse.

Another inquiry

Mrs Slea, the Matron of the separate Female Factory Nursery, at this stage still in Liverpool Street, gave many insights into the running of the nursery to the major 1841 inquiry into female convict discipline. Many assignable women refused to act as nurses because they disliked the work and it was often the other mothers who were used to look after the children. By this time women did not have to wean their children until the age of nine months. Matron Slea felt that the majority were good mothers and when they had been assigned they often behaved particularly well in order to

Dynnyrne Nursery

Photograph courtesy of Archives Office of Tasmania

maintain regular contact with their children, which was stopped if they offended against the regulations. Some mothers were able to get a certificate of their good behaviour and ability to support the child which meant that they got custody rather than the child being sent to the Orphan Schools.

At the same 1841 inquiry, Dr Dermer, the current medical officer, was only one of a long line of critics, both medical and lay, who over many years had severely criticised the extreme overcrowding and lack of proper ventilation in wards and rooms set aside for the infants. Both he and the Matron felt that the children were reasonably healthy and he attributed the higher mortality rate amongst the Nursery children compared to his private practice to the effects of poor ventilation and congenital 'diseased constitutions'. When it closed in 1842, the Liverpool Street Nursery had 57 women and almost 100 children crammed into one very small house.

Dynnyrne House Nursery

The Female Factory Nursery at Dynnyrne House was established in 1842. Four or five hundred metres closer to the town than the Cascades Factory and on the other side of the Rivulet, it was the site of the first distillery built in the colony, and had been known as Midwood's Sorell Distillery. In 1830 it was bought by Robert Lathrop Murray who rebuilt and extended the main house and renamed the complex Dynnyrne Distillery.

Murray was the prominent newspaperman who as foreman of the Coroner's jury in 1838 had forced an inspection of the Female Factory which had led to the disclosure of the conditions in which the women and children were being held. During the late 1830s he started subdividing his property and later moved to his other property about one and a half kilometres away, and renamed this second house Dynnyrne House as well. It was these later estates which were in the area to which they later gave the name Dynnyrne.

Conditions did not improve at the Dynnyrne Nursery for though the site was marginally more sunny and salubrious, it drew its water from the Rivulet below the Cascades Factory and that water was partly polluted by effluent from the Factory. There is no evidence of any attempt by the authorities to isolate or quarantine the very young children arriving with their mothers from the convict transports. Although Dynnyrne House was a substantial stone gentleman's house comprising the matron's quarters and another eight rooms, there was at the end of 1846 forty five women as well as an unspecified number of babies and young children in residence there. Far better than the circumstances had been ten years before in the Cascades Factory, but substantially overcrowded nevertheless.

Throughout the 1840s the female convict establishment in Hobart was widely scattered. The Factory at Cascades was still the largest and most important single institution but women and their young children were also held in the Nursery at Dynnyrne House, newly arrived probationers were held aboard the hulk *Anson* which was moored off Dowsings Point just north of Prince of Wales Bay, and probationers for hire and those available for assignment were held at the Brickfields Branch establishment in North Hobart. At times there were also Hiring Depots at New Town and in Liverpool Street in the centre of town.

The Dynnyrne Nursery had not been an improvement on either the Liverpool Street house or the original Cascades accommodation. The high

---

Such impudent creatures

As for doing anything about the women here, in the factory, it seems next to impossible huddled as they all are together, and such impudent creatures, almost all of them, there in order that they may lie in [give birth] and then go to service again.

Jane Franklin, letter to her sister Mary Simpkinson,
4 October 1838

The agreeable casualty

[A convict woman at the Nursery] has plenty of companions, plenty of food, no work, and moreover is liable to the agreeable casualty of being selected … [as] a wet nurse [breast feeding another woman's child], to enter in that capacity into a private family, a rich one perhaps … where she meets with the usual bribes by which tender mothers strive to secure to their children the care of their hired substitutes. In ordinary cases, however, the child being weaned, at the end of 9 to 12 months, the mother either is removed into the nursery as a nurse … of weaned children … or she goes back to the factory … to be punished [for having been pregnant].

Jane Franklin, letter to Elizabeth Fry,
3 August 1841

---

infant death rate continued in both places. In order to alleviate the problem and to once again centralise the administration of female convicts, in 1849 the Government started work on expanding the Cascades establishment. It was if the problems connected to the old site had been completely forgotten.

Back to Cascades

In June 1849 plans were drawn up for a new purpose-built Nursery on the eastern side of the Factory wall. Designed to accommodate 88 women and innumerably more babies, the site was to form the fourth yard of the Factory. Built of stone, brick and timber, the yard was alongside the third, separate apartments yard. It was surrounded by a wall 61m by 33m, with the main, mostly two-storey Nursery building 49m by 8m along the western wall facing east. There was also a matron's house, 135 square metres, single-storeyed with a bow-window. As well as the main building which was well-endowed with open verandahs, there was also a large open shelter shed, described by the traveller Colonel Mundy when he visited the new Nursery on 1 January 1851, not long after its completion:

In a large exercise yard, with an open shed in the centre to afford shelter from the sun, we found sixty women, with as many babies from two years to as many days old - women and children all silent! One would have thought them all deaf and dumb … Some of the females, I found were the hired nurses of the establishment - not the mothers of the children … many of the wretched little ones, in the hands of the nurses, will never know either parent. The public consoles itself with the dry fact, that they will all come into the labour market. A large ward was allotted to the mid-day sleep of the poor little babes. It was rather a pretty sight for a father (of none of them) to contemplate. There were a score or so of wooden cribs, in each of which lay two, three or four innocents, stowed away head and tail, like sardines … while others were curled about like a litter of kittens in a basket of straw.

However cute Mundy found the young children, what he was describing was a factory process for dealing with babies most efficiently on grounds of cost. Piling babies into cots like sardines in a tin is not a reasonable way of dealing with infants and ensures that if one contracts an illness, many others will fall prey to it as well. These precepts were well known and accepted by the medical men dealing with the children, but they were largely helpless in the face of the system put in place twenty-two years before by Governor Arthur and continued by his successors.

The new Nursery buildings were by far the best designed up to this date. They had large airy rooms and wards, with verandahs designed to catch the maximum sunlight. But the location had not changed and so there was precious little sunlight for much of the year, and probably only sufficient for health in the height of summer. Mundy visited the Factory at New Year, when the surrounding area would have been green with summer growth, the sun high in the sky, and the boggy morass around the institution would have dried out in the warm air.

We don't know whether Mundy had been told of the bleak history of the Female Factory Nursery; he certainly doesn't acknowledge it. Nor could he know that what he was seeing was merely a seasonal break in a continuing disaster. The new buildings did not work, the site and the overcrowding were the culprits, not the style and efficiency of the buildings. Arthur's poor original choice of the site and the Government's huge subsequent outlays on the buildings and infrastructure meant that later administrations were committed to extending at Cascades or risk censure by abandoning a large capital investment. It was not until the 1880s, over fifty years from the original decisions and thirty years after the cessation of Transportation that government officials gained the courage of their

Cascades Female Factory. The 1850 Nursery is Yard 4, the first yard at the left.

Photo courtesy of Archives Office of Tasmania.

156

convictions and began to demolish and abandon parts of the Cascades complex. Meanwhile, in spite of Mundy's praise and the vain hopes of the designers and officials of the new Nursery, the death toll continued. There was no choice within a few years of its completion but to abandon the new buildings. What makes the situation even more poignant, was that the answers to the problems were known and proven, and in the Ross Female Factory there was an exemplar of how to organise a Nursery so that the death toll within an institution might drop to something approaching that of the outside society.

During the two years 1851 and 1852 following Mundy's visit to the new Nursery, the mortality rate amongst the infants was not reduced, and just over a hundred young children died. Government officials reacted with a number of short term attempts at a solution by first transferring the babies to New Town and then later that same year to the Brickfields. However the Nursery returned to the Cascades in 1854. After an investigation in the following year, 1855, during which one doctor put the main blame on bad administration, the children were again returned to Brickfields. Finally, the efforts of officials began to bear some fruit, though it should be remembered that by this stage, Transportation had ceased more than two years earlier and both the number of female convicts and the numbers of their newborn infants were dropping steeply as people left the system. The Brickfields situation was more favourable to the children's health, and finally the death rate of Nursery children in the Hobart Town area was considerably reduced

The infant deaths

We actually have some statistics of the deaths of infants in the female factories. These were compiled by Dr ES Hall for the period 1851-1855 and compared children from the Hobart District with children from the Factory Nursery. Historian Bryan Gandevia compared some of the figures: 'The annual age-specific mortality rates (0-3 years) were approximately 10% for Hobart district and 30% for the nursery children.'

Of the 366 children who died in the Factory nurseries, 51% died of dysentery, diarrhoea or enteritis, compared to 13% amongst those who died in the general population. In the Factory 13% of child deaths were due to influenza, bronchitis or pneumonia compared to less than 5% in the general population. Since these are diseases of infection or environment, it is reasonable to ascribe a large part of the difference between the town and the nursery death rates to overcrowding and poor facilities for isolating those children who were already suffering from illness.

Premature birth and convulsions, easily identified and likely to have similar death rates whatever the environmental conditions, did in fact have similar rates per thousand children, but made up 29% of the general population deaths as against only 11% of the Nursery deaths. These figures suggest very strongly that the excessive death rate in the Factory Nursery was two to four times higher than that of the general population and was directly caused by the environment, probably by overcrowding, possibly contributed to by the reduced quality of food, water and care.

Chapter 14. Life at Cascades Factory

Although the effect of probation was to create more institutions to house and control female convicts, this was also occurring at a time of huge increase in total numbers of convicts and their children being sent from Britain. With the cessation of transportation of convicts to New South Wales in 1840, there was no let up in the numbers of female convicts being sent. One newspaper described the circumstances in the Cascades Female Factory in October 1841:

> The capacity of the building is so unequal to the number of the wretched inmates, that their working rooms resemble the hold of a slave ship; what their sleeping rooms must be, shut up during the whole night [with only buckets for human wastes]... So foetid, so wholly unfitting for the human being is the atmosphere after the night's halations, that if we are correctly informed, the turnkeys when they open the doors in the morning, make their escape from the passages with the utmost expedition to avoid semi-suffocation.
>
> *Austral-Asiatic Review*, 29 October 1841

What, one may ask, ever happened to the idea, promulgated initially by Superintendent Drabble, that no more than four women should be sleeping in each room? It is obvious no real attempt beyond the building of the hundred or so separate apartments had ever been made to attain this goal. Whilst the suggestion of the newspaper writer that the sleeping rooms resembled the hold of a slave ship was probably exaggerated, it was equally probably not too far from the mark. A description by one of the women convicts of the conditions within one of the wards about this time shows that the hammocks used were so tightly packed that a woman couldn't get out to use a bucket at night without disturbing all the others in the ward. Beds were used in other circumstances, but it is clear that these were often shared.

As Kay Daniels points out, although the rhetoric about the factories, and in the case of the Launceston Factory even the outward appearance, reflected nineteenth century ideas of penal reform, the actual 'chaotic' conditions in the factories much more closely resembled those of the eighteenth century English prisons, but in which 'some of the new ideas of the prison reformers and their urge for discipline, order and the reformation of the individual were pursued'.

The second yard: more space, not better conditons

When Arthur turned his mind to the problems inherent in the Cascades Female Factory it was not to the health, hygiene and unnecessary deaths amongst the inmates and particularly the children. It was to the problem of overcrowding and the consequent problems of keeping discipline in the institution. On 5 December 1829, at the end of the first year, Principal Superintendent of Convicts Josiah Spode wrote to Colonial Secretary Burnett that following a recent official and public notification that the Factory was also to become a place 'of reception for free persons' [that is for free women found guilty and sentenced to a period in gaol], together with the constant and ever increasing pressure of new convict arrivals, the Factory could no longer cope. At the end of January 1830, Assistant Surgeon Bryant was writing that the conditions in the Factory were far too crowded and that additions were urgently needed for sanitary and health reasons, especially because increased numbers of new arrivals were expected imminently. Arthur authorised the planning and construction of a second yard including solitary working cells a few days later.

However, it was to be two and a half years later until the new yard was completed. By this time the new yard was little help in easing the overcrowding from the conditions that had existed when they were originally planned, the numbers of inmates having increased in the interim. The new section was designed to enable better classification and separation of individuals and groups; and to help control refractory elements amongst the women. The cells were also designed to assist in the reformation process, though how far that was possible is unknown. But given that they were described at the time as 'dismal and sepulchral' it appears that there was little likelihood of success. The rest of the yard was to be used for washtubs and drying lines.

The deaths of many children and the general poor conditions in general led to a debate between the Principal Superintendent and another Assistant Surgeon Dr ESP Bedford about the possibility of improvements. Later a hospital section was built in the second yard, but neither plans nor details of when it was built appear to have survived. Certainly as far as Bedford was concerned, having the hospital in the second yard was unlikely to help; he had wanted new buildings away from the site of the Factory

160

altogether, and he believed that as long as the women were kept in the environs of the Factory their health would suffer.

The second yard was smaller than the first, for although it was the same length from front to back, 60 metres (200 feet), its width at 30 metres was almost 30% less. Solitary cells two storeys high were erected along the front wall closest to the Rivulet, and a yard within a yard consisting of more solitary cells was built along the back wall. By the end of 1832 the masonry work of 100 solitary working cells was finished. In the following year they were roofed and fitted out ready for occupation. The total cost of construction was almost £1900. The more buildings that were added to the Cascades site the less likely the female convicts were to ever obtain healthy and reasonable quarters in the Hobart Town area. With every development the government was increasingly committing itself to the site.

Not enough staff

For most of their histories the female factories were seriously understaffed. During the 1820s and most of the 1830s the only females were the matron and her assistant to control hundreds of women. Since most of the female staff had large families (the Hutchinsons had twelve children altogether) much of their time must have been spent looking after their own households. This meant that wardswomen, chosen from among the inmates themselves were the main organisers and controllers of work and discipline, with the superintendent and overseer only able to provide an arms-length form of control. No doubt presents of food and contraband made life a lot easier for the wardswomen and task-mistresses. Nor was it just the convicts who benefited from presents and winked an eye at irregularities. Staff members were dismissed or resigned over corruption. There seemed to be almost constant rumours and allegations that the wardswomen and sometimes the staff were easily and frequently corrupted. The enquiry of 1841 revealed that a considerable amount of food, tobacco and liquor found its way into the factories.

Not enough to eat

The rations provided to all convicts, whether male or female, were scarcely sufficient to keep body and soul together, particularly in the cold, dank conditions and hard unremitting labour of the Cascades Factory. Arthur's Rules and Regulations specified rations that were completely inadequate. One pound of bread, a pint of gruel for breakfast, and a pint of soup for both dinner and supper were the total ration for the day. A pound of bread is 450 grams or roughly 2/3 of a modern loaf; a pint of gruel or soup is 20 fluid ounces, a little more than half a litre; and gruel is a liquid food made from steeping oatmeal in water. The soup for each meal contained only two ounces of meat and was thickened with either vegetables or barley. A two ounce ration of meat is the equivalent of using a kilogram to feed seventeen people.

The ration was later increased to eight ounces (less than ¼ kilogram) of meat, eight ounces of potatoes or a pound of cabbage; and an ounce each of sugar and roasted wheat (a coffee substitute), as well as a pound of

---

It's such a good story, what a pity it *probably* never happened

The story is told by Robert Crooke in his book *The Convict* of an incident where Sir John Franklin, Lady Franklin, some ladies (presumably the Ladies Committee) together with the Colonial Chaplain Bedford addressed three or four hundred women at the Cascades Factory. According to Crooke the governor was listened to with respect, and Jane Franklin spoke of Mrs Fry's work, causing murmurs and hissing presumably for her presumption and hypocrisy. But when Bedford started preaching:

> the three hundred women turned right around and at one impulse pulled up their clothes showing their naked posteriors which they simultaneously smacked with their hands.

In spite of the incident being reported by virtually every historian (including myself) who has written on female convicts it is highly unlikely to be factual. Alison Alexander is particularly dubious about its authenticity. Crooke was writing ten years after the supposed incident and had no particular access to information. Some sort of indecent display accompanied an attack on Bedford in 1833 at Sunday Service in the Factory but only a very few women were involved and it was three years before the Franklins' arrival. The action describes a standard working class women's insult of the time that was still current in the slums of North Hobart as late as the 1940s. There is simply no other evidence that the incident ever occurred. If it had, it would not only have been widely publicised at the time it would also have attracted at least some degree of recorded punishment to the female convicts involved.

bread. In 1830 the newspaper *The Tasmanian* refers to the meat ration as only a nominal half pound:

> ... by the time it reaches the Factory, it is cut up, divided, the bone is extracted, etc., if it nets a quarter of a pound it is the utmost at which it can be taken...

Dr RC Hutchinson, a descendant of the Superintendent and matron of the same name and an expert in nutrition, has written at length of the improved food scale:

> ...it would not have provided a satisfactory diet. To prevent the onset of various nutritional disorders, it would have been necessary to supplement it with other foods, particularly fresh fruits and dairy products. The provision of an inadequate diet would have resulted in various degrees of malnutrition which in their mildest forms, would have made the inmates of the Factory nervous, irritable, and difficult to manage.

'Nervous, irritable and difficult to manage' sounds like a good description of the women in all the factories. Malnutrition should be seen as at least part of the explanation of the general behaviour of the women, and it also explains the great lengths they went to in order to obtain contraband tobacco and foodstuffs. Bread, cheese and butter sparked off the riot in early 1829. Arthur's desire that the food be dull and monotonous created the situation where the diet was entirely inadequate. There can be little doubt that at the back of his mind was the idea that a bland and minimal diet would significantly reduce the cost of running the Factory.

And no underclothes

The standard of the clothes was much like that of the food. Arthur went much further than Mrs Fry's drab suggestions when he decided which clothes were to be issued. He stipulated that they be made of cheap coarse materials. A gown or petticoat, an apron, a jacket, a strong straw hat (mob caps were later worn), socks and shoes. No underclothes were provided but the women were to be allowed two handkerchiefs with their two changes of clean clothes every week.

Jane Franklin and the Female Convicts

Jane Franklin was the second wife of John Franklin, Governor of Van Diemen's Land 1837 to 1843 and successor to Governor Arthur. She is a major historical and mythological figure in Tasmania, with many current major institutions either named after her, or officially referring to an historical connection with her. These links are sometimes substantial but frequently tenuous. She has indeed become an institutionalised hero, and not just in the popular imagination.

It is perhaps inevitable that the mere fact that Jane Franklin referred in her correspondence to the issues relating to female convicts and the female factories, was in touch with the extraordinarily famous Quaker prison reformer Elizabeth Fry on these matters, and was the official founder and head of a Ladies Committee for visiting the Female Factories, that she should have been considered to have been one of the few official figures who tried to 'help' the female convicts. The actual facts suggest that this is probably a highly oversimplified and distorted view. Although she had some interest in them it was more likely from a desire to forward her own interests rather than theirs and could hardly be called helping them.

Jane Franklin was not sympathetic to the circumstances of the female convicts. If anything, she was decidedly unsympathetic. In spite of being in Hobart at the time of the 1837-8 infant death-rate scandals, she never in any of her correspondence about the factories and the nurseries, referred to the plight of the little babies. It's not as though her attention was never drawn to the issue. It quite clearly was. In 1839 the Hobart newspaper, the

Queen's Orphan School, New Town (Hobart)

By permission of State Library of Tasmania, Allport Library and Museum of Fine Arts

164

Tasmanian and Austral-Asiatic Review, generally known as *Murray's Review*, launched a bitter personal attack on Jane Franklin for going off to explore the western Tasmanian wilderness rather than investigating and improving the conditions at the Cascades Female Factory, 'the dreadful abode of wretchedness and death'.

That the attack was ever made at all is quite extraordinary. The Governor's wife had no official duties; it was not her job to investigate or to interfere in the business of government. But as the editor of the newspaper was fully aware, the governor's wife was in fact constantly interfering in matters that were her husband's domain, except in one of the few acknowledged areas that the public and government at home might expect a governor's wife to be involved, and possibly even to interfere. On the matter of infant deaths Jane Franklin's voice was silent, her hand stilled.

Jane Franklin and the Cascades Female Factory

Considering that she and her husband were in Hobart Town for six years, and that she had an avowed and publicly known interest in the female convicts, Jane Franklin seems to have rarely visited the Cascades Female Factory and seems to have shown no interest at all in the Launceston Female Factory. She seems to have had only a little more interest in the Queen's Orphan Schools at New Town.

British penal reformer Elizabeth Fry continued to keep an interest in the convict system in the Australian colonies and there is substantial evidence that she had hoped that Jane Franklin, rather than the governor himself, would feature as her chosen instrument to forward her attempts to reform the circumstances of the female convicts. Before Lady Franklin left England, Mrs Fry asked her to care for the female convicts and to write back to her with an on-the-spot report of the conditions in Van Diemen's Land. It seems that Lady Franklin was both flattered and swept up by Fry's encouragement but without really considering what such involvement would entail. Elizabeth Fry's fame, reputation and extraordinary status in England was enviable to any woman in public life. With the exception of Queen Victoria, Fry was the most prominent woman of the age and she was a legendary figure of British public life. After being in Van Diemen's Land for almost two years Jane Franklin wrote confidingly to her sister in October 1838:

I have never written to Mrs Fry and am afraid I must be very low in her estimation … As for doing anything with the women … in the factory, it seems next to impossible … I think the whole system of female transportation, and particularly of female assignment in service, so faulty and vicious, that to attempt to deal with the women … seems waste time and labour [sic]. I have been always looking to have a little leisure to give this subject more mature consideration, and as soon as I can do so, I will write to Mrs Fry.

It was to be another two and a half years before Jane Franklin found the 'little leisure' to write to Elizabeth Fry. When she did so it seems most likely that rather than attempting to ameliorate the conditions for the women in the Factory, the letter and her consequent actions were designed more to aggrandise her position with the notable female philanthropists in England.

It was the arrival of two friends and confidants of Mrs Fry on board the female convict transport *Rajah* on 19 July 1841 which finally precipitated Jane Franklin's desire to write to Fry. Dr James Donovan who is mentioned in the letter, was Surgeon-superintendent on board the ship, and although he was only visiting for a few days, Jane Franklin knew that he would inform Mrs Fry of the poor conditions for female convicts in the factories of the colony. Miss Kezia Elizabeth Hayter on the other hand, had arrived to stay. An intensely religious though somewhat neurotic woman, she intended to assist the female convicts in much the same way her mentor and patron Mrs Fry had assisted the prisoners in the gaols of England.

The letter Jane Franklin wrote to Elizabeth Fry on 3 August 1841, two weeks after the arrival of the *Rajah*, was absolutely remarkable. Rambling, disorganised, contradictory, hypocritical and full of wild allegations, the letter both attacked and defended the assignment system, condemned the female convicts as contaminators of everything decent in society and, ignoring her husband's pivotal role for the previous four years, flayed the whole colonial female convict administration:
> … all the women convicts who come out here are still sent into assignments. And not a single voice that I know of has been raised in England to save them from this tyranny and this degradation… The assignment of the women is an infinitely worse thing than the assignment of men… it has all the evils … and still more… [Sexual transgression] is fostered by the association of male and female prisoners in the same family… and it is unchecked by any sufficient penalties of the law… [and encouraged] by a mistaken philanthropy

...by the Institutions which exist in this colony to relieve the prisoner parents from all burden of their offspring.

The institutions she was referring to were principally the Female Factory Nursery and the Queen's Orphan Schools. The Nursery, as she represented it to Mrs Fry, was a home away from home, where convict women enjoyed the companionship of their friends, abundant food, no work and the possibility of getting all the good things in life through the 'agreeable casualty' of becoming wet-nurses. She complained that the six months sentence for pregnancy was not enough as the women were not even: 'subjected to that most harmless yet most efficacious of female punishment... being deprived of the ornament of her hair...' They were not punished by being sent to the wash-tub nor given solitary confinement and half-starved but were instead:

> ... put into that class or yard in the Factory, which has the best ration, are in no way separated from the rest, have no harder labour than the picking of a little oakum and sleep in the same common room with the other women of their division. The only shadow of punishment they receive is detention in the Factory itself which is of six months duration.

This extremely hard line taken by Lady Franklin on punishment has been noticed by historians before. Six months imprisonment for having been pregnant would be considered to be a reasonably severe punishment in any period or era. But not to Jane Franklin; she obviously wanted the women to be abjectly shamed by having their heads shaven, put into punishment cells on rations even less than the little they already received and put to labour at something more than 'the picking of a little oakum.' Oakum picking was a standard punishment in gaols in the nineteenth century. It was designed to be boring and painful, with old ropes from ships, often stiffened with tar and encrusted with salt, being torn apart with the prisoners' bare hands in order to use the fibres for matting and caulking seams on ships. It was considered to be a good punishment because the individual's daily work could be easily measured against a set task, but it did not affect all equally, being particularly onerous for those with weak or soft hands.

Life in the Factory during the probation period

The Reverend HP Fry was the rector of St George's Church, the parish covering Battery Point, Sandy Bay, South Hobart and Cascades. He lived ᴏne corner of Macquarie and Gore Streets almost half way between the City and the Cascades Factory. In 1850 he wrote that the Factory:

...is a scene of feasting, complete idleness and vicious indulgence. They are occasionally let into the town, and have free communication with their associates. When they bring forth illegitimate children they are received into a nursery... with nothing to do but to nurse their infants... the common practise of the convict women is to get into service, in order to obtain money by theft or prostitution... [they] lead most flagitious lives...

This vision of life in the Cascades Factory was widespread amongst the highest classes in Van Diemen's Land, and was at least partially subscribed to by Jane Franklin and a number of other commentators. Significantly no-one who knew the circumstances of the Factory and its inmates intimately, including the Hutchinsons, the various investigating committees, regular visitors like clergymen, surgeons, magistrates and coroners, ever suggested that the Factory was anything other than a fairly awful place to be. Much was made of the female convicts' apparent willingness to go to the Factories. This was presumed by some, especially those who wanted an even more rigorous and harsher system at the factories, to reflect the lack of discipline, the presence of corruption, and the failure of the institutions to operate as an adequate deterrent. Since the introduction of the Probation System, the main punishment and deterrence for misbehaviour was the threat of being sent to the factories. It must have been particularly galling that many of the women thumbed their noses at authority and even publicly embraced the idea of being sent to the factory.

When sentenced to six or twelve months at the wash tub in one of the factories women were known to exclaim: 'I'll do that standing on my head.' Or words to that effect. However, it is likely that many of these instances may represent bravado rather than complacency, a spirited immediate reaction rather than a cool appraisal of life in the Factory. Damp, cold surroundings, wearing dresses made of drab coarse cloth, combined with constant immersion of hands and arms in washing water for between eight and twelve hours a day is scarcely a fate to be desired or welcomed. It is nobody's idea of a good time.

However, the Factory did offer some consolations. In the midst of misery, poor and inadequate amounts of food, enforced silence and constant discipline, the women found companionship and were amongst their own

168

kind. To the authorities it was inexplicable that the lowest order of society preferred their own degraded and downtrodden kind rather than serving as a household drudges for 'respectable' families. For the officials it was part of the convicts lot to take on the morality and external appearances of respectability, but to nevertheless never be respectable. They were doomed to a lower world where they were expected to shun their fellows but nevertheless were in turn shunned themselves. Companionship and friendship were not perceived to be an ordinary and necessary part of living for the lowest class in colonial society.

Even so the Factory was hardly a bed of roses for any of its inmates. Although they might look forward to companionship, good fellowship was not automatically engendered by common adversity. If many of the convicts were relatively harmless and fairly ordinary, it is just as well to remember that some amongst them were disposed to criminality and violence. Violence, threats of violence, theft and sexual assault were known to have been perpetrated on a number of occasions, sometimes by a group ranged against an individual. These problems were unlikely to have been continual and pervasive but nevertheless there are frequent references that suggest the Factory contained an underlying climate of fear and bullying. For a while at least there was a group known as the 'Flash Mob' who sported forbidden frills on caps and petticoats, flaunting their finery in the face of authority.

A much more believable commentary on life in the Factory than that of the Reverend Fry was written at roughly the same time as his book was published. Colonel GC Mundy visited the establishment on New Years Day 1851:

We were received at the entrance by the matron, a dignified lady who looked quite capable of maintaining strict discipline whether in a public or merely a domestic establishment. From her hands we received, in due military form, 'the morning state' of her garrison - which, as it appeared amounted to 730 women and 130 infants. In turn we visited the several courts [yards], solitary cells, the hospital, refectories [dining rooms], dormitories, and lavatories [washing rooms]. In one yard was formed up for our inspection, in hollow square, seventy or eighty women - open to be hired as servants. 'These', as we were informed, 'were the better conducted, and the pregnant women'. In another court were a strong division of more troublesome and notorious characters, who were under restraint and not permitted to go into service. The uniform, a very unbecoming one to the person, however becoming to the station of the wearer, is a white mob cap and a dress of grey duffle. As we passed down the ranks the poor creatures saluted us with a running fire of curtseys, and a dead silence was everywhere observed...

One of the yards of the Factory was devoted to laundress-work. Squads of women were up to their elbows in suds, - carrying on the cruel process of wringing, - or displaying their thick ankles as they spread the linen over the drying lines. The townsfolk may have their washing done here at 1s 6d [one shilling and sixpence] per dozen, the money going towards the expenses of the institution. I was pained to see so many very youthful creatures in this yard - delinquents in their earliest teens - debauched ere the pith had hardened in their little bones.

We had next a glimpse of a room full of sempstresses, most of them employed on fine work. It was not impossible the matron admitted, that some of the elaborate shirt-fronts we should see at the Government house ball this evening had been worked up in this, and washed and got up in the last ward. A rougher fabric done by the less-skilled prisoners is a coarse kind of woollen tweed, only used for the material of prison-dresses.

A job in her own right for Mrs Hutchinson

On 31 March 1851, the Hutchinsons resigned in their twentieth year of superintending the Cascades Female Factory. This was part of a general shake-up of staff at all the female factories. Reverend John Hutchinson had been suffering from ill health for a considerable period and now his eyesight was also failing. He was approaching retirement age, being 59 years old, and it was clear that he could no longer manage the job. His wife, Mary, being only 41, was still in her prime. She was appointed to manage the much smaller Launceston Female Factory, to replace Major and Mrs Frazer, whose regime had not been entirely approved of by the government. Mary Hutchinson, as Matron-in-Charge of the Launceston Female Factory, a senior managerial position held in her own right, thus became a notable first in Van Diemen's Land's convict administrative history in being appointed to another institution. Something similar had happened to Mrs Bowden after her husband had died, but in that case it was a matter of staying with the *Anson* and continuing in the same institution. Mrs Hutchinson was paid an annual salary commensurate with her skills, experience and abilities of £140 plus an extra £10 for rations. The average number of female convicts at the Launceston Factory at that time was about 160, approximately 15% of the numbers held at the Cascades. She held that position until 31 August 1854, when after a total of more than 22 years in the convict service and at the relatively young age of 44 she was retired on an annual pension of £60. John Hutchinson died in 1866, Mary died in 1880.

J.M. May, previously Assistant Superintendent with the Frazers at the Launceston Female Factory, was appointed superintendent of the Cascades complex. Breaking the previous pattern of appointing married couples to the two most important positions at Cascades, C. McCullough was appointed Matron. By the middle of 1851 the Factory had been extended to accommodate a nominal 700 inmates but actually held 1020 women and 176 children, though many of the children only made a fleeting appearance on the rolls with over 100 dying during 1851 and 1852. The staff had also been increased and included an Assistant Matron, a clerk, a storekeeper, seven overseers and a gatekeeper. There were also two catechists for teaching religious studies and a needlework teacher.

During the early 1850s the Cascades Female Factory was significantly extended by the construction of a fifth yard on the southwest side of the second yard and major reconstruction works within the second yard itself. The new yard was enclosed by a brick wall and contained a large two storeyed dormitory approximately 60 by 8.5 metres along the wall of the second yard. Within the earlier yard the large open washing shed described by Colonel Mundy was also converted into a two storey dormitory. It is most likely that they were constructed in late 1851 or early 1852 when the complex housed approximately 1200 people.

No women waiting for work

By the end of 1852 significant changes had occurred since Superintendent May had taken over from the Hutchinsons. The proportion of women in institutions to those working for private employers had dropped from a third to a quarter of the female convict population in the colony. Whereas eighteen months before there had been over 600 women awaiting hire, now there were no women waiting for jobs at Cascades, and few elsewhere. The numbers of children in the factories and orphan schools had also dropped considerably. What had increased dramatically were the number of women under punishment, a rise from around five hundred to almost eight hundred.

In his half-yearly report to the Comptroller-General of Convicts, May explained the changes. Female labour was in such demand that one hundred women from the *Sir Robert Seppings*, and fifty women from the *Martin Luther* were hired on the first available day alone, and that requests from all parts of the colony for female servants were unable to be fulfilled. In spite of the fact that most of the women were untrained and unskilled they were being readily employed at £8 pa, and cooks and laundresses were fetching £10 to £14 pa. Over the colony as a whole, twelve hundred women had been absorbed by the employment market during the previous year, and at the end of the year only twelve remained for hire. This had enabled the hiring depots at the Brickfields and New Town Farm to be closed. On 17 November 1852 Brickfields was closed as the principal hiring depot with its role being transferred to Cascades, and the Nursery was transferred there, the institution having been proclaimed a House of Correction, but as a branch of Cascades. It was hoped that:

…its open situation and salubrious air, together with spacious airing and exercise grounds, is much better adapted for the purposes of a nursery.

During the six months covered by the report only three adults had died at the combined Cascades and Brickfields establishments, but horrifically 57 babies had died. During the half year 51 children were admitted with their mothers, 41 had been born in the institution and 94 remained: a total of 207. Twenty-two children had been sent to the Orphan Schools, 34 had been discharged with their mothers. More children were leaving the Nursery through death than by reaching the age of three or being taken out by their mothers. More than two babies a week were dying.

Chapter 15.   Winding down of the System

Finally, after many false hopes, the decision was made to cease transportation from Britain to the Eastern colonies of Australia. With that came another decision, that no more women convicts would be sent out. Henceforth, only male convicts were to be sent, and they only to Western Australia, which altogether received around 9,000 male convicts between 1850 and 1868.

Of the last three convict ships to Van Diemen's Land, two were carrying women. The *Midlothian* arrived at Hobart 24 February 1853 carrying 167 Irish women embarked at Dublin, one of their number having died on the voyage. Two months later on 21 April 1853 the *Duchess of Northumberland* arrived with 216 women embarked from Woolwich in London. In this case three women had died on the voyage. The last male convict ship to the Eastern colonies, the *St Vincent* was to arrive five weeks later.

By the end of 1853 the effects of the cessation of Transportation were being felt in the organisation of the female convict institutions. After the tremendous overcrowding of 1851, when there were a total of twelve hundred people at the Cascades Female Factory, the situation had been partly eased in 1852 by the removal of the infants and their Nursery staff firstly to New Town and then to Brickfields. However, with the reduction in total numbers brought about by a combination of no new arrivals and the continuing process of women exiting the system through gaining pardons, becoming free by servitude or by dying, the total numbers of women in the system dropped dramatically. But these factors alone can not explain the huge drop in numbers.

Purging the system

In spite of the fact that between 1847 and early 1853, a total of 5027 female convicts arrived in Van Diemen's Land, by the end of 1854 the government figures for the total number of female convicts in the colony was only 3310. Only a year later, by the end of 1855, the number had dropped by almost a thousand to 2342. Fifteen months later, 31 March 1857, a little less than four years after the *Duchess of Northumberland* brought the last of the female convicts to the Vandemonian shores, the total females still in the convict system was a mere 869. Of these 339 were either invalids or still serving their sentences, with a further 530 possessing tickets-of-leave and being self-supporting. Since most of the transported women had been sentenced to seven years transportation and many had been sentenced to 14 years and Life, these figures suggest that the imperial and colonial authorities were profoundly embarrassed by the convict system and were doing their utmost to expedite the removal of the women from the system as soon as was humanly and administratively possible.

This situation was parallelled to some extent with male convicts. Within less than four years from the arrival of the last ship there was a total of only 3008 convicts in the system: 2139 men and 869 women, forty five percent of whom had tickets-of-leave. There were only 1312 men under the direct control of the system and nearly all of them were on the Tasman Peninsula. The men had a much larger percentage under sentence than the women.

Nobody cared very much

The mere cessation of Transportation to Van Diemen's Land and the lack of new arrivals does not explain the huge drop in total numbers of those in the system and in particular those facing sentences for minor infractions of the convict system. Other factors were obviously at work. It is as if with the decision to cease Transportation the whole heart went out of the system. Minor infractions must have been ignored. Probationers must have been consistently awarded tickets-of-leave at the first possible opportunity. Ticket-of-leave holders must have been allowed to drop out of the system almost at will, presuming they could keep clear of the authorities. Furthermore, employers of probationers and ticket-of-leave holders must have connived at turning a blind eye to behavioural problems and regulatory infractions and reverted to the traditional methods of keeping servants under control. Perhaps with the sniff of freedom in the air all but the most refractory convicts suddenly en masse decided to behave themselves.

There were broader inducements to good behaviour as well. Whereas formerly exile to the colony had been perceived as being sent to the ends of the earth, Van Diemen's Land was now next door to some of the most exciting and attractive places on earth. With the discovery of the New South Wales and Victorian goldfields it was much more possible to be optimistic about the circumstances in which the convicts found themselves and the future to which they might aspire. Whilst there is no hard evidence to support the assertion that women of whatever civil status were welcome on the goldfields, it is interesting that the main focus of the colonial authorities' screening at the ports of entry to Victoria was on preventing the immigration of Vandemonian male convicts and ticket-of-leave men. There does not seem to have been any concerted effort to impose similar restrictions on women.

However the disappearance of the vast mass of the convicts did not mean that the system stopped immediately, and in fact bits and pieces, and the major institutions, were to persist for another twenty years. Any individual convict or ex-convict who was so foolish as to bring themselves to the notice of the authorities or who flaunted their new-found freedom in socially unacceptable ways soon found that the system still had teeth and the ability to devour its victims. Besides those who were caught committing a fresh crime, alcoholics, those acting suspiciously, vagrants, prostitutes, and the occasional obstinate servant still found that the law applied differently to ex-convicts than it did to those who had always been free.

Nevertheless, the cessation of Transportation had an almost immediate effect in relieving the overcrowding in all the female convict establishments, and most of the minor institutions were almost immediately broken up.

By June 1856 the numbers at Cascades had dropped so dramatically that part of the complex was proclaimed a gaol under the control of the Sheriff and the Factory became officially *The Hobart Town Gaol and House of Correction for Females*. The Launceston Factory had been similarly proclaimed partly a gaol nine months earlier. This meant that free women could now be committed to Cascades by the colonial courts either for sentences or on remand (a situation that had occurred in earlier days but which, with the introduction of the new form of colonial government, probably needed to be officially reauthorised and separately sanctioned). This had the effect, when combined with the falling numbers of female convicts in the system, of steadily reducing, year by year, the proportion of convicts amongst the inmates.

At about the same time as the 1856 proclamation, there appears to have been a complete overhaul of the most important staff members of the Cascades Factory. Ringrose A Atkins was appointed Superintendent and Susan Wigmore was appointed Matron in early April 1856. Atkins had considerable experience and had first been appointed to the Convict Department in 1841. The changes were possibly a governmental reaction to allegations of mismanagement which had emerged from the 1855 enquiry into the Convict Department, although it is more likely that they merely reflected the change of status of the institution from being under the old imperial administration to being partially under the new colonial administration. To reflect this, whilst the staff remained employed under the auspices of the Convict Department, the new superintendent Atkins received one third of his salary from the new Colonial Government.

"Absconded"

It is quite clear that as the system ran down in VDL after 1853, the formerly rigorous oversight of the Convict Department also deteriorated. Unlike the situation for males, where for instance the new colony of Victoria tried every avenue to exclude "Vandemonians", and even the rebels at Eureka refused to have them in the stockade, there was not the same level of exclusion for the women. Its hard to believe that the Van Diemen's Land authorities didn't connive to some degree with the disappearance to other colonies of the Ticket-of-Leave and married women.

Mary Ann Patterson was not hiding in Sydney when her husband registered the birth of their daughter Mary Jane on 4 July 1856. They didn't try to obscure any data that identified her quite clearly as the former Mary Ann Nowlan whose convict record had been marked just eighteen weeks earlier as: *Absconded 19/2/56.*

Mary Ann had been convicted at Kildare, Ireland 18 July 1849 and sentenced to Transportation for Life for arson in burning down a house. The arson was her first conviction, she was a 22 year old confectioner by trade, and quite oddly she had been born in Yorkshire, a reversal of the usual migratory pattern. Ten months later she arrived in VDL on board the *Earl Grey* 143 days out of Dublin with 236 shipmates, four having died on the voyage. She married ten months later, and when she received her Ticket-of-Leave after another three and a half years she already had three children.

During her time as a convict she wasn't punished for any offences and she was recommended for an early conditional pardon, which is when the authorities realised she had already departed with her husband.

The last victims

By 1860 the Cascades Factory was also being used to house female pauper invalids who, as ex-convicts, had their upkeep paid by the Imperial Government. Conditions had improved in some measure, but the rooms were still dull, damp and cold. In July 1860, in the worst period of the winter when the sun rarely shone on the yards, five female pauper invalids were asphyxiated by the fumes from the stove in their room. The wards being so damp and cold, they had shut up their room and used rags to close off all the draughts. Unwittingly they had also closed off all possible ventilation. There was a coronial inquest and the jury brought in a verdict which absolved Atkins and his staff from any blame or responsibility in the matter. This was yet another case of death caused by the poor location and bad construction of the institution. Even after more than 30 years, Governor Arthur's drive for economy was still reaping its grim rewards.

Only four prisoners left

Two years later, in 1862, a part of the Female Factory complex was offered to the Committee of the Hobart Town Female Refuge as a reformatory. However, they were not deceived by the apparent beneficence and magnanimity of the offer and replied that the establishment was not suitable for their purposes. They preferred to go elsewhere, even at considerable cost. The offer for part of the complex to be made available to non-governmental charitable institutions was repeated in the 1890s, though on the later occasion the offer was gratefully accepted. That the government was willing and able to actively seek tenants reflects the rapid running down of the female part of the convict system and indeed of the convict establishment as a whole.

The Factory was already far more of a colonial gaol than a convict system House of Correction. By August 1864 there were only 116 women and 29 children in the establishment. Of these only 26 women and six children had their upkeep paid for by the British Government reflecting their convict status, and all except four of these were invalids rather than serving sentences for misbehaviour. By the end of the year the Colonial Government was prepared to take control of both the male and female convict systems and establishments. The convict days were almost over.

Consequently, on 1 January 1865, less than twelve years after the last

A sad, tragic and pitiful tale

Margaret Cochran arrived on the *Duchess of Northumberland* in 1853, the last female convict ship to come to Van Diemen's Land. She was 39 years old, married with one child when convicted at Glasgow of stealing. After less than three years in the colony, she had spent almost half of the time at hard labour or in solitary confinement, mostly for alcohol related offences.

In July 1856 she was granted a Ticket-of-Leave, and in September gave birth to a son, avoiding the usual punishment of losing her Ticket and serving up to 12 months in the Factory by marrying George Martin, a former NSW bushranger. The child, Walter Small, was not Martin's. He was the son of a black convict from Bermuda, Jacob Small. Later newspaper reports would refer to young Walter as 'a little coloured boy'.

By 1866 they were all at Recherche Bay in the far south of Tasmania. The boy said his stepfather often threatened to drown him, but Walter, even at the tender age of nine, was mindful that his stepfather was 'a poor man and found it difficult to earn a living'. The local publican said Martin 'has the reputation of being a quiet hardworking man, not given to quarrel' whilst the mother 'was of drunken habits'. On the evening of 18 January the publican, Mr WL Donnelly, ordered Margaret from the pub at 9:30pm, but not for drunkenness. He had found her in the 'men's bed room'.

Donnelly didn't see Margaret Martin again until 7:30 next morning when she came into his kitchen, befuddled, her dress torn, missing a boot, and with obvious wounds on her face. He asked what had happened but she only replied: 'Oh give me some beer'. He let her rest on a sofa before getting her out of the pub, but two hours later at 11am she was brought back by two women who had found her slumped down behind a tree stump, weak, cold and only partially conscious. Donnelly put her into bed but she died within a few minutes.

Evidence was given by Walter Small and Thomas Bentley, a 15 year old neighbour. The boys had been roused by cries of murder and saw George Martin beating and kicking his wife on the beach at midnight. Together they had pulled him off. The couple had been fighting over her conduct with a man named Mackay at the pub. Charged with murder, Martin was found guilty of manslaughter. Perhaps the jury agreed with the defence that Martin was an honest, hardworking man with a life made miserable 'from his wife's intemperate habits'. He was sentenced to twelve years imprisonment.

convict transport had arrived at Hobart Town, all the Convict Department staff were transferred to the Tasmanian Colonial Government. At the Cascades Factory, Atkins and Wigmore still held the positions of Superintendent and Matron respectively. John Serviss who had first been appointed to the Convict Department in 1843, two years after Atkins, and to the Female Factory as Overseer in 1857, was now designated Gatekeeper. His new salary was so much higher than previous gatekeepers that it is reasonable to assume that his work now involved a combination of the duties formerly carried out by the overseer and gatekeeper. Three female warders, Margaret Galt, Elizabeth Hodkins and Mary Montgomery; and a nurse-midwife Margaret Sterling comprised the rest of the female staff. Francis Smith the night officer, and John Hogan the carpenter/messenger completed the male staff. A Church of England chaplain, the Reverend Samuel Parsons, was also attached to the Factory.

Invalids, paupers and boys

By 1869 the numbers of inmates at the Cascades Factory had dropped to such an extent that the government introduced a number of new institutions. The situation of the female ex-convict invalids was regularised by officially creating a Female Invalid depot. A Male Invalid depot and a Boys Reformatory were also introduced. The Female Gaol and House of Correction were now housed in only the first, second and part of the fifth yard. Atkins was appointed Superintendent of the whole complex including the new institutions.

With the arrival of the non-convict institutions in 1869 many of the conditions were improved. The male invalids (male paupers) were housed in the 1850 Nursery Yard and one section of the Third or separate apartments yard. The boys reformatory was in the other half of the separate apartments yard. The female invalids (female paupers) were in the front half of the Fifth and most recent Yard. An example of the improvement in conditions was the creation of a library with six of the more able male invalids appointed book wardsmen. The food ration was improved though there were still problems with poor quality meat.

A *Mercury* reporter visited the establishment in 1873. He reported that the Female Invalid Depot held 114 inmates and eleven nurses, the Male Invalid Depot 160 inmates and the reformatory 40 boys. The invalids would have been mostly ex-convicts. The invalid women were almost completely helpless, although some degree of assistance to the nurses was given by

179

the female prisoners in the Gaol and House of Correction. Many of the male invalids were blind and consequently few of them could work. Those that could were employed as wardsmen and were paid a tiny allowance. The boys worked from 6am to 3.30pm, at which time they were expected to do an hour and a half's schoolwork. The newspaper criticised the government for making the boys do a full day's work and then expecting them to be able to concentrate on their lessons. They were certainly worked hard - they were the only group of able-bodied inmates. Their labours had turned the stony ground into a model farm with vegetable gardens, a piggery and a dairy.

Truganini

The Cascades Female Factory was officially moved to the Campbell Street gaol in central Hobart in April 1877 eleven months after Truganini was buried in the centre of the original Factory just in front of the chapel.

Truganini was not the last of the Tasmanian Aborigines but she was the last of those held in the government Aboriginal establishment first set up in the 1830s in the Bass Strait islands, most notably at Wybalenna on Flinders Island and from 1847 at Oyster Cove twenty-five kilometres south of Hobart in Truganini's tribal lands.

As her compatriots died their bodies were plundered from the hospitals and graves for sale to European institutions. Truganini lived in fear of this happening to her body. The public made it clear that they would not stand by and see Truganini's body abused and the government arranged for the burial at the Female Factory.

Two years later, after extracting a promise that they would not display her remains, permission was given to the Royal Society of Tasmania to exhume her body for scientific study. The flesh had largely parted from her skeleton due to the minerals in the boggy ground and only the bare skeleton was removed. The flesh and coffin were left behind. Like most solemn promises made to the Tasmanian race, this last was also broken and Truganini's skeleton was displayed to the public at the Tasmanian museum until 1947.

A hundred years after her death the skeleton was cremated and the ashes scattered over the waters near her homeland of Bruny Island.

An extra blanket, but nothing to read

The pauper invalids received better treatment than the female prisoners in the Factory, receiving an extra blanket and a few luxuries in their still far from adequate diet. Although those invalids who were partially able-bodied were expected to do odd jobs, most of them appear to have spent their time in a state of crushing boredom. Atkins pleaded with the readers of *The Mercury* to send old newspapers, however outdated. Apparently the inmates read them avidly, and the illiterate and blind sat around one of their fellows, listening and querying every item, even the advertisements, from newspapers often three months old.

Sleeping on the floor

When a reporter from the *Tasmanian Tribune* visited the Cascades Female Factory in December 1874 he compared the conditions unfavourably with the situation for the men in the Hobart Town Gaol, previously the Male Prisoners' Barracks and Male House of Correction. At the Gaol, in Campbell Street, central Hobart, the men slept in dormitories and had access to day rooms for recreation. By contrast, the women at the Factory had to sleep on the floor in their cells. The Nursery was situated to the right of the main entrance to the first yard, a much smaller area than was formerly the case. The women had now been in the colony for a minimum of twenty-one years. Most were no longer of any concern to the authorities and of those who were, many were no doubt past childbearing age.

The Factory had reached such a state of decline that it only contained 70 women and 15 children up to eight years of age. Previously the children had been removed to the Queen's Orphan Schools when they were three years old. Some other aspects had also improved. The staff called the prisoners by their first names and on the whole the children looked happy and healthy. The section of the complex that housed the Female Factory was over twice the size of the original Factory for fewer inmates than it was originally meant to hold.

End of the dark cell, start of washing machines

The dark cell with its triple doors, depriving a prisoner of all light and sound, was no longer used. The work was of much the same general description: sewing, washing and ironing. The work however was much easier, the worst of the convict days were a thing of the past, modern technology helped: the women now had washing machines and mechanical wringers. However, these were still very primitive machines and the work would still have been uncomfortable, boring and onerous.

In 1877 the Cascades Female Factory and Female Factory Nursery were finally closed down. Superintendent Atkins and the remainder of the staff, together with all the inmates, were all transferred to a section of the Campbell Street Gaol. The move was undertaken in order to make way for the male convict 'lunatics' who were in turn to be transferred from Port Arthur following the final closure of that station.

The last female convicts leave Cascades...

The female invalids were transferred to New Town in early 1874 to make way for male paupers and invalids from Port Arthur. Adolarius H Boyd was transferred from his position as Commandant at Port Arthur to become the Superintendent of the Female Factory and Boys Reformatory. Atkins was transferred to be the Gaoler at the Campbell Street Gaol in Hobart. The government intended to create a new gaol for the worst of the Port Arthur men at Cascades and work was started on enclosing the third yard for this purpose. The work proved much more costly than was at first thought and was eventually abandoned due to the impossibility of constructing such a large building in the boggy ground. Eventually in early 1885 the two separate apartment blocks in the Third Yard were demolished. The offices at the front of the yard were left intact and were to remain until 1967.

Boyd remained Superintendent at Cascades until Atkins took over once again on 1 April 1877 when the Female Factory was transferred to the Campbell Street Gaol. The reorganisation was in order to create a new Hospital for the Insane at Cascades for the so-called 'Imperial Lunatics', which did not refer to any illusions of grandeur amongst the inmates but to the fact they were convicts or ex-convicts from Port Arthur whose costs

---

Melancholy madness

"Situated in a hole, which in winter becomes a swamp, it is cold, damp and gloomy ...[in] winter time the sun is excluded except...for about two hours ...instead of being a fit place for the care of mental disease, [it] is rather calculated to produce melancholy madness in the sane."

Dr Turnley, 1885, describing the Cascades Female Factory site

---

were to be paid for by the British Imperial Government. By May 1877 the reorganisation was complete. The range of cells at the rear of the Second Yard built in 1832 were used to restrain refractory patients, while the old triple-doored cell, for years disused or used as a privy was restored to the height of its glory for use as a 'dumb cell'. There were only male inmates for the present: the insane, male paupers and the Boys reformatory. The superintendency was taken over by Dr John Coverdale, previously Boyd's successor at Port Arthur, on 1 January 1878.

But not the last women

However, this was not to be the end of the story of women at Cascades. In 1879 the Male Invalid Depot was transferred to New Town and the Boys Reformatory was closed.

The Tasmanian Government was not going to allow perfectly good buildings to go to waste. On 18 November 1879 a Contagious Diseases Hospital was established to treat reputed prostitutes suffering from venereal disease. *The Contagious Diseases Act* had been passed earlier in the year after a campaign of threat and cajolery by the British Navy. They threatened not to call at Hobart again unless legislative acts along similar lines to British laws were passed and enforced. Nobody seemed to notice that the British laws (which only referred to garrison towns) were currently being repealed. The legislation was once again more of a reflection of Victorian hypocrisy than a real attempt to come to grips with the basic problem. Women were to be forced into the Lock Hospital (as it was generally known) who were neither prostitutes nor diseased. Of course there was no parallel law to force men with venereal disease to be compulsorily treated.

In more ways than one the new institution reflected the same attitudes as those held by Governor Arthur about the convict women. Designed by the Act to be a hospital rather than a prison, the institution operated in ways uncommonly like the old Female Factory, though the Superintendent had even more power and was able to order solitary confinement for breaches of discipline. Some of the early patients were actually sentenced by the magistrates with the words 'to the Factory'. The British Navy continued to interfere and actually wanted the Act to be extended to include any woman who had more than one lover. Shades of the convict discipline system! However, the Tasmanian Government baulked at this rather incredible suggestion.

The Contagious Diseases Hospital was obviously expected to have a huge influx of women and was originally allocated almost the entire first and second yards. However in the first few years there was only an average daily occupancy rate of ten, with an annual admission rate of around 100. Two years later the numbers had been reduced by two thirds. The hospital was closed in 1900.

This was the end of the imprisonment of women, any women, for any reason, at the Cascades Female Factory.

A strange road to freedom

Maria Middleton arrived in Hobart Town on 8 October 1828 on the *Borneo* together with 69 other female convicts 150 days out from London. Three had died on the voyage. Eighteen year old Maria had been a slave in Honduras living with her mistress, Mary White, as a servant of all work. When William Mair, a local builder, attacked her and they struggled with his knife it was Mair who died. Found guilty of murder, Maria was sentenced to Transportation for Life. The records describe her as "a woman of colour". Two years later she married John Murray. By 1832 she and her husband were running a lodging house and she had a female convict servant herself. The servant claimed that Maria had stolen property from their previous lodgings but the evidence was complex and disputed and Maria was acquitted. This was her only record of possible wrongdoing in the colony. She had a daughter in 1837 and it seems most likely she died of tuberculosis in June 1839. As a number of recent historians have pointed out, Australia's cultural diversity is of long standing and there were considerable numbers of blacks other than Aborigines in colonial society, though it's possible that Maria was the only female convict who was actually a slave at the time of Transportation.

Chapter 15. Conclusion

Having immersed myself as a historian in the stories of female convicts for twenty-three years, I look back on the words that make up this book with a form of dismay. Like so many other historians, I have largely failed to give you the overall story of the female convicts with all the generalities and particularities that are so necessary to allow the general reader to make up their minds as to how things turned out for most of the more than 13,000 female exiles forced to make a new life in Van Diemen's Land.

Many, perhaps the vast majority of the total, spent a few years directly under the convict system of which we know so much, and then disappear into the rest of their real lives of which we know so very little. The majority of these appear to have married or settled into stable relationships, had children and become wives and mothers. Their husbands, more often than not, were small landholders in Tasmania. Other husbands were labourers and farmers on the large landed estates or workers, tradesmen or small entrepreneurs in Hobart, Launceston and smaller centres.

But it would be a mistake to see these women as 'merely' wives and mothers, though it needs to be pointed out that when they did have children they tended to have many more children on average than their sisters they had left behind in the United Kingdom. Many of them brought with them skills or trades that were of great assistance to their joint family endeavours; others were young and learned new skills that went beyond the environs of their household; and not a few of these skills may have been learnt during their convict days. Perhaps they assisted their husbands by taking in laundry, sewing or lodgers, or earning money by working part-time in neighbouring houses or businesses. But more often they would have assisted directly in the household economy running the cottage garden, orchard, dairy and chicken run, assisting in heavy jobs in the barn or in seasonal high times like planting, harvesting or droving if they were on a small holding, or keeping an eye on the shop, storeroom, forge, workshop, bar or horses if they were in business.

With the children grown, or the youngest being looked after by the older siblings, these skills would often come into their full fruition and many families of the sturdy English yeomanry tradition in Tasmania between 1840 and the early 1950s owed the ability to purchase their land or to extend their holdings or build a better house to the added value of the wife and mother's direct contribution to the family economy.

Others had a similar story to tell, but its place was to be elsewhere. The founding mothers of Victoria, New Zealand, Queensland and Western Australia were often ex-convicts or the daughters of ex-convicts from Van Diemen's Land, as were no doubt quite a few though a proportionately small number who escaped the system altogether to South Australia, California or even back to Great Britain and Ireland. Sydney and New South Wales of course would have attracted quite a few, though there it would have been a little more difficult to ignore or escape the implications of their convict origins.

No doubt a few of the female convicts from Van Diemen's Land ended up working in the brothels of the goldfields of Victoria, though the authorities of both colonies regularly exchanged information about ex-convicts and the Victorian Government was leery of all ex-Tasmanians, male and female. But if this was anything more than a rare occurrence we would expect to have quite a lot more evidence of it. Though we can't overlook that much prostitution was unofficially condoned, nevertheless we would expect that had ex-convict Vandemonians been a large percentage of prostitutes on the diggings, the periodic clean-ups would have led to a significant number of scandals and exchanges of dispatches on the matter. Far more likely and far more numerous would have been women who worked in the laundries, food shops and stalls and the pubs and who entered a form of respectability no different to that of other working class women, met up with diggers and settlers, shrugged off their origins and disappeared amongst the mass of other newer immigrants.

Many others amongst the female convicts - not a majority but nevertheless a very substantial minority, of perhaps a third of the total who came to Van Diemen's Land - never married or had a family. They lived out their lives in lonely exile far from their families and childhood friends. Amongst these were the ones who lived out their final days in the pauper institutions and mental asylums of the colonies, who lived isolated lives in small huts on the edges of towns and villages, or who wandered the colony from place to place, homeless and friendless, desperately trying to keep out of the pauper institutions that were hardly different to the convict institutions they had replaced. Between 1860 and 1885, 95% of the inmates of the Invalid Depots were ex-convicts and in 1898, close to the turn of the century and the creation of the new country of the Commonwealth of Australia, slightly over half (52%) of all the inmates at the New Town Charitable Institution (a combined invalid depot and aged persons' facility in the old Queen's Orphan Schools) were ex-convicts.

The rations were better, the staff may have been a little more kindly, the discipline would have been a little looser, but nevertheless for these people the convict system was still in place fifty to sixty years after they had left the shores of Great Britain and Ireland, consigned to exile on the other side of the globe, never to see their loved ones and homeland again.

Forgotten but not gone

With the arrival of the *Duchess of Northumberland* in Hobart Town in 1853, the exile of female convicts from Britain to Australia ceased, but did not mark the end of the convict system nor the end of the exile experience. The last arrivals still had to serve their sentences: typically of seven, ten and fourteen years or Life. The convict institutions still had to serve their purposes well into the 1870s; and convict records were still being used into the twentieth century to remark on such everyday occurrences as an application by an ex-convict for the old age pension.

Literally thousands of ex-convicts would have voted in the first Australian elections following Federation in 1901. Possibly as many as a hundred Tasmanian ex-convicts and thousands of Western Australian ex-convicts waved goodbye to their grandsons and great-grandsons as they sailed away to fight at Gallipoli and in the trenches of France and Belgium in the First World War.

On board the *Duchess of Northumberland* in 1853 were quite a few women who lived to see the twentieth century. Among them was Sarah Hornsey, who despite being aged in her late thirties when she arrived, nevertheless lived to see the Federation of the Australian colonies, dying in Hobart on 27 January 1901. Of her two children who accompanied her on that last female convict transport, John who was five when he arrived at Hobart Town didn't die until 1918; and Elizabeth, who was six or seven on her arrival in 1853 died in 1923.

But these children sharing their mother's exile fate were outlasted by a number of the female convicts themselves. Elizabeth Wood from Leith, Scotland, was only seventeen when she arrived in 1853. Married three times, Elizabeth had eight children altogether. She didn't die until 3 March 1923, almost seventy years after her arrival. Her youngest son, Axton O'Neal lived until 1946, and it is possible that some of her other children lived into the 1950s and 1960s. At the time of writing this book in 2003 there is a woman in the northern suburbs of Hobart who as a child knew her grandfather very well as an old bearded man, and whose genealogist grandchildren forbear to inform her that he arrived not as a free settler as she believes, but as a convict in chains

Women wanted

Almost as if to get as many women sent away before a looming catastrophe, in the last thirteen months of sending female exiles to Australia, from October 1851 to when the *Duchess of Northumberland* left England in November 1852, the convict authorities in Britain dispatched to Van Diemen's Land 1,191 female convicts on six ships. The *Anna Maria*, *Sir Robert Seppings* and the *Duchess of Northumberland* sailed from England carrying a total of 639 female convicts, and the *John William Dare*, *Martin Luther* and *Midlothian* departed from Irish ports carrying 552 Irish women. Twelve women died on the voyages and altogether 1,179 were landed at Hobart Town. For a small colony this was an enormous influx of young mainly eligible young women.

And, of course, so it was meant to be. It was hoped that every increase of young women from Britain, whether convict or assisted immigrant, would help to reduce the huge disproportion of the sexes in Van Diemen's Land created by the convict system. This, and not their original crime, was the reason that many of the female convicts were sent to the island now known as Tasmania.

The nature of these women, viewed from the standpoint of a fairly unbiased observer, has been part of the subject of this book. But what a terrible price had to be paid by the individual young women who were caught up in this vicious piece of social engineering.

"That will not hurt me either"

Ann Wilson, five feet two-and-a-half inches tall, with brown hair and grey eyes, was 22 years old when she was transported to Van Diemen's Land on the *Morley* in 1820, having received a life sentence of exile for 'Larceny from the person'. She could read and write.

Ann is one of the rare women who speaks for herself. Most of the women are known to us only by the facts recorded by disapproving authorities, but this young woman's remarks were noted down. After seven years as a female convict, with a history of absconding, she was again in trouble on 30 April 1827 for being absent from her master's house overnight. She was sentenced to sit in the stocks for two hours the next day and to spend a week in a cell on bread and water.

On May 7, the day of her release, she broke the window of the apartment of Mr Drabble, Superintendent of the Hobart Town Female Factory, and was "insolent and abusive" to him. For this her sentence was to be "confined in George Town Factory 12 months". Phillip Tardif, in *Notorious strumpets and dangerous girls*, quotes the record:
> On receiving sentence the prisoner in an insolent and improper way said 'I thank you it is the very place I wish to go to.' On being brought back and sentenced to sit in the stocks for 4 hours said 'That will not hurt me either. You shall not have my hair off for all that.' She was then ordered to have her hair cut and then said 'That will not hurt me either. I don't care if it was cut off fifty times.'

For years she continued to abscond, to be "shameful in the extreme", feign sickness, or to be drunk and insolent. The lengthy list of her misbehaviour includes the notable offence, in September 1834, of "Giving tobacco to prisoners on the settlement (Port Arthur) and being under the influence of liquor" for which she was punished with 6 months in Cascades Female Factory. Ann was one of the few female convicts we know of at Port Arthur. Women were only sent there as assigned servants. Ann was working for the Commandant.

In May of 1836 there is recorded one last offence and one last punishment: "Absconding. 5 days solitary confinement." Then four months later: "Died in the service of G.C. Clarke Esq". She never quit fighting, or ignoring, her designated role as female convict in Van Diemen's Land, and after 16 years of refusing to be a prisoner, Ann Wilson had finally escaped.

Bibliography

Alison **Alexander (1999)** *Obliged to submit: Wives and mistresses of colonial governors* Montpelier, Hobart, 1999

Alan **Atkinson** & Marian **Aveling (1987)** *Australians 1838* Fairfax, Syme and Weldon, Sydney, 1987 *Australians: A historical library* series

Marian **Aveling (1992)** "Imagining New South Wales as a gendered society, 1783-1821" in *Australian Historical Studies*, v25n98, 1992:1-12

James A **Backhouse (1843)** *A narrative of a visit to the Australian colonies* London, 1843

Anne **Bartlett (1994)** "The Launceston Female Factory" in *Tas Hist Research Association P&P*, v41n2, June 1994: 115-124

Charles **Bateson (1974)** *The Convict Ships 1787-1868* Reed, Sydney, (First Australian Edition) 1974

JM **Beattie (1974)** "The pattern of crime in England: 1660-1800" *Past and present*, n62, 1974:47-95

JM **Beattie (1975)** "The criminality of women in eighteenth-century England" (originally published in *Journal of Social History*, v8, 1975) reprinted in D Kelly Weisberg (ed): *Women and the law: the social historical perspective,* Schenkman, Cambridge, Mass., 1982:197-238

JM **Beattie (1977)** "Crime and the courts in Surrey 1736-1753" Chapter 7 in JS **Cockburn (ed) (1977)** *Crime in England 1550 - 1800* Methuen, London, 1977:155-186

JM **Beattie (1986)** *Crime and the courts in England: 1660-1800* Princeton University Press, Princeton NJ, 1986

JM **Beattie (2001)** *Policing and punishment in London, 1660-1750: Urban crime and the limits of terror* Oxford University Press, Oxford, 2001

PW **Boyer (1974)** "Leaders and helpers: Jane Franklin's plan for Van Diemens Land" in *Tasmanian Historical Research Association, Papers and Proceedings* June 1974, v21n2: 47-65

GTWB **Boyes (1985)** Edited by **Peter Chapman** *The diaries and letters of GTWB Boyes; Volume 1: 1820-1832* Oxford University Press, Melbourne, 1985

JG **Branagan (1980)** *George Town: History of the town and district* Mary Fisher, Launceston. 1980

Ian **Brand (1978)** *Penal Peninsula,* Jason, West Moonah Tasmania, 1978

Ian **Brand (1990)** *The convict probation system: Van Diemens Land 1839-1854* Blubber Head Press, Hobart, 1990

Ian **Brand** and Mark **Staniforth (1994)** "Care and control: Female convict transportation voyages to Van Diemen's Land, 1818-1853" *Great Circle*, v16n1, 1994:23-42

Joan **Brown (1972)** *Poverty is not a crime* THRA, Hobart, 1972

Eleanor C **Casella (1999)** *Dangerous girls and gentle ladies: Archaeology and nineteenth century Australian Female Convicts* Unpublished Ph.D dissertation, University of California, Berkeley Ca., 1999

Eleanor C **Casella (2002)** *Archaeology of the Ross Female Factory: Female incarceration in Van Diemen's Land, Australia* Queen Victoria Museum, Launceston, 2002

Sandra **Champion (1994)** "Prostitution, hardened offenders or gratuitous immigrants? Irishwomen of the *Greenlaw* and the *Midlothian*" *Tasmanian Historical Studies*, v4n2, 1994:20-24

CMH **Clark (ed.) (1950)** *Select documents in Australian history 1788-1850* Angus & Robertson, Sydney, 1950

CMH **Clark (1973)** *A history of Australia, Volume III* Melbourne UP, Melbourne, 1973

JS **Cockburn (ed) (1977)** *Crime in England 1550 - 1800* Methuen, London, 1977

R **Crooke (1958)** *The convict* University of Tasmania, Hobart, 1958

Joy **Damousi (1997a)** *Depraved and disorderly: female convicts, sexuality and gender in colonial Australia* Cambridge University Press, Melbourne, 1997

Joy **Damousi (1997b)** " 'What punishment will be sufficient for these rebellious hussies?' Headshaving and convict women in the female factories, 1820s-1840s" Chapter 11 in Ian **Duffield** & James **Bradley** (eds) *Representing convicts: New perspectives on convict forced labour migration* Leicester UP, London, 1997:204-214

Kay **Daniels** *et al* **(eds.) (1977)** *Women in Australia* AGPS, Canberra, 1977

Kay **Daniels (ed) (1984)** *So much hard work: women and prostitution in Australian history* Fontana/Collins, Sydney, 1984

Kay **Daniels (1997)** "Convict Women- The view from Tasmania" in Ian **Terry** & Kathryn **Evans**, *Hobart's history: the first two hundred years* Professional Historians Association of Tasmania, Hobart, 1997:2-6

Kay **Daniels (1998)** *Convict Women* Allen & Unwin, Sydney, 1998

AP **Davidson (1975)** *"An analytical and comparative history of master and servant legislation in Tasmania",* Master of Laws thesis, University of Tasmania, Unpublished, 1975

Richard **Davis (1974)** *The Tasmanian gallows: A study of capital punishment* Cat & Fiddle Press, Hobart, 1974

Richard **Davis (2000)** *"Not so bad as a bad marriage": Irish transportation policies in the 1840s* Tasmanian Historical Research Association offprint, Hobart 2000 (previously published in *THRA P&P*, Hobart, March 2000, v47 n1:9-64)

Ian **Duffield** & James **Bradley**, (eds) **(1997)** *Representing convicts: New perspectives on convict forced labour migration* Leicester UP, London, 1997

Barrie **Dyster (1985)** "A new view - convicts as working people" in *Westerly*, n3, September 1985:57-61.

Barrie **Dyster (1989)** *Servant & master: building and running the grand houses of Sydney 1788-1850* New South Wales University Press, Sydney, 1989

PR **Eldershaw (1965)** *Guide to Public Records of Tasmania: Section 3: Convict Department Record Group* State Library of Tasmania, Hobart, 1965

VR **Ellis (1976)** *Truganini: Queen or traitor?* OBM, Hobart, 1976

Clive **Emsley (1983)** *Policing and its context, 1750-1870* Macmillan, London, 1983

Clive **Emsley (1991)** *The English police: a political and social history* Harvester Wheatsheaf, Hemel Hempstead Herts., 1991

Clive **Emsley (1996)** *Crime and society in England, 1750-1900* Longman, London, 2nd Edition 1996

Kathleen **Fitzpatrick (1949)** *Sir John Franklin in Tasmania* Melbourne UP, Melbourne, 1949

Michael **Flynn (1993)** *The Second Fleet: Britain's grim convict armada of 1790* Library of Australian History, Sydney, 1993

WD **Forsyth (1970)** *Governor Arthur's Convict System: Van Diemens Land 1824-36* Sydney University Press, Sydney, 1970 (Originally published in 1935)

Lucy **Frost (1999)** *"singing and dancing and making a noise": spaces for women who speak* University of Tasmania Occasional Paper No. 52, Hobart, 1999

Lucy **Frost** and Hamish **Maxwell-Stewart (2001)** *Chain letters: narrating convict lives* Melbourne University Press, Melbourne, 2001

Bryan **Gandevia (1978)** *Tears often shed: child health and welfare in Australia from 1788* Pergamon Press, Sydney, 1978

VAC **Gatrell (1994)** *The hanging tree: execution and the English people, 1770-1868* Oxford University Press, Oxford, 1994

VAC **Gatrell** and TB **Hadden (1972)** "Criminal statistics and their interpretation" Chapter 8 in EA **Wrigley (ed)** *Nineteenth-century society: Essays in the use of quantitative methods for the study of social data* Cambridge University Press, Cambridge, 1972: 336-396

Robin **Haines (2003)** *Life and death in the age of sail: the passage to Australia* UNSW Press, Sydney, 2003

Douglas **Hay (1975)** "Property, authority and the criminal law" Chapter 1 in Douglas **Hay** and Peter **Linebaugh**, (eds) *Albion's Fatal Tree: Crime and society in eighteenth century England* Allen Lane, London, 1975: 17-63

EF **Haynes (1976)** "Edward Swarbreck Hall: medical scientist and social reformer" Unpublished MA Thesis, University of Tasmania, 1976

Laurel **Heath (1978)** "The Female Convict Factories of New South Wales and Van Diemens Land: An examination of their role in the control, punishment and reformation of prisoners between 1804 and 1854" Unpublished MA Thesis, Australian National University, 1978

JB **Hirst (1983)** *Convict society and its enemies* George Allen & Unwin, Sydney, 1983

Warwick **Hirst (2003)** *Great convict escapes in colonial Australia* Kangaroo Press, Sydney, 2003

RC **Hutchinson (1961)** "The Reverend John Hutchinson" in *Tasmanian Historical Research Association, Papers and Proceedings* August 1961, v9n3:93-108

RC **Hutchinson (1963)** "Mrs Hutchinson and the Female Factories of early Australia" in *Tasmanian Historical Research Association, Papers and Proceedings* December 1963, v11n2:51-67

Robert **Hughes (1988)** *The fatal shore: A history of the transportation of convicts to Australia 1787-1868* Pan, London, 1988

Michael **Ignatieff (1978)** *A just measure of pain* Macmillan, London, 1978

David **Jones (1982)** *Crime, protest, community and police in nineteenth century Britain* Routledge and Kegan Paul, London, 1982

James S **Kerr (1984)** *Design for convicts* Library of Australian History, Sydney, 1984

James S **Kerr(1988)** *Out of sight, out of mind* SH Erwin Gallery, Sydney, 1988

Peter **King (2002)** "War as a judicial resource. Press gangs and prosecution rates, 1740-1830" Chapter 5 in Norma **Landau;** *Law, crime and English society, 1660-1830* Cambridge UP, Cambridge, (2002): 97-116

Marilyn **Lake (1988)** "Convict women as objects of male vision: an historiographical review" *Bulletin of the Centre for Tasmanian Historical Studies*, v2n1, 1988:40-48

Norma **Landau (2002)** *Law, crime and English society, 1660-1830* Cambridge UP, Cambridge, (2002)

MCl **Levy (1953)** *Governor George Arthur* Georgian House, Melbourne, 1953

David **Lieberman (2002)** "Mapping criminal law: Blackstone and the categories of English jurisprudence" Chapter 7 in Norma **Landau;** *Law, crime and English society, 1660-1830* Cambridge UP, Cambridge, (2002): 139-164

Peter **Linebaugh (1993)** *The London hanged, crime and civil society in the eighteenth century* Penguin, London, 1993

Kristine **McCabe (1999a)** "Discipline and punishment: female convicts on the Hunter River, 1830-1840. 'What can we do with her?' " in *Journal of Australian Colonial History*, v1n1, 1999:38-61

Kristine **McCabe (1999b)** "Assignment of female convicts on the Hunter River, 1831-1840" in *Australian Historical Studies*, n113, 1999:286-302

John **McDonald** and Ralph **Shlomowitz (1990)** *The cost of shipping convicts to Australia* Flinders University research paper 90-9, Adelaide, (1990)

Randall **McGowen (2002)** "Making the 'bloody code'? Forgery legislation in eighteenth century England" Chapter 6 in Norma **Landau;** *Law, crime and English society, 1660-1830* Cambridge UP, Cambridge, (2002): 117-138

George **Mackaness** (editor) **(1947)** *Some private correspondence of Sir John and Lady Jane Franklin* in 2 volumes, volumes XVII & XVIII (new series) Australian Historical Monographs, Sydney, 1947

Judy **Mackinolty** and Heather **Radi (1979)** *In pursuit of justice: Australian women and the law 1788-1979*, Hale and Iremonger, Sydney, 1979

Lyn **McLeavy (1998)** "Jane Cook" *40 degrees South*, Hobart, 1998: 48-49

GA **Mawer (1997)** *Most perfectly safe: The convict shipwreck disasters of 1833-42* Allen & Unwin, Sydney, 1997

CG **Mundy (1852)** *Our antipodes* 2nd Edition, London, 1852

Mary **Murnane** & Kay **Daniels (1979)** "Prostitutes as 'purveyors of disease': Venereal disease legislation in Tasmania, 1868-1945" in *Hecate*, v5n1:5-21, 1979

Stephen **Nicholas** (editor) **(1988)** *Convict workers: reinterpreting Australia's past* Studies in Australian History Series; Alan Gilbert and Peter Spearitt editors Cambridge University Press, Sydney, 1988

John **Nicol (1822)** *Life and adventures of John Nicol mariner 1776-1801* Edited and introduced by Tim Flannery Text Publishing, Melbourne, 1997

Tamsin **O'Connor (1997)** "A zone of silence: Queensland's convicts and the historiography of Moreton Bay" Chapter 7 in Ian **Duffield** & James **Bradley (eds)**, *Representing convicts: New perspectives on convict forced labour migration* Leicester UP, London, 1997:124-141

Deborah **Oxley (1988)** "Female Convicts" Chapter 6 in **Nicholas (1988)**:85-97

Deborah **Oxley (1996)** *Convict maids: the forced migration of women to Australia* Cambridge University Press, Melbourne, 1996

Deborah **Oxley (1997)** "Representing convict women" Chapter 5 in Ian **Duffield** & James **Bradley (eds)**, *Representing convicts: New perspectives on convict forced labour migration* Leicester UP, London, 1997:88-105

Jennifer **Parrott (1994)** "Agents of industry and civilisation: The British government emigration scheme for convicts' wives, Van Diemen's Land 1817-1840" *Tasmanian Historical Studies*, v4n2, 1994:25-30

Jennifer **Parrott (1996)** "Elizabeth Fry and female transportation" in *Tas Hist Research Association P&P*, v43n4, December 1996: 169-186

HS **Payne (1961)** "A statistical study of female convicts in Tasmania, 1843-53" in *Tas Hist Research Association P&P*, v9n2, June 1961: 56-69

Kim **Pearce (1993)** *North Hobart historical research* Hobart, 1993

Kim **Pearce (1997)** "The Queen's Orphan Asylum - New Town" in Ian **Terry** & Kathryn **Evans**, *Hobart's history: the first two hundred years* Professional Historians Association of Tasmania, Hobart, 1997:19-34

Monica **Perrott (1983)** *A tolerable good success: economic opportunities for women in New South Wales 1788-1830* Hale & Iremonger, Sydney, 1983

Leon **Radzinowicz (1948)** *A history of the English Criminal Law and its administration from 1750: Volume 1, The movement for reform* Stevens and Sons, London, 1948

Leon **Radzinowicz** and Roger **Hood (1986)** *A history of the English Criminal Law and its administration from 1750: Volume 5, The emergence of penal policy* Stevens and Sons, London, 1986

Tony **Rayner (1979)** "Historical survey of the Women's Prison Historic Site, Cascades, Hobart" Unpublished report to National Parks &Wildlife Service Tasmania, Hobart, December 1979, largely reproduced as 1981a

Tony **Rayner (1980)** "Master and Servant in the New Norfolk Magistrates Court 1838" in *Push from the Bush*, n6, May 1980:34-41

Tony **Rayner (1981a)** *The female factory at Cascades, Hobart* National Parks &Wildlife Service, Hobart, 1981

Tony **Rayner (1981b)** "Historical Survey of the Ross Female Factory Site, Tasmania" Unpublished Report, National Parks & Wildlife Service Hobart, 2 February 1981

Tony **Rayner (1988)** *The Hobart Rivulet: historical study* City of Hobart, Hobart, 1988

Tony **Rayner (1994)** "Historical Report: 38 McFarlane Street, South Hobart" Unpublished Report to the Developers for submission to the Hobart City Council Hobart, 25 May 1994, copies held by the HCC and SLT Tasmanian Collection

Bob **Reece (2001)** *The origins of Irish convict transportation to New South Wales* Palgrave, Basingstoke Hampshire, 2001

Sian **Rees (2001)** *The floating brothel: The extraordinary story of the* Lady Julian *and its cargo of female convicts bound for Botany Bay* Hodder, Sydney, 2001

Kirsty **Reid (1995)** *Work, sexuality and resistance: the convict women of Van Diemen's Land, 1820-1839* Unpublished PhD Thesis, University of Edinburgh, 1995

Kirsty **Reid (1997)** "Contumacious, ungovernable and incorrigible: Convict women and workplace resistance, Van Diemen's Land, 1820-1839" Chapter 6 in Ian **Duffield** & James **Bradley (eds)**, *Representing convicts: New perspectives on convict forced labour migration* Leicester UP, London, 1997:106-123

Kirsty **Reid (2003)** "The assignment system and female convict labour in Van Diemens Land, 1820-1839" in *Historical Studies*, v34n121, 2003:1-25

Thomas **Reid (1822)** *Two voyages to New South Wales and Van Diemen's Land with a description of the present condition of that interesting colony: including facts and observations relative to the state and management of convicts of both sexes also reflections on seduction and its general consequences.* Longman, London, 1822

Henry **Reynolds (1969)** " 'That hated stain': the aftermath of Transportation in Tasmania" in *Historical Studies*, v14n53, October 1969:19-31

Portia **Robinson (1979)** "The First Forty Years" in Judy **Mackinolty** and Heather **Radi**, *In pursuit of justice: Australian women and the law 1788-1979*, Hale and Iremonger, Sydney, 1979: 1-16

Portia **Robinson (1988)** *The women of Botany Bay: A reinterpretation of the role of women in the origins of Australian Society* Penguin Books, Ringwood, Vic., Revised Edition, 1993

LL **Robson (1963)** "The origin of the women convicts sent to Australia, 1787-1852" in *Historical Studies*, v11n41, November 1963:43-53

LL **Robson (1965)** *The convict settlers of Australia* Melbourne University Press, Melbourne, 1965

LL **Robson (1983)** *A history of Tasmania: Volume I, Van Diemens Land from the Earliest Times to 1855* Oxford University Press, Melbourne, 1983

Lloyd **Robson (1988)** "The convict cargo re-inspected" *Bulletin of the Centre for Tasmanian Historical Studies*, v2n1, 1988:29-39

Michael **Roe (1963)** "HP Fry: Four letters from Hobart Town, 1839-1845" in *Tasmanian Historical Research Association, Papers and Proceedings* September 1963, v11n1: 20-28

Margaret **Rolfe (2004)** "The Rajah Quilt" in *The Tasmanian Bicentenary Rajah Quilt Project* Female Factory Historic Site, Hobart, 2004

George **Rudé (1978)** *Protest and punishment: the story of the social and political protesters transported to Australia 1788-1869* Oxford UP, Melbourne, 1978

Lyndall **Ryan (1990)** "The governed: convict women in Tasmania, 1803-1853" *Bulletin of the Centre for Tasmanian Historical Studies*, v3n1, 1990/1:37-51

Lyndall **Ryan (1995)** "From stridency to silence: the policing of convict women, 1803-1853" Chapter 5 in Diane Kirkby, *Sex, power and justice* Oxford University Press, Melbourne, 1995:70-85

Annette **Salt (1984)** *These outcast women: the Parramatta female factory 1821-1848* Hale & Iremonger, Sydney, 1984

Irene **Schaffer (1997)** "The forgotten women convicts of Macquarie Harbour 1821-1826" in *Tasmanian Ancestry*, v18n2, September 1997:94-98

JA **Sharpe (1990)** *Judicial punishment in England* Faber & Faber, London, 1990

AGL **Shaw (1955)** *The story of Australia* Faber and Faber, London, 1955 (Revised Edition 1972)

AGL **Shaw (1966)** *Convicts and the colonies* Faber and Faber, London, 1966

AGL **Shaw (1986)** "Sir George Arthur after ten years" *Bulletin of the Centre for Tasmanian Historical Studies*, v1n2, 1986:4-14

WJ **Sheehan (1977)** "Finding solace in eighteenth century Newgate" Chapter 10 in JS **Cockburn (ed) (1977)** *Crime in England 1550 - 1800* Methuen, London, 1977:229-245

JR **Skemp (1956)** *Letters to Anne* Melbourne UP, Melbourne, 1956

Babette **Smith (1988)** *A cargo of women: Susannah Watson and the convicts of the Princess Royal* New South Wales University Press, Sydney, 1988

Coultman **Smith (1941)** *Shadow over Tasmania* Hobart, 1941

James Montagu **Smith (2001)** *Send the boy to sea: the memoirs of a sailor on the goldfields* Edited by Peter Cuffley Five Mile Press, Melbourne, 2001

Roy **Smith (1962)** *John Lee Archer: Tasmanian architect and Engineer* THRA, Hobart, 1962

Michael **Sturma (1978)** "Eye of the beholder: The stereotype of women convicts, 1788-1852" in *Labour History*, n34, May 1978: 3-10

Michael **Sturma (1983)** *Vice in a vicious society: Crime and convicts in mid-nineteenth century New South Wales* University of Queensland Press, St Lucia Qld, 1983

Christopher **Sweeney (1981)** *Transported in place of death: Convicts in Australia* Macmillan, Melbourne, 1981

Phillip **Tardiff (1990)** *Notorious strumpets and dangerous girls: convict women in Van Diemen's Land 1803-1829* Angus & Robertson, Sydney, 1990

Ian **Terry & Kathryn Evans (1997)** *Hobart's History: The first two hundred years; papers and proceedings of the conference held by the Professional Historians Association of Tasmania on 4 October 1997* Professional Historians Association, Hobart, 1998

Marjorie **Tipping (1988)** *Convicts Unbound: The Story of the Calcutta Convicts and their settlement in Australia* Viking O'Neil, Ringwood Vic., 1988

NL **Tranter (1985)** *Population and society 1750-1940: Contrasts in population growth* Longman, Harlow Essex, 1985

EP **Thompson (1968)** *The making of the English working class* Penguin, Harmondsworth, 1968

Clive **Turnbull (1965)** *Black war* Landsdowne, Melbourne, 1965

Hilary **Weatherburn (1979)** "The Female Factory" in Judy **Mackinolty** and Heather **Radi**, *In pursuit of justice: Australian women and the law 1788-1979*, Hale and Iremonger, Sydney, 1979: 18-30

John **West (1852)** *The history of Tasmania* Edited by AGL Shaw, A&R Australian Classics Edition Angus & Robertson, Sydney, 1981

John **Williams (1972)** "Irish convicts and Van Diemen's Land" in *Tas Hist Res Assn P&P*, v19, n3, September 1972:100-120

History, n44, May 1983:1-17

John **Williams (1994)** *Ordered to the Island: Irish Convicts and Van Diemen's Land* Edited by Richard Davis; Crossing Press, Sydney, 1994

Christine **Woods (2004)** *The last ladies: female convicts on the Duchess of Northumberland, 1853* Woods, Hobart, 2004

EA **Wrigley (ed) (1972)** *Nineteenth-century society: Essays in the use of quantitative methods for the study of social data* Cambridge University Press, Cambridge, 1972

EA **Wrigley** and RS **Schofield (1981)** *The population history of England 1541-1871* Edward Arnold, London, 1981

Notes and References

While the references here will enable the general reader to locate source material, those with a further or professional interest may wish to obtain more detail through the publisher's website: <esperancepress.com.au>.

Abbreviations

ADB: Australian Dictionary of Biography
AOT: Archives Office of Tasmania
BPP IUP: British Parliamentary Papers in the Irish University Reprint Transportation Series
HRA: Historical Records of Australia

Chapters 1, 2, and 3 are based on the work of the following people: Bateson 1974, Beattie 1974, 1975, 1977, 1986 and 2001; Cockburn 1977; Emsley 1983, 1991, 1996; Flynn 1993; Gattrell & Haddon 1972; Gattrell 1994; Hay 1975; Hughes 1988; King 2002; Landau 2002; Lieberman 2002; Linebaugh 1993; McGowan 2002; Radzinowicz 1948; Radzinowicz & Hood 1986; Sharpe 1990, Sheehan 1977; Shaw 1966; Smith 1988; Thompson 1968; Wrigley 1972; Wrigley & Schofield 1981

1. Young, noisy and light-fingered

p1. The story of the *Duchess of Northumberland* is told in Woods, 2004

2. City of Terror

p9-12. Based on Radzinowicz, 1948, Gatrell, 1994; Linebaugh, 1993; Beattie, 1974, 1975, 1977, 1986, 2001; Gatrell & Haddon, 1972
p10. The young man was Samuel Rogers quoted in Gatrell, 1994: 11
p11-12. Gatrell, 1994: Radzinowicz, 1948:

3. The Bloody Code

p13-14. Gatrell, 1994: Radzinowicz, 1948:
p15-16. Radzinowicz, 1948: 211-215 on the burning of women
p16-17. Radzinowicz, 1948: Beattie, 1986: 509-10, 565 n.78
p18. Beattie, 1986: 503, 565
p20-21. Beattie, 1986: 477, On Gipps Heath, 1978:152-3
p22. Black Box... JM Smith, 2001:27
p24. Refusing to eat... JM Smith, 2001:29, on Millbank Penitentiary see Shaw, 1966:133

4. The Women

p26. Knopwood 3/4/1820: HRA s4v3: 271-289:285; Youl 27/4/1820: HRA s4v3: 442-445:445
p27-28. Stanley to Franklin, 25 Nov 1842 in

BPP, IUP, Transportation, v7:114-117
p28. Young and beautiful... Nicol, 1822:
p28-33. Robson, 1965: Scottish the worst... Robson, 1965:76
p30. Sweethearts... JM Smith, 2001:27
p32. Robson, 1965:75, Love and rivets... Nicol, 1822:
p33. Violent offences... Robson, 1965:179,187
p34-5. Had to walk... Bateson: 1974:58-66, no taming her... Nicol, 1822:

5. Perils at Sea

p.36. JM Smith, 2001:25-27
p.37-38. Reid, 1822: 93-133
p39. The fourteen who died... Tardiff, 1990:15
p39-42. Bateson:1974:94-119, 120-171
p40. *The Lady Shore* Bateson:1974:151-7
p42. *The Emu* Bateson, 1974:191-2
p43. improved conditions... Haines, 2003:25
p44. *The Amphitrite* Bateson:1974:246-248
p45-47. Bateson:1974, Shaw, 1966.
p46. *The Neva* Mawer, 1997, Bateson, 1974:248-52
p49. Bateson: 1974:87-90
p50. *Frances and Eliza* Bateson, 1974:188-193

6. Entering Exile

p51. Ryan, 1990, 1995; Daniels, 1998: 64-5
p54. Jane Franklin to Elizabeth Fry, 3 August 1841 in Mackaness, 1947, v2:22-29
p54. Comparatively free... JM Smith 2001
p55. Brand, 1990:15-17, 17-18
p56. Flagitious lives... HP Fry quoted by Clark, 1950
p56. Forfeit savings... Brand, 1990:17-20, HP Fry, *A system of penal discipline*, 1850 quoted in Clark, 1950:119-120
p57-61. Heath, 1978; Rayner, 1981a; Salt, 1984
p58. Marriage and freedom... Reid, 1822:
p59. A husband's provocation, *Hobart Town Courier*, 8 May 1830, as quoted in Tardiff, 1990: 321-2
p62. Evidence of Knopwood to Commissioner Bigge, 3 April 1820, see note for p26 above
p63. *Hobart Town Courier*, 21 February 1829 as quoted in Tardif, 1990:274-5

7. Colonial Crime and Punishment

p64. Humphrey to Bigge 13 March 1820, Lenahan to Bigge, 21 April 1820 in HRA s3v3:410; Boothman to Cimitiere, 18 May

1820 in HRA s3v3: 877-878;
p65. Reid, 1822:
p66-7. Eliza Dowling in Tardif, 1990:57-9
p67. Sarah Lascelles in Tardif, 1990:81;
Isabella Noble in Tardif, 1990:133-4
p67-8. Schaffer, 1997; Rachel Chamberlin and
the surgeon's comments in Tardiff, 1990:
531-2; p68. Mary Furze in Tardiff,
1990:386-7; Phillips, 1997:18
p69. Elizabeth Murphy in Tardif, 1990:62-3;
Radzinowicz, 1948:578 n35
p70. Owen to Bigge, 8 July 1820, HRA s3v3:
408
p70. Cimitiere to Bigge, 8 June 1820, HRA
s3v3: 877-878
p71. Rachel Wright in Tardif, 1990:100;
Eleanor Doyle in Tardif, 1990:91-2;
Margaret Hughes in Tardif, 1990:95-6;
Mary Hart in Tardif, 1990:542-3
p72. Tardif, 1990:98-9, 117, 136-7, 112-3, 141-
2, 132-3
p73. Tardif, 1990:114-5, 133-4, 120,
p73-4. Tardif, 1990:120, 138
p74. Davis, 1974:20, 25, 49; Tardif, 1990:1565-
6
p75. Ann Pirie AOT LC375/2:16; Sarah Talbot
AOT LC375/2:550
p76. Mrs Ludgater AOT CSO5/182/4331:143-7;
Flynn, 1993

8. A New World

p79. Quote is from Reid, 1822:305; Knopwood
HRA s3v3:366; Youl HRA s3v3:445
p80. Youl HRA s3v3: 442-445:442; Owen HRA
s4v3: 405-408:407
p81. Bigge, 1966:105; Fry to Marsden, 23 May
1832 quoted in B Smith, 1988:68
p82. Julia Mullins. Tardif, 1990:919-921 and
frontispiece
p84. Dyster, 1989:45; Bridget Nolan AOT
CSO1/555/12, 221: 23ff; CON 40v7,31
p85. Davidson, 1975
p86. Boyes, 1985
p87. Mary Revlet in Tardif, 1990:504-5; Phoebe
Allen in Tardif, 1990:1048-51
p90. Rebecca Kerr AOT LC375/2
p94. Payne, 1961:62-7
p95. Report of the select committee on
Transportation Molesworth Committee
1837, in Clark, 1957:195; New Norfolk
courts AOT LC375/2
p96. Mary Carter in Tardif, 1990:115-6

9. The Female Factories

p98. Heath, 1978: 14; 15-17
p99. Heath, 1978: 9-17
p101. Heath, 1978: 309, 325
p101. Heath, 1978: 310
p101. Heath, 1978: 309-310
p102. HRAs3v3:850-1

p103. HRAs3v4: 689
p103. Heath, 1978:164
p103. Heath, 1978:310
p103. Phillips, 1997:15
p103. Hobart Town Gazette, 23 March 1822;
quoted in Phillips, 1997:15
p103. Phillips, 1997:16
p104. Phillips, 1997:16-17
p104. Phillips, 1997:17
p104. Phillips, 1997:19
p104. Phillips, 1997:18-9
p104. Phillips, 1997:19
p104. Phillips, 1997:20; Heath, 1978:170-1
p105. Heath, 1978:171
p105. AOT CSO1/19/340:28
p105. Launceston Advertiser 24 July 1832,
quoted in Phillips, 1997:21
p106. Bartlett, 1996; Daniels, 1998:147
p107. BPP, 1969, v9:123
p108. Despatch: Lord Stanley to Lt-Governor
Franklin, 25 November 1842; BPP, IUP,
Transportation, Volume 7:114-117
p109. Rayner, 1981b passim, 14
p111. Rayner, 1981:14
p112. Hampton to Lt-Governor Denison, 15
October 1847
p112. John Hampton, Comptroller-General's
Report 3, 30 April 1848: 253

10. Hobart Female Factory

p113. HRAs3v2:290, 8 December 1817
p114. HRAs3v2:292
p114. HRAs3v3:71 6 December 1820
p114. Hobart Town Gazette quoted in Tardif,
1990:533-4
p115. Heath, 1978:325
p115. HRAs3v3:278
p115-116. Macquarie to Sorell, 30 June 1821,
HRAs3v4:18; Heath, 1978:165
p116. AOT, GO1/1 Dispatch 2:19-20
p116. Tardif, 1990:339-341; passim, but
Margaret Morgan was one of the activists
p117. Heath, 1978:165-6
p117. AOT, GO25 Enclosure 1 to Dispatch 75,
25 October 1827, Report on the Female
Factory, Hobart Town, 13 Jan 1826
p118. Hobart Town Gazette, 6 January 1827,
quoted in Tardif, 1990:182-4
p119. p3c3 1829; Rayner, 1981a:12; Colonial
Times 2 January quoted in Tardif, 1990:663

11. The Man with the Black Books

p120. Rayner, 1981a:25; Daniels, 1998:28
p122-4. JV Barry, Alexander Maconochie of
Norfolk Island, Melbourne University Press,
1958; quoted in Forsyth, 1970:vii
p124. Forsyth, 1970:56
p125. Government Notice, 3 December 1829
quoted in Forsyth, 1970:58-59
p125-9. Rayner, 1981a:8-11

p126. AOT CSo1/364:71-80
p127. AOTcs01/241/5820:1-16

Chapter 12. Cascades Female Factory

p134-142. Rayner, 1981a:3-16
p142. Sarah Simmons. Tardif, 1990:1196-7
p143. *Colonial Times*, 16/10/1829:p3c3
p144. Tardiff, 1990:1196-7

Chapter 13. Pity the Children

p145. AOT CS01/358/8215:287
p146. *Colonial Times*, 7 August 1829:3-4;
     Colonial Times, 16 October 1829 p3c3
p147. AOT CS01/366:50, CS01/
     895:19,025:174ff
p148. Rayner, 1981a:17-18
p149. Rayner, 1981a:18
p150. AOT CSO5/114/2608
p151. *True Colonist*, 30 March 1838
p151. Rayner, 1981a:17-8; AOT CSO 5/114/
     2608:183ff; Atkinson & Aveling, 1987:284
p152. Gandevia, 1978:27
p153. Gandevia, 1978:27
p153. Rayner,1988:29; 1994:5.2
p153. Rayner, 1994:5.2
p153. Brand, 1990:141-2
p154. Mackaness, 1947 v1:37-8
p154. Mackaness, 1947 v1:23-4
p155. Munday, 1852:15-16
p157-8. Gandevia, 1978:27

14. Life at Cascades Factory

p159. *Austral-Asiatic Review*, 29 October 1841
     quoted in Hutchinson, 1993:62
p159-60. Daniels, 1998:176
p160. Rayner, 1981a:15-16
p161. Rayner, 1981a:8-11
p161-3. Rayner, 1981a:19-20; Hutchinson,
     1962:59
p162. Crooke, 1958
p162. Alexander, 1999:143; Daniels, 1998:149
p165. *Tasmanian and Austral-Asiatic Review*,

15 October 1839, Rayner, 1981a:29-36
p166. Jane Franklin to Mary Simpkinson, 4
     October 1838 in Mackaness, 1947:I:37-8
p167. Jane Franklin to Elizabeth Fry, 3 August
     1841 in Mackaness, 1947:I:22-9
p168. HP Fry quoted by Clark, 1950
p169-70. Mundy, 1852:15-16
p170.Hutchinson,1961:93-107;
     Hutchinson,1963:65-6
p171. Hutchinson, 1961:93-107;
     Hutchinson,1963:65-6
p171-2. Report, 31 December 1852:343, 366

15. Winding down of the system

p173-4. Bateson, 1974; Rayner, 1981a:38-40;
     Statistics of Tasmania 1855-65, 1855:5;
     1856:5. *Hobart Town Gazette*, 30 October
     1855 & 17 June 1856:82
p175-6. *Statistics of Tasmania 1855-65*,
     1857:62, 67-8. AOT:CSD1/93/2479
p176. Mary Ann Nowlan per *Duchess of
     Northumberland*, Woods, 2004
p177. *Mercury*, 28 July 1860
p177. AOT:CSD4/51/819
p178. Woods, 2004; AOT: CSD4/37/455; 156
p179. *Statistics of Tasmania, 1855-65,
     1865:104
p179. Brown, 1972:98-9; Lands Department,
     Map 94 Buckingham, 26 June 1869
p180. Rayner, 1981a:44-5
p181. *Tasmanian Tribune*, 11 December
     1874:3c4
p182. Turnley was quoted in Brown, 1972:98
p182-183. Brown, 1972:99; AOT: *Statistics of
     Tasmania, 1877*: Blue Book 1877:17
p178. Woods, 2004:51-54
p184. Maria Middleton in Tardif, 1990:1442-3;
     Bateson, 1974:360, 386; Frost and
     Maxwell-Stewart, 2001:127-132]
p188. Lyn Rainbird; story of old man
p189. Ann Wilson in Tardif, 1990:468-71

Index

Also available from Esperance Press

Ordinary Women , an epic novel by Edward Kynaston

The story of an anti-Nazi family who survive the Gestapo, the infamous destruction of Dresden by Allied fire-bombing, and then the brutalities of Russian invasion. This is also a truly Australian story of post-WWII migration. Based on the life of the author's wife and meticulously researched, the book refuses to be put down.

Four Quarters , poetry by Edith Speers

If you love poetry, or think you hate it, this is the book for you: rhymes, free verse, and love sonnets. Les Murray and Mark O'Connor have commended this collection by a widely published and prize-winning poet.

Rattling the Cage , short stories by Morag Kirk

Mysterious deaths and murderous mothers; treachery, lies and liars; strange visitations by a turkey, a robin and a flock of white cockatoos; plus an absolute gem of a housekeeper. Quirky, compelling, witty and utterly readable.

A Writer's Tasmania , Edited by Carol Patterson & Edith Speers

Fourteen of Tasmania's finest writers describe their island state in essays filled with humour, affection, personal reminiscence and historical background. Contributors include Margaret Scott and Senator Bob Brown. Foreword by Amanda Lohrey.

The Time It Rained Fish , a novel by Philomena van Rijswijk

The first Ellen is a Carmelite nun, born near Skibbereen during the Great Hunger. The second Ellen is a New Age convert, born in Sydney. They are soul-sisters in this family saga spanning over 100 years of land rights and republicanism in Ireland and Australia.

Over the Fence - Tasmanian Bush Yarns , by Geoff Dean

Old Willum Haas is the only man in the district who won't pray for rain; Phylis Barnes, the baker's wife, offers more than just an extra cream bun; Elsa Gernhart finds that a coffin makes life worth living. Meet the people of Montvale, a typical country town.

Esperance Press
Dover, Tasmania
Australia 7117
esperancepress.com.au